Human Rights and Democracy

Human Rights and Democracy

The Precarious Triumph of Ideals

TODD LANDMAN

B L O O M S B U R Y

LONDON · NEW DELHI · NEW YORK · SYDNEY

Bloomsbury Academic

An imprint of Bloomsbury Publishing Plc

50 Bedford Square	1385 Broadway
London	New York
WC1B 3DP	NY 10018
UK	USA

www.bloomsbury.com

Bloomsbury is a registered trade mark of Bloomsbury Publishing Plc

First published 2013

British Library Cataloguing-in-Publication Data
A catalogue record for this book is available from the British Library.

ISBN: PB: 978-1-8496-6345-8
HB: 978-1-8496-6346-5
ePub: 978-1-8496-6347-2
ePDF: 978-1-8496-6486-8

Library of Congress Cataloging-in-Publication Data
A catalog record for this book is available from the Library of Congress.

Typeset by Deanta Global Publishing Services, Chennai, India
Printed and bound in Great Britain

CONTENTS

Acknowledgements viii
List of tables and figures x

1   Introduction 1
   Suggested reading 10
   Notes 10

2   Abundance and freedom 11
   Introduction 11
   The correlates of democracy 11
   Political actors and political processes 18
   Examining the 'outliers' 20
   Summary and implications 22
   Suggestions for further reading 23
   Notes 23

3   Democracy and human rights 25
   Introduction 25
   'Thick' and 'thin' definitions of democracy 26
   Human rights: Evolution and protection 31
   Human rights: Definition and content 33
   Democracy and human rights 38
   Summary and implications 41
   Suggestions for further reading 42
   Notes 43

4   Waves and setbacks 45
   Introduction 45
   Democracy's journey 46

Democratic setbacks 51
Summary: The fifth wave? 57
Suggestions for further reading 59
Notes 59

5   Evidence and explanations 61
Introduction 61
Modernization 62
Macro-historical change 66
Games of transition 70
The making of democracy 74
International dimensions 76
Summary 80
Suggestions for further reading 81
Notes 82

6   Agents and advocates 83
Introduction 83
Domestic mobilization 84
International mobilization 89
Summary 95
Suggestions for further reading 96
Notes 96

7   Truth and justice 97
Introduction 97
Choice of truth mechanism 99
Mandate and scope of a truth process 102
Methods for uncovering the truth 105
Types of justice and the impact of truth processes 107
Summary 111
Suggestions for further reading 111
Notes 111

8   Threats and pitfalls 113
Introduction 113
Conflict 114
Terrorism 116

Economic globalization 121
Climate change 125
Summary 126
Suggestions for further reading 127
Note 127

9   Benefits and outcomes 129

Introduction 129
Democracy qua democracy 130
Democratic peace 136
Economic benefits 137
Environmental outcomes 140
Summary 142
Suggestions for further reading 142
Note 143

10 Hopes and challenges 145

A tale of three women 145
Abundance and freedom 148
Democracy and human rights 149
Waves and setbacks 151
Evidence and explanations 152
Agents and advocates 153
Truth and justice 155
Threats and pitfalls 155
Benefits and outcomes 157
A precarious triumph 157

References 159
Index 171

ACKNOWLEDGEMENTS

This is a book that has been many years in gestation, as I have taken my academic research and teaching interests into a variety of international consultancies in over 35 countries around the world. My teaching and research in the areas of development, democracy and human rights provided a foundation in theories, comparative methods and strategies for measurement and assessment that have proved useful for a large number of international governmental and non-governmental organizations. My work has taken me to countries across Europe, Latin America, Africa, Asia and the Middle East. I have met wonderful people in all these countries and many who are passionate about politics, changing their own societies and fighting for democracy and human rights. I have taught hundreds of students at the University of Essex, the European Master's Degree in Human Rights and Democratization, a Romanian summer school in research methods, a research design course at the Ludwig Boltzmann Institute in Vienna, a Chinese human rights research methods training programme and numerous other seminars, workshops and conferences around the world. I am grateful to the main inter-governmental, governmental and non-governmental organizations with whom I have worked, including the International Institute for Democracy and Electoral Assistance (IDEA), the United Nations Development Programme, the United Nations Office of the High Commissioner for Human Rights, the European Commission, the Westminster Foundation for Democracy (and the Westminster Consortium for Strengthening Parliaments and Democracy), the UK Department for International Development, the German Development Institute, InWEnt International Capacity Building and Minority Rights Group International.

As ever, some people I meet have assumed a special place in my professional as well as personal life and who are worth thanking here for all their support, ideas, collegiality and friendship: Tom Thomas, Edzia Carvalho, Ingrid Wetterqvist, David Beetham, Stuart Weir, Jonathan Crook, Balthasar Benz, Maria Leissner, Ruth Emmerink, Keboitse Machangana, Jaime Baeza Freer, Miguel Angel Lopez, Jaime Fierro, Joe Foweraker, David Howarth, Bent Flyvbjerg, Sanford Schram, Anita Gohdes, Jule Krüger, Terence Huw Edwards, David Kernohan, the late Kevin Boyle, Patrick Ball, David Cingranelli, David Richards, Neil Mitchell, Bethany Barratt, Marco Larizza, Marku Suksi, Attracta Ingram, Horst Fischer, Kirsten Harstrup,

Hans Otto-Sano, Joachim Nahem, Julia Häusermann, Matthew Sudders, Meghna Abraham, Michael Freeman, Fred Grünfeld, Neil Robinson, Heather Smith-Cannoy, Thomas Wolnick, Alejandro Anaya Munoz, Carlos Lascarain, Sergio Montaño, Manuel Palma, Tomislav Lendo, Irma Mendez, Joerg Faust, Thomas Plümper, Tom Scotto, Rene Lindstadt, Bill Simmons and Rhona Smith.

I'd like to offer deep thanks to Dr Dorothea Farquhar, executive officer of the Institute for Democracy and Conflict Resolution (IDCR) at the University of Essex. Dorothea has shown unstinting dedication to the work of the IDCR and has been an instrumental part in providing me the little bits of time to work on this book. Finally, special thanks go to my mother Laura Landman, my bother Drew Landman and his wife Kate Landman and my brother Hank Landman and his wife Kelli Landman. In my home, much love and thanks to my dear wife Melissa Landman, my daughter Sophia Laura Landman, my stepson Oliver Daniel Heginbotham and young Briony Rose Landman, all of whom patiently indulged in my ruminations, discussions, absences, strange reading habits and magic. It is to them that I dedicate this book.

LIST OF TABLES AND FIGURES

Table 3.1   Procedural democracy 27

Table 3.2   Liberal democracy 28

Table 3.3   Social democracy 29

Table 3.4   List of human rights protected under international law 34

Table 3.5   Main international human rights treaties 37

Table 4.1   Waves of democracy: regions and countries 47

Figure 1.1   The growth of democracy (number and percentage) 4

Figure 2.1   Development and democracy 12

Figure 2.2   Democracy and development 14

Figure 2.3   Support for and satisfaction with democracy by region, 1998–2002 18

Figure 2.4   Development and democracy revisited 21

Figure 3.1   Thin and thick definitions of democracy 30

Figure 3.2   Democracy and human rights 39

Figure 4.1   Waves of democracy 47

Figure 4.2   Mean democracy scores by region 51

Figure 4.3   Mean human rights score by region 52

Figure 5.1   Modernization and revised modernization 65

Figure 5.2   Routes to the modern world 68

Figure 5.3   Pathways to initial democratization 69

Figure 5.4   Democratic transformation: A revised 'Dynamic Model' 72

Figure 5.5   Democratic transformation 77

Figure 8.1   Armed conflicts by type, 1946–2011 116

Figure 9.1   Voter turnout for parliamentary and presidential elections and the level of democracy, 1981–2010 131

Figure 9.2 Physical integrity rights and democracy, 1981–2010 132
Figure 9.3 Human development and executive competiveness,
1980–2010 138
Figure 9.4 Caloric intake and competiveness, 1980–2010 139
Figure 9.5 Water pollution and competiveness, 1980–2010 141
Figure 9.6 Fossil fuel consumption, wealth and competiveness,
1980–2010 141

CHAPTER ONE

Introduction

It was late June 2005 when my plane swooped down into Ulaanbaatar, Mongolia, and I was struck by the sparse landscape, looming power stations (labelled conveniently and in huge numbers as 1, 2 and 3) and ring of **ger** villages encircling the city. The drive from the airport to the Chinggis Kahn Hotel is short and bumpy, while traffic chaos is typical of any transitional country. Mongolia is a country three times the size of France with a population of under 3 million, the majority of whom live in the capital. Its average per capita income level is $3,300 USD (indexed in 2010), while its growth rates for the last decade have fluctuated between 6 per cent and 8 per cent per year. It is one of the fastest growing economies in the world mostly due to its rich deposits of natural resources. This is a country that was the land of the conquerors and is now sandwiched between Russia to the North, China to the South, North Korea to the East and the post-Soviet countries of Central Asia – Kazakhstan, Kyrgyzstan, Tajikistan, Uzbekistan and Turkmenistan – to the West.

As I reflected on Mongolia's size, geographical position, relative economic wealth and unbelievable natural beauty, I asked myself, 'How and why did its people in 1991 decide to overthrow the Communist regime and establish a multi-party democracy? And how has it managed to sustain this democracy against all odds?' In the short space of less than two decades, Mongolia overthrew the past regime with comparatively little violence (although key dissenters were killed), established a functioning party system, carried out successive elections in which power has been transferred between different political parties and passed its own 9th Millennium Development Goal (MDG) on democracy, zero tolerance of corruption and human rights that joined the eight other well-known MDGs. Throughout the 20 years of this new democratic period, Mongolia has suffered challenges to its systems and democratic institutions (including some violent contestations over electoral results and a corruption scandal preceding the 2012 elections), but it has not experienced a reversal, or 'rollback' of democracy to the degree that has occurred in other similar new democracies (see Diamond 2008).

In late 2010, I once again found myself descending into a mountainous and sparsely populated country with its own looming power stations that has also been building democratic institutions since the end of the Cold War. The site of my arrival was Santiago de Chile. In contrast to Mongolia, Chile had had a long experience with democracy from the nineteenth century until 1973, when President Salvador Allende was overthrown by the military and the country endured 18 years of dictatorship under General Augusto Pinochet. But Chile underwent a rapid transition to democracy after Pinochet's 1988 defeat in a plebiscite, rather than a popular uprising that sought to unseat him from power. Like Mongolia, Chile has been able to avoid a return to authoritarianism and an alternation of power between the broad leftist coalition **Concertación** (which won all the post-1989 elections until 2009) to the rightist National Renovation party led by former LAN Chile CEO Sebastian Piñera. In my meeting with former President Patricio Aylwin (or Dom Patricio as his supporters call him), he said 'it does not matter to me that the right has won in Chile, since it is a great sign of the health of our democracy'. These are very wise words indeed and will be reiterated throughout this book.

Chile has now had five democratically elected governments since Pinochet and has joined the Organisation for Economic Cooperation and Development (OECD) along with other wealthy and stable democracies. It rose to international fame with the military coup of 1973, sending dissidents and exiles throughout the world and becoming a pariah state for many years as the international community mobilized around its frequent and serious abuse of human rights. International pressure on the issue of human rights continued after Pinochet's departure from formal power with his 1998 detention in London based on a request for extradition to Spain from a judge seeking redress for past crimes against humanity. While Pinochet never saw justice, the principle of 'universal jurisdiction' (the idea that jurisdiction over crimes extends beyond the boundaries of the prosecuting state) was buttressed as the Law Lords in the United Kingdom agreed that a former head of state was not immune from prosecution for crimes against humanity. The story of Chile is thus one of successful democratic transition and one of advance (albeit incremental) for the human rights movement.

Contrast these pictures with those of Mexico. Again, as we approached Mexico City – a sprawling metropolis of 20 million people – I reflected on the process of democratization in a country that had undergone a prolonged revolution between 1910 and 1917, a period of contestation between the end of the Revolution and the consolidation of authority under the **Partido Revolucionario Institucional** (Institutional Revolutionary Party, PRI), and one of the most successful periods of authoritarian rule that effectively ended in 2000 with the election of the main opposition party **Partido Acción Nacional** (National Action Party, PAN) to the Presidency. Mexico is an upper-middle-income country that has developed to the stage that it is now a full member of the World Trade Organization (WTO), a member of the OECD (like Chile) and one of three partners in the North American Free Trade Agreement (NAFTA) along with the United States and Canada. Over the last decade, it has seen remarkable rates of economic growth, decreasing rates of inflation, greater trade links with other countries, and it is the leading producer of smart phones (especially the Blackberry), television sets and automobile parts.[1]

Long before its 'official' transition to democracy in 2000, Mexico has struggled with classic problems of economic development, including successful state-led growth and stagnation between the 1950s and 1970s, economic liberalization and a debt crisis in the 1980s and integration into the world economy in the 1990s. Throughout these decades, political representation was dominated by the PRI as it gradually liberalized its political system, established the **Instituto Federal Electoral** (Federal Electoral Institute, of IFE) and conceded defeat at the Presidential level in 2000 with the election of Vicente Fox from PAN.

These twin processes of economic modernization and political liberalization have been marred by political and social disturbances such as student and teacher mobilizations in the 1970s and 1980s; an armed rebellion in Chiapas in the 1990s that struggled against Mexico's participation in processes of economic globalization; and a highly profitable and increasingly violent drug trade that since 2006 has led to tens of thousands of killings and disappearances.[2] The federal structure of Mexico with 32 states and more than 3,000 municipalities has provided a set of incentives for corruption and impunity that have had profound human rights implications and undermined democratic development in a country that has competitive elections, well-developed political parties and the alternation of political control of government. Moreover, the process of democratization itself is seen by many as a possible reason for the instability since it has transformed the informal and authoritarian form of rule in ways that have not yet been consolidated and provided opportunities for conflict, violence, corruption and impunity (see, e.g. Snyder 2007; Philip and Berruecos 2012).

This **contrast of contexts** between Mongolia and Chile on the one hand and Mexico on the other provides the starting point for this book. Democracy and human rights have an inherent appeal that has inspired human communities around the world to throw off their authoritarian past and to embrace a set of institutions and values that at their heart place the idea of human dignity and human well-being. The desire for democracy is strong, and it is one that has increased dramatically in the latter half of the twentieth century. Indeed, since 1974, more than 90 countries have embraced democracy in 'waves' that have spread from Southern Europe, to Latin America, to Eastern Europe and to parts of Africa and Asia (Huntington

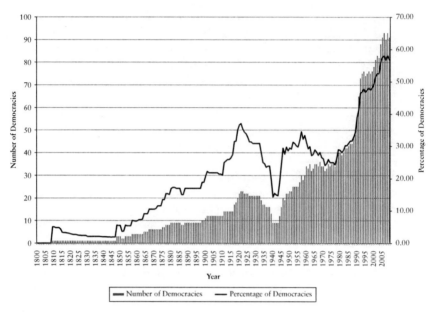

FIGURE 1.1 *The growth of democracy (number and percentage).*

Source: Polity IV.

1991; Doorenspleet 2005). Figure 1.1 shows the historic trends in the growth of democracy, both in terms of the number and percentage of democracies in the world and the various 'waves' that characterize the trends. The period between the middle of the nineteenth century to 1920 saw a large increase in democracy. The interwar period saw a dramatic decrease, with democratic gains in the immediate post-World War II period, but democratic collapse during the 1960s (partly explained by the growth in newly independent countries after decolonization and partly the turn towards authoritarianism in Latin America). But it is clear that from 1974, the world has witnessed an impressive and steady growth of democracy such that by today, roughly 60 per cent of all countries in the world are ruled by democratic governments.

In late 2010 and early 2011, countries across the Middle East and North Africa have shown dramatic popular mobilizations that led to regime change and new elections in Tunisia and Egypt, international intervention and regime change in Libya, challenge and oppression in Yemen and Bahrain and prolonged and violent conflict in Syria. While not a 'Fifth Wave' of democracy, there is much expectation among observers and concerned parties in the region as these countries undergo rapid political changes that were unimaginable only a few years ago. The self-immolation of a student in Tunis led to a mass uprising that toppled the Ben Ali regime; a style of social mobilization that spread quickly to Cairo and in time led to the collapse of the Mubarak regime after 30 years in power. Similar to social protest under authoritarianism in other contexts, the popular mobilizations in these two countries adopted a language of rights that started with an economic critique and expanded to include a demand for the protection of civil and political rights (see Foweraker and Landman 1997; Breuer et al. 2012). Early concessions by the regimes in both Tunisia and Egypt were simply not enough as the protest movements remained steadfast in their determination to rid their countries of unsavoury rulers. Time will tell as to whether these processes will usher in solid and stable democratic regimes, but the appeal of democracy and human rights and the inability of the leaders to bottle up their people are testimony to the ideas put forward in this book.

Alongside the development of democracy, the appeal of human rights formalized and codified legally after the mass atrocities of World War II is one that has become increasingly accepted as a global moral discourse that has intuitive appeal to millions of people around the world. But despite its appeal, there are many and diverse paths to democracy, and despite their acceptance, the ways in which human rights are given expression at the local level vary tremendously. Moreover, and this is the cautionary element of the entire argument presented in this book, the maintenance of democratic institutions and the protection of human rights remain **precarious** even in the best of times. Economic fluctuations, the rise of undemocratic forces in society, 'uncivil' movements, terrorism and natural disasters carry with them the serious potential to undermine hard fought freedoms and cherished institutions in the oldest and the newest democracies in the world. But this is not a book about so-called illiberal democracy, where the improvement in rights protection has not kept with the development of democratic institutions (See Zakaria 2003); an idea that seems to focus rather too much on the deficiencies of new democracies and remains unreflective on the many problems in so-called established democracies. It is ultimately a cautiously optimistic book about the triumph of ideals and how these ideals have found expression through the development of international and domestic institutions and have been supported through the vigilance of mass publics inspired by the basic idea that **government ought to be subject to the will of the people.**

Since World War II, when the world emerged from one of the most appalling periods of violence and human suffering, democracy and human rights have become a set of successful political ideas that challenge oppression, celebrate humanity and protect us from the worst forms of our own behaviour; what Susan Mendus (1995) has called 'bullwarks against the permanent threat of human evil'. Democracy and human rights channel and shape popular preferences into governing programmes, and they construct an endurable architecture for sustainable and long-term self-rule. But despite their appeal and their power, democracy and human rights are precarious and subject to significant challenge on a daily basis by governing elites tempted to undermine rules and institutions for enhanced personal power and by mass publics disenchanted with the partial and incremental satisfaction of popular demands (see Chapter 2).

At a more abstract and theoretical level, the book's argument is founded on assumptions about human nature found in Thomas Hobbes, but seeks to show that the world has sought to construct solutions for everyday governance that are based on institutions found in the work of John Locke and notions of justice found in John Rawls. Hobbes assumes that the 'state of nature' (a mental construct or thought experiment constructed for theoretical purposes) is comprised of rational individuals who pursue their own self-interest through any means, including the use of violence or 'warfare' in the terms he uses in **Leviathan**. Locke, on the other hand, shows how constraints on the rational pursuit of self-interest are possible without the existence of an all-powerful leviathan and that institutions and the rules that govern them can be constructed in ways that prevent otherwise self-interested individuals from engaging in the worst forms of behaviour towards one another. Rawls, however, reminds us that even within (and between) societies with well-developed forms of these institutions, there is still the need to think about how the fruits of development and benefits of society are distributed in ways that benefit the least well off. The establishment and maintenance of democracy combined with the protection of human rights across all their dimensions provide a contemporary solution for realizing these key ideas from Hobbes, Locke and Rawls.

To sustain these claims, this book takes a thematic journey through a complex set of global developments over the last 60 years. Rather than chart the history of democratic and normative achievements, the book examines different sets of 'thematic couplets' that frame our thinking about current and future trends in the world. These couplets include **abundance** and **freedom** (Chapter 2), **democracy** and **human rights** (Chapter 3), **waves** and **setbacks** (Chapter 4), **evidence** and **explanations** (Chapter 5), **agents** and **advocates** (Chapter 6), **truth** and **justice** (Chapter 7), **threats** and **pitfalls** (Chapter 8), **benefits** and **outcomes** (Chapter 9) and **hopes** and **challenges** (Chapter 10). Each couplet addresses a natural set of tensions between themes and the balanced, cautionary approach of this book.

Chapter 2 examines the global expansion of economic wealth and the quest by ordinary people to achieve greater freedom in their own countries, while at the same time arguing that much of the expanse in wealth remained in the global north (although is beginning to be challenged from the BRIC countries) and much freedom has come under threat during the so-called war on terror since 11 September 2001. For the latter half of the twentieth century, development practitioners and policymakers have debated whether economic **abundance** is compatible with political **freedom** or whether the real route to rapid economic development is through authoritarian and non-democratic means. Far from arcane debates or stale academic discussion, this topic is once again at the forefront of discussion with the rise of China as an economic powerhouse which has tremendous economic capacity and very little political freedom. China has overtaken the World Bank as the largest donor to developing countries, is now the second largest economy in the world and is likely to overtake the United States in the next 10 years. The chapter examines this debate and the current understandings of the relationships between economic development (i.e. abundance) and democracy (i.e. freedom) with fresh eyes as policymakers in the OECD countries look for linkages between their aid policies and political institutions, and the United Nations system looks past 2015 and the new 'sustainable development goals'.

Despite the impression that democracy and human rights are inherently compatible concepts and ideas, Chapter 3 examines the tension between them in order to show that the two are not completely intertwined and can in some ways be contradictory. To do so, the chapter maps out 'thin' and 'thick' definitions of democracy, outlines the main contours of contemporary human rights and what they mean and then shows how the two concepts overlap and explains why such an overlap is important. It argues that any attempt for human rights to 'hegemonize' the concept of democracy is unhelpful for bringing about democratic reform, since the idea of democracy is grounded in **accommodation** and **agreement,** while the idea of human rights has been codified through international law, which carries with it an inherent sense of **judgement** against a well-defined standard. I illustrate these discussions with graphical representations of the main ideas and the connections between them to show that some idea of 'partial overlap' is the most fruitful way to conceive of them.

In the 1990s, Samuel Huntington's notion of 'waves' of democracy was a popular way to describe democratic developments in the world from the nineteenth through to the twentieth century. Chapter 4 uses this idea of **wave** as a foil and device to examine democratization in comparative perspective. It argues that the waves of democracy in the twentieth century were indeed unprecedented as this 'tantalizingly strange' (Dunn 1993) idea has caught the imagination of more and more people around the world. But it also shows that the later waves have been accompanied by an unexpected decline in the protection of human rights within many 'new' (third and fourth waves) democracies (see Smith-Cannoy 2012); a trend that has not been helped by the fact that many historically won rights protections have been compromised in many 'old' (first and second waves) democracies as the threat of terror raised alarm about too much 'openness' and freedom (see Brysk and Shafir 2007). Moreover, the erosion of rights commitments has been accompanied in some cases with democratic **setbacks,** in countries such as Peru, Ecuador, Russia, Fiji, São Tome and Mali.

One function of this book is to describe and categorize the many developments the world has witnessed since World War II, and the other function is to examine how such developments can be **explained** using systematically collected **evidence.** Using the so-called modernization school as a backdrop, 'straw man' and starting point, Chapter 5 reviews the main conceptual and explanatory frameworks used to explain the variation in democracy and human rights across countries and over time. The chapter discusses the structural (or economic), rational (or self-interested) and cultural (or ideational) explanations for patterns in democratization and the variation in human rights protection. In other words, the chapter examines the degree to which economic development (and the broad sets of social changes that it entails), the interplay of power politics (at the national and international level) and the appeal and construction of ideas explain why democracy comes about, how it can be sustained and why human rights are better protected in some parts of the world than others.

While Chapter 5 looked at the broad explanations for the patterns in democracy and human rights, Chapter 6 focuses on how people and states (also known as **agents**) seek to bring about democracy, build democratic institutions and **advocate** for the promotion and protection of human rights. Such agents include domestic elites in government and opposition, international actors such as the United States and the European Union, as well as the relative power and impact of networks of non-governmental organizations (NGOs) fighting for human rights and justice. These so-called transnational advocacy networks (Risse et al. 1999) connect agents at the domestic level who confront their regimes to international actors that put pressure on those regimes to bring about reform. Over time, it is possible to say that the appeal of democracy and human rights has been 'socially constructed', or built out of a long series of interactions that combine the rational pursuit of material self-interest and the normative values associated with the promotion and protection of human dignity.

The process of democratic transition and the construction of institutions for the guarantee of human rights in many countries carry with them the need to confront the atrocities of the past. Authoritarian governments commit crimes against humanity as part of their overall strategies to maintain stability, security and control over their societies. Their atrocities include the use of arbitrary detention, torture, 'disappearance', exile and assassination. In countries that have emerged from prolonged periods of civil conflict (as in Peru between 1980 and 2000) or foreign occupation (as in East Timor), similar such atrocities have been committed. In over 30 transitional and post-authoritarian countries, there have been formal institutions, commissions or other bodies that have sought to capture the 'truth' about past wrongs as a means to bring about democratic longevity and respect for human rights. Chapter 7 shows that the focus on the past, memory work and truth commissions has sought public recognition of atrocities that were committed and justice and reconciliation for the victims and their families. But the chapter also shows that the verdict after many years of such bodies carrying out their different mandates is that we now have much more truth about what has happened (e.g. under Augusto Pinochet in Chile, under Apartheid in South Africa and during the conflict in Peru) than real justice for the victims. But great lessons have been learnt and the constraints of democracy and human rights continue to be seen as suitable political and legal solutions to move countries forward.

Despite the advance of democracy and human rights charted in the first chapters of the book, there remain significant **threats** and **pitfalls** to their long-term sustainability. Chapter 8 argues that these can be understood in the following four groups: (1) inter-state and intra-state conflict, (2) economic globalization and inequality, (3) global terrorism and its response and (4) environmental degradation and climate change. Democracy and the protection of human rights (as well as the international connections that result) are generally good for reducing international and domestic conflict, but war between and within states can and does break out in ways that can destroy democracy and lead to gross human rights violations. Prolonged and deeply embedded patterns of land and income inequality have a negative relationship with the protection of certain human rights. The threat from terrorism and its response in the twenty-first century continue to undermine the very rights commitments that were the hallmarks of the twentieth century. Finally, the challenge of sustainable development is at the forefront of policymakers' minds as the world finds ways in which to increase economic abundance and raise overall levels of welfare without long-term adverse effects on the environment, while a large proportion of the world continues to be vulnerable to environmental change.

A popular refrain in political discussions is 'so what?' 'What are the benefits and positive outcomes associated with democracy and human rights?' Chapter 9 explores the idea and burning question as to whether democracies and 'rights-protective' regimes, to use a phrase from Jack Donnelly, actually deliver tangible benefits to the people. It examines the benefits that are intrinsic to democracy and the value for individuals living under democratic conditions. It looks at the 'pacific' benefits of democracy at the international and domestic levels of conflict prevention. Drawing primarily on the development literature, the chapter shows that democracies are no worse at pursuing economic development, actually enhance the human-related dimensions of sustainable development and provide a set of institutions that are best equipped to guarantee the protection of human rights.

Chapter 10 concludes with a survey and summary of the main points of the book and maps out the both the **hopes** about and **challenges** for the future, taking into account the demographic shifts in different parts of the world, the continuing problem of religious extremism, discrimination, ethnic and other violence, as well as the many social, political institutions that remain weak in the world. Taken together, I hope the chapters in this book will allow you to think critically about developments in the world with respect to democracy and human rights so that the next time you fly into a capital city and try to get a feel ofyour surroundings, you will have a deeper understanding of the precariousness of the human conditions but also the remarkable ways in which we have sought to struggle for better systems of governance that at their heart have a genuine concern for human dignity.

SUGGESTED READING

Dahl, Robert (2000) *On Democracy*. New Haven: Yale University Press.
Diamond, Larry (2009) *The Spirit of Democracy: The Struggle to Build Free Societies in the World*. New York: Holt and Rinehart.

Notes

1 These and other macro-economic indicators formed part of a keynote presentation by the Minister of Finance of Mexico Ernesto Cordero at the London School of Economics on 21 March 2011.

2 Data released by the government and published by the Guardian newspaper in the United Kingdom suggest that the total killed between 2006 and 2010 is more than 31,000, but the figure may be even higher as these killings are only those that can be documented, while many others remain unreported.

CHAPTER TWO

Abundance and freedom

Introduction

The 'Arab Revolutions' of 2011 have reopened a set of age-old questions about economic and political modernization. These questions centre on the relative complementarity between economic abundance and political freedom. Are the richest countries in the world also the most politically free? Are they politically free because they have economic abundance? Or are they rich because they are politically free? If the rich democracies of the world got there in following a certain path, is that path still available for other countries? Are there alternative pathways to economic abundance that do not involve political freedom? Has the global spread of democracy since the 1970s brought with it greater economic abundance? Do Singapore and China offer examples of successful economic development in the absence of political freedom? Or do the development models being followed by democratic Brazil and India offer better examples? Do certain phases of capitalist development require authoritarian rule? Does it make sense to say that some countries are not yet rich enough to embrace democracy? These and related questions are key to understanding developments in the world today and are likely to captivate the public imagination for many years to come, particularly after the financial crisis of 2007 and all that is has brought with it, as well as the dramatic re-emergence of democracy on the global political agenda since the Arab Spring.

The correlates of democracy

The first set of answers to these key questions emerged in the late 1950s as scholars started to look at systematic evidence that compared levels of economic wealth and the type of regime. Those that looked at many countries at once sought to collect data on a range of economic indicators that were meant to measure economic wealth (such as rates of urbanization, paved roads, electricity, newspaper circulation, etc.) and then compared them across different kinds of government. The most famous study of this kind was conducted by Seymour Martin Lipset (1959) and was framed with a simple question: 'are wealthy countries more democratic?' He compared economic indicators across what he called 'stable democracies', 'unstable democracies', 'unstable dictatorships' and 'stable dictatorships'. He found that his collection of 'stable democracies' had on average higher values across his collection of indicators than any of his other regime types. He concluded from this evidence that 'the more "well-to-do" a nation, the more likely it will be to sustain democracy'. Using data from the contemporary world, his basic insights can be demonstrated easily. Figure 2.1 is a plot between democracy (on the vertical axis) and development (on the horizontal axis) in which it is clear that those countries with higher levels of development (measured here in terms of per capita GDP) are indeed those countries with higher scores for democracy (measured here in terms of the presence of basic democratic institutions).[1]

While his comparisons (and those illustrated in Figure 2.1) presented compelling evidence for a positive relationship between economic abundance

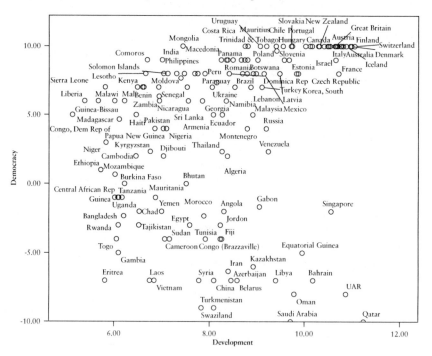

FIGURE 2.1 *Development and democracy.*

Sources: Mean combined democracy score from Polity IV data for 2007–2009; natural log of mean per capita GDP from the World Bank 2007–2009.

and political freedom, many questions remained, since his findings said nothing about whether this relationship is causal or in which direction that it goes. In other words, does development cause democracy or does democracy cause development? Many commentators thought that he had made a causal claim, while many others thought he had not. Lipset himself published a follow-up article in 1994 and argued that he never meant to make a causal argument. Nevertheless, academic research and policy prescriptions that built on his early work often assumed that he had made a causal argument and then sought ways of refining his analysis or setting out policy objectives that made a direct link between economic abundance and political freedom. Using different definitions of democracy (see Chapter 3) and different ways of measuring democracy and development, there are two competing views about the causal relationship. The first argues that Lipset was broadly correct and that the types of large-scale social changes that accompany economic development lead to democratization (see, e.g. Boix 2003; Boix and Stokes 2003). The second argues that any positive and statistically significant relationship between levels of economic development and democracy comes from the fact that when countries make a transition to democracy under conditions of relatively high economic development, then they tend to remain democratic (see e.g. Przeworski et al. 2000). These are fundamentally different claims. One claims that development causes democracy while the other claims that development sustains democracy once it has been established. The proponents of each view claim to have settled the question with statistical evidence, but like all analyses, the results depend very much on how things are defined and measured. The debate thus continues.

But Lipset's work also inspired another line of research that examined the economic benefits of democracy. Here, analysis flips the causal question around and asks if democracy is good for economic development. The idea here is that the democratic institutions reflect and respond to citizen preferences and make leaders accountable for their economic decisions, and thus key feature of economic development ought to be better realized through democracy than through non-democracy. Indeed, the United Nations has long advocated that democracy is the better political system for realizing the Millennium Development Goals; a set of measurable goals with eight targets that ought to be met by 2015. The answers to this question, like those above, vary depending on what is meant by economic development. In terms of annual changes in Gross Domestic Product, it appears that democracies are no better than non-democracies in promoting economic growth (see e.g. Przeworski et al. 2000). **But they are no worse either.** When different indicators of development are used, such as the distribution of income and human development (itself a combination of per capita GDP, life expectancy and literacy), democracies perform much better than non-democracies, and among the world's poorest countries, democracies outperform non-democracies (Halperin, Seigle and Weinstein 2010; and see Chapter 9). In

Development as Freedom, Amartya Sen (1999) claims 'No famine has ever taken place in the history of the world in a functioning democracy'. Since democracies are based on the accountability of leaders through the electoral process and other institutions, Sen argues, it is not possible for leaders to ignore the plight of their population to the point where people are actually starving. At a more general level, it is possible to see the positive association between democracy and human development (see Figure 2.2).[2] On balance, the figure shows that those countries with higher levels of democracy have higher levels of human development. In addition to these kinds of positive benefits relating to different features of development that go beyond mere consideration of growth rates, democracy also brings other benefits, such as greater freedom, protection of human rights (see Chapter 3) and accountability of government. Democracy thus offers a collection of 'goods' that make it a preferable political system even if other systems have shown higher rates of economic growth.[3]

But these different sets of findings have led to a range of expectations that are based on, in my view, a false equivalence between democracy and development, or abundance and freedom. On the one hand, there is an expectation that abundance will necessarily lead to freedom and on the other hand, there is the expectation that once freedom has been obtained

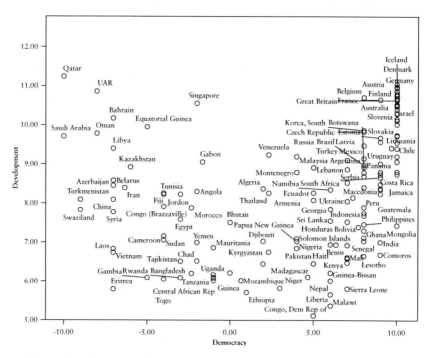

FIGURE 2.2 *Democracy and development.*

Sources: Mean combined democracy score from Polity IV data for 2007–2009; human development index (per capita GDP, litereacy, life expectancy), UNDP.

abundance will follow shortly thereafter. For many states in the developed world, investment in economic development that carried with it the promise of political modernization and democratization was a very attractive way of conducting foreign policy and overseas aid strategies. From John F. Kennedy's 'Alliance for Progress' in Latin America in the 1960s to current aid strategies, there is an in-built assumption that economic modernization breeds democracy and thus 'pumping' money into less developed countries has a good chance of encouraging democracy.[4] Indeed, in the context of the Cold War, such a strategy was seen as a way to avoid 'any more Cubas' and subsequently as a way to encourage democracy in the Soviet Bloc and satellite countries. For some, the logical extension of this 'modernization' perspective is that not only do such strategies yield democracy, but **they can be accelerated** through either the 'export' of democracy, as it was understood by the Reagan Administration in the 1980s, or the **forceful imposition** of democracy through foreign invasion as understood by George W. Bush and his neo-conservative advisors between 2000 and 2008, such as Donald Rumsfeld, Dick Cheney and Paul Wolfowitz. Interestingly, this latter position on the forceful imposition of democracy supported by neoconservatives is based on the early modernization logic of Lipset and on the belief that particular outcomes can be 'socially engineered' (see Fukuyama 2006).

The modernization logic, as forceful as it is, is subject to a number of remarkable exceptions. Indeed, at precisely the time modernization theory was being articulated, a number of countries in Latin America that had reached particular phases of capitalist development experienced profound democratic breakdown. In 1964, Brazilian democracy was overthrown by the military, which ushered in a period of authoritarian rule that lasted until 1989. In 1966 and again in 1976, the military in Argentina ousted its democratic leaders and oversaw two brutal periods of authoritarian rule. The latter period lasted from 1976 until 1983 and featured the infamous 'Dirty War' that led to thousands of people 'disappearing'. The militaries in Uruguay and Chile overthrew their democracies in 1973, where authoritarian rule as in the other cases led to large-scale human rights violations and subsequent international condemnation. A popular argument at the time was that these military coups were part of the modernization process and that particular phases of capitalist development 'required' authoritarian rule to oversee the developmental process (see O'Donnell 1973). Modernization, it would seem, did not necessarily lead to democracy in every case.

The idea that different modes of capitalist development required particular regime types also influenced policy in the 1980s and 1990s in the era of World Bank and IMF 'structural adjustment' programmes (economic models that sought to allocate good and services primarily through price mechanisms). Based on a series of comparative studies that examined the relative economic success of the 'East Asian Tigers', the World Bank and IMF became convinced that export-led growth (i.e. the export of finished capital goods such as cars, household appliances, electronics, etc.) was both desirable for long-term economic development and that it required some form of labour control or repression (see Geddes 1990; Brohman 1996; Stiglitz 2002). Indeed, many of the Tigers were not democratic and a combination of state control and coordinated development of the export capacity had produced remarkable growth rates. One long-term consequence of this experience, it could be argued, is that authoritarian states today such as China can claim that they are in the middle of precisely such a phase of development and not yet ready for democracy. In contrast, Brazil and India are democracies and 'emerging economies' that are in the middle of a period of impressive economic growth that challenges this authoritarian view.

Another consequence of the analysis of the relationship between abundance and freedom is that there is some sort of 'threshold' of development after which the survival of democracy is nearly 100 per cent guaranteed. In rejecting the notion that development necessarily leads to democracy, Przeworski et al. (2000) nevertheless conclude that such a threshold exists and that it is possible to put a value on it. For the global data that they analysed, if democracy is established in a country that has a level of per capita GDP greater than $5,500 (as measured in 1995), then the probability of democracy collapsing in that country is very close to zero. In other words, new democracies in rich countries have a greater chance of survival than in poor countries. The idea that greater economic abundance provides governments with latitude to supply goods, services and the benefits of economic development to potential opposition makes sense; particularly, if one has an instrumental view of politics and political power. Elected elites have won power and will distribute economic benefits to stay in power through the electoral process. If opposition groups receive enough economic benefit from such elites, then the motivation to disrupt democracy is low, and democracy survives. Such narrowly constructed arguments in the political economy of democracy have been very popular in accounting for its survival (see Przeworski 1991; Bates 2001; Bueno de Mesquita et al. 2003; Bueno de Mesquita 2010).

But many countries in the world have established democracy under economic conditions that are well below this threshold figure of $5,500 per capita GDP. Indeed, the beginning of this book provided a short summary of the case of Mongolia, which at the time of its transition had a per capita GDP of less than $1,000. Recall that the argument is not that democracy cannot be established in poor countries but that the probability of survival is much lower for poor democracies. For the Mongolians and on this reading, democracy was a precarious venture since the economic conditions for survival were not in place. But democracy did survive as it has done in many other countries that have made democratic transitions under such conditions of economic scarcity, where per capita GDP figures are unlikely to reach the threshold values for some time to come. The fact that these democracies have survived does not discredit the argument from Przeworski et al. (2000), but it does give hope to those poor democracies struggling to develop and maintain their democratic institutions. It is thus important to recognize that democracy can survive in poor countries and that democracy does not need to wait for high levels of development.

There is one final consequence of the assumed affinity between abundance and freedom that involves the raised expectations about the speed with which democracy can deliver greater economic benefits. We saw above that democracy does deliver better developmental outcomes, but many in new democracies expect these to take place rather more quickly than they do in practice. Citizens are eager for change and expect higher levels of economic development and fairer distribution of the benefits of development. The simple causal link between development and democracy, which often ignores complex sets of intervening factors, can ultimately threaten the process of democratic consolidation if citizens expect too much of their new democracy. This is particularly the case if the lack of economic performance or a slow pace in economic growth during the new democratic period leads to a certain nostalgia for earlier periods of economic prosperity under conditions of non-democratic rule (see Landman 1999: 626). Such cases of 'democratic disillusionment' are not rare. In Eastern Europe and the Former Soviet Union, mass publics in some countries showed disenchantment with democracy as economic liberalization in the absence of regulation became associated with market distortions, speculation, corruption and new inequalities that undermined basic standards of living. Supermarkets with a narrow selection of goods during the Communist period gave way in some countries to low availability of any goods during the new democratic period. Such scarcity, if prolonged, can lead to increased levels of political support for former communist leaders, new nationalists and other authoritarian actors. In the late 1990s, analysis conducted by Marta Lagos (1997) showed that Latin American mass publics were indeed disenchanted with democracy. Measures of 'satisfaction with democracy' were as low as 11 per cent in Mexico (itself undergoing a prolonged period of democratic transition) to high of only 52 per cent in Uruguay, which by that time had been democratic for over 10 years. She subsequently showed (Lagos 2003) that between 1996 and 2002, satisfaction with democracy in the region peaked in 2000 at 37 per cent and declined by a few percentage points in the ensuing years.

But democratic satisfaction is not low only in Latin America. Figure 2.3 shows mass public support for democracy 'as an idea' and satisfaction with democracy as a system that delivers goods and benefits to the public. The differences between the two are striking as across the world support for democracy is consistently higher than satisfaction with democracy, while across the different regions it is apparent that there is great variation in both measures. Support for democracy is highest in the European Union at nearly 80 per cent, but satisfaction is only 53 per cent. For Africa, support is less that in the European Union but satisfaction is higher at 58 per cent. The difference between support and satisfaction is the least for East Asia at 61 per cent and 55 per cent respectively. For India, Eastern Europe and

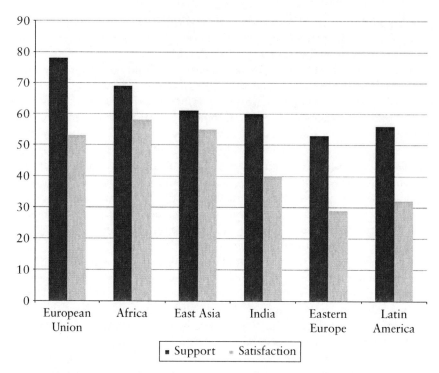

FIGURE 2.3 *Support for and satisfaction with democracy by region, 1998–2002.*
Source: Lagos (2003).

Latin America, the differences between support and satisfaction are large, where satisfaction is the lowest in Eastern Europe at just 29 per cent.One reading of these figures suggests that despite the advance of democracy and despite different levels of economic development, democracy receives mixed reviews as an idea and as a system for delivery of benefits, which is consistent with the idea that too much expectation about what democracy can deliver may lead to popular dissatisfaction. Another reading suggests that despite geographical and economic position, democracy receives levels of public support greater than 50 per cent worldwide and that democracies themselves have a lot of work to do to improve levels of satisfaction. Both readings are consistent with the main argument of this book about the inherent appeal of democracy.

Political actors and political processes

If the natural affinity between abundance and freedom (or development and democracy) is upheld at the global statistical level, there are certainly enough regional and single-country exceptions that suggest we need to look more closely at other factors that may play an intervening role, such as political actors, processes, structures and institutions. Analysis of these kinds of features have typically been conducted on smaller sets of countries and have focused more on the **evolution of processes** over time and **pathways** followed by different groups of countries. In such studies, economic development is seen as an external factor that drives other changes and characteristics within countries, such as the emergence of new social classes and the conflicts or alliances that form between them; the power and stability of the state domestically and how it is affected by international factors; and the ways in which new social groups find representation and inclusion in new political institutions. Since socio-economic development differs across a different array of what economists call 'factor endowments' (i.e. the relative distribution of land, labour and capital), different paths to modernity are possible that may not necessarily include democracy. Dependencies on small sets of factor endowments can create oligarchies with vested interests (e.g. in agriculture or industry) whose political interests may not favour democratization. Industrializing countries generate large urban working classes that can mobilize for inclusion and challenge existing power structure that in certain cases lead to democratization, while in others some form of clampdown, co-optation or authoritarian control. The state apparatus, originally seen as an **organic** result of modernization and a way to raise taxes for maintaining stability and security, can be 'captured' by different vested interests that vary in the degree to which they are supportive of democracy. These and other intervening factors that lie between economic development and political regimes suggest that democracy is but one possible outcome and not the only outcome despite the compelling arguments found in the modernization school.[5]

In *Industrialization and Democracy*, de Schweinitz (1964) compared the cases of Britain, the United States, Germany and Russia and found that the 'stable' outcomes in Britain and the United States (i.e. democracy) were largely owing to a set of unique features in those countries that were not available to Germany and Russia, which were considered 'unstable' and 'not democratic', respectively. While he concluded that the 'Euro-American' route to democracy was likely to be closed, there certainly remains open the possibility for other paths to democracy. In *The Social Origins of Dictatorship and Democracy*, Barrington Moore (1966) compared 'routes to modernity' in countries that had bourgeois revolutions (France, Britain and the United States), communist revolutions (Russia and China) and fascist revolutions (Germany, Italy and Japan) to show that particular configurations of features in these cases (such as class alliances and the role of violence) were associated with the political outcomes that were obtained. His conclusion that some sort of 'violent break' from the past was a key factor in bringing about democracy was subsequently challenged by Rueschemeyer et al. (1992), who looked at a much larger collection of countries to examine the relationship between capitalist development and democracy. Like their predecessors, their analysis focused on configurations of factors (such as the state, the nature of development, the relationships and alliances between different social groups and relative political power of different interests) and concluded that there is not an automatic association between economic development and democracy. Rather, capitalist development is varied according to initial factor endowments and that emergent groups capture the state and or demand inclusion in the national political system differently and thus affect the possibility, timing and pace of democratization.

As we shall see in Chapter 5, popular explanations for the emergence of democracy also focus on the role the political actors play in choosing and 'crafting' democracy (DiPalma 1992). Such choice-based frameworks focus on the elites within the authoritarian regime and the elites within the opposition. The analysis is confined to a range of choices open to these elites in ways that allow them to reach significant political accommodation in moving their society towards democracy. But like the comparative studies outlined above, the analysis of elites often reveals that democracy is but one outcome among many available and that a specific set of choices across cases has been taken that has yielded an initial commitment to democracy. For such studies, democracy is a fairly narrow but stable outcome based on the idea of the 'institutionalization of uncertainty' (Przeworski 1991), where elites play the game of democracy without knowing the outcomes of electoral competition but with the knowledge that they may be successful in obtaining power in the future. The promise of power is enough to buy allegiance to the new rules of the game and that with time, democracy becomes 'the only game in town' (Linz and Stepan 1996). Such a narrow view of democracy and a narrow focus on elites allow for a more precise set of analyses on interests, choices and relative power. It also includes the possibility that democracy will not come about, or that it could be reversed at a later date; something popular explanations often exclude. But such a focus also tends to exclude attention to masses, social movements and popular mobilization for democracy that has characterized many democratic transitions since the third wave in the 1970s. Any discussion of democratization ought to consider both the so-called bottom-up processes and top-down processes to provide a fuller account of what has happened and how.

Examining the 'outliers'

The discussion of actors and processes complements our discussion of the overall relationship between development and democracy. In many ways, such a focus seeks to get inside the 'black box' of modernization and look at the different ways in which processes of development affect different groups, how groups create and/or respond to different sets of incentives and how democracy is but one outcome out of many possible outcomes for the ways in which a society will be governed. Now, if we revisit the relationship depicted in Figure 2.1 and focus on the Arab world, we discover a selection

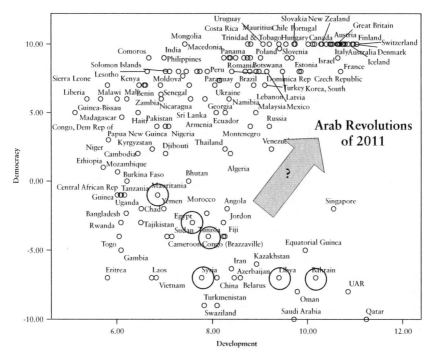

FIGURE 2.4 *Development and democracy revisited.*

Sources: Mean combined democracy score from Polity IV data for 2007–2009; natural log of mean per capita GDP from the World Bank 2007–2009.

of countries that are relatively wealthy (certainly in the top half on the scale of development) and yet not at all democratic. Such exceptions to a general rule are referred to as 'outliers' (a term made popular by Macolm Gladwell in a book by the same name) and challenge us to think of explanations for the exceptional position. It also allows us to consider the broader questions posed in this chapter alongside the question about actors and processes. Figure 2.4 reproduces the relationship from Figure 2.1 but highlights these outlier cases, such as Egypt, Tunisia, Libya, Syria, Bahrain and Yemen. These countries all experienced significant challenges to their governments from popular protests and rebel movements, and in the case of Libya, military action from the North Atlantic Treaty Organization (NATO). As outlier countries, analysts tend to see them as paradox cases of democratization. On the one hand, they have high levels of economic development (measured in terms of per capita GDP) and yet they have had prolonged periods of authoritarian rule where dissent has not been tolerated. It is clear that many of them enjoy vast sources of wealth based on their rich oil and natural gas deposits. The natural resources, however, tend to be highly concentrated within particular regions of these countries and controlled by a very small percentage of the population. Moreover, tribal and clan groupings have based their power on these resources and have relied on the strong arm of the state to maintain stability and authority.

But across many of the cases, the events of early 2011 started as economic critiques of a model of development that is highly dependent on a concentrated set of natural resources and then evolved into a broader political critique and demand for basic freedoms (see Foweraker and Landman 1997). It is not clear whether these movements and political transformations are analogous to the movements that shook Eastern Europe in 1989, but it is fairly clear that it will be impossible for these countries to revert back to the **status quo ante** (see Carothers 2011). The Ben Ali regime in Tunisia and the Mubarak regime in Egypt have been ousted in relatively rapid fashion. Events in Egypt ushered in a political process that includes presidential elections in November 2011 and a number of associated political reforms. Based on what we do know about development and democracy outlined in this chapter, if democracy does become established in many of these cases, then the material conditions for its survival are already present. The key challenge will be the democratization of economies that are so highly dependent on one or two major exports, and the emergence of new forms of political representation that are less reliant on tribal links and traditional clans. This is not to say that there is some 'western' route to democracy, but as we shall see in the next chapter, democracy is founded on the fundamental principles of popular sovereignty and collective decision-making that is inclusive, participatory and accountable. The route to such an outcome is not predetermined but will be crafted by those who seek a different form of political regime supported by a level of economic abundance that bodes well for democracy.

Summary and implications

The simple association between abundance and freedom, whether through an intuitive sense about how the world 'works' or through the examination of comparative data has captured the imagination of scholars, commentators and policymakers for many years. But as I have shown in this chapter, the relationship is not as simple as it seems. There are large questions about whether the relationship is directly causal, indirectly causal or mutually reinforcing, and it is clear that it leads to a number of raised expectations about likely outcomes if one or the other changes dramatically. For me, the two **are** associated to the degree that higher levels of economic wealth provide governments with a resource base that allows them to deliver public goods to their populations, but that the impulse for democracy comes from much more than a simple set of underlying socio-economic changes that somehow culminate in democracy. The evidence presented that democracy survives if it is established in a wealthy country is very convincing and logical. It has been equally clear that not only are there many routes to democracy but that democracy itself is one of many possible outcomes.

The chapter has also shown that democracy tends to be a system that provides a better quality of development. It is a political system that is **no worse** than non-democracy in delivering economic growth, but it is markedly better across a broader set of macro-economic indicators that measure **human** development and inequality. Development does not require a period of authoritarianism to ready a society for democracy, and there are numerous examples of democracy having been established and having survived in poor countries. But such poor democracies may well have a number of additional challenges in maintaining their democratic institutions over the long run since resources are relatively scarce and the possibility of satisfying potential democratic 'spoilers' is much lower. We have also seen that beyond development, democracy brings with it other benefits, including a greater protection of human rights, a reduction in state violence such as genocide and or 'politicide' and even less violence with other countries.

The discussion presented in this chapter focused on abundance and freedom and left open the question of what constitutes democracy. The chapter did not define the concept but rather focused on its relationship with patterns of economic development. The next chapter sets out to define democracy and human rights and examines the conceptual and empirical relationship between the two.

SUGGESTIONS FOR FURTHER READING

Diamidis, Peter H. (2012) *Abundance: The Future is Better Than You Think.* New York: Free Press.
Lipset, Seymour Martin (1960) *Political Man: The Social Bases of Politics.* New York: Anchor Books.
Norris, Pippa (2011) *Making Democratic Governance Work: The Impact of Regimes on Prosperity, Welfare and Peace.* Cambridge: Cambridge University Press.

Notes

1　Statistically, the relationship is positive and significant (Pearson's $r = .295$; $p < .001$), which means that wealthier countries tend to be more democratic and that if we collected the same data on the same sample of countries at a different point in time, then we would be more than 99 per cent certain that a similar positive relationship would be found.

2　As in the relationship depicted in Figure 2.1, the relationship depicted in Figure 2.2 is positive and statistically significant (Pearson's $r = .357$; $p < .001$). But this relationship is somewhat stronger than the one depicted in Figure 2.1.

3 Even the evidence that non-democratic governments are better at overseeing economic growth has been challenged on the grounds that democracies survive economic downturns, while many authoritarian states do not, and thus on aggregate, average levels of growth will be lower for democracies than for non-democracies (see Przeworski and Limongi 1997).

4 For an overly optimistic view about the natural association between economic development and democracy, see Singer (1997); and for a brilliant and insightful critique of policies based on this assumption, see Cammack (1997).

5 **Foreign Affairs** has a resource on The Modernization School, see http://www.foreignaffairs.com/features/readinglists/what-to-read-on-modernization-theory.

CHAPTER THREE

Democracy and human rights

Introduction

The twin ideas of democracy and human rights that frame this book have long histories. Democracy has its origins in Ancient Greece and since then has been a relatively **rare** and **recent** form of political rule (see Finer 1997) compared to other political systems that have characterized the history of the world, such as monarchy, oligarchy and authoritarianism. Despite its growth in popularity (see Chapters 1 and 4 in this volume), however, as an idea, it remains an 'essentially contested concept' (Gallie 1956) and much debate continues over the definitions, components and meaning of the term democracy.[1] Certainly, the renewed attention to democracy in light of the events in the Middle East and North Africa will once again invite commentary on definitions and 'models' of democracy (Held 1996). Some have argued that human rights have an equally long history (see, e.g. Ishay 2004), but most scholars and practitioners see human rights as a modern 'construction' (e.g. Donnelly 1999) that developed out of the tradition of **citizenship rights** and was then universalized through a set of practices and agreements that have yielded the international system for the promotion and protection of human rights that we now have today.

The history of citizenship is one of a **struggle** for rights, as subjugated populations increasingly articulated their grievances in the language of rights and as modern states formed, rights became extended through law and enforcement mechanisms that provided greater legal protections to an increasingly wider range of rights concerns (see, e.g. Barbalet 1988; Foweraker and Landman 1997). The current system for the promotion and protection of human rights is thus an international version of rights that had long been grounded in the nation state, which are now seen as an inherent feature of all human beings **by virtue of them being human** (Donnelly 1989).

They thus transcend the nation state in terms of individual entitlement to an enjoyment of these rights wherever a person may find him or herself. But like democracy, the idea of human rights and its purported universality are still open to debate with respect to contested philosophical foundations for their existence (see Ingram 1994; Mendus 1995; Freeman 1994; Landman 2005b) and the different ways in which they are understood across different political contexts found in the world today.

Despite these different historical trajectories, there is much overlap between democracy and human rights, as both are grounded in shared principles of accountability, individual integrity, fair and equal representation, inclusion and participation and non-violent solutions to conflict. This chapter provides different definitions of democracy, outlines and discusses the wide range of contemporary human rights and explores the linkages between democracy and human rights both in theory and in practice. What we shall see is that democracy and human rights are highly complementary to one another, but **they are not equivalent** and they are not are perfect substitutes. Rather, each of the concepts retains its own set of core features while also exhibiting certain shared features. It will also be made clear that there are certain tensions between democracy and human rights, which reside in conflicting principles upon which they are founded and the pragmatic ways in which they are realized, as well as the kinds of politics that they make possible.

'Thick' and 'thin' definitions of democracy

As outlined above, democracy is arguably the oldest concept of the two under consideration here and it was first formulated in the work of Aristotle, whose notion of 'polity' most closely matches the modern conception of democracy used today. While polity refers to the 'good' form of **rule by the many**[2], modern conceptions of democracy are based on the fundamental ideas of **popular sovereignty** and **collective decision-making** in which rulers are in some way held to account by those over whom they rule. But beyond this basic consensus on what is otherwise a highly contested concept, there are many variations of democracy, or 'democracy with adjectives' (Collier and Levitsky 1997) that have been in use by scholars, practitioners and policymakers. These definitions can be grouped broadly into (1) procedural democracy, (2) liberal democracy and (3) social democracy, the delineation of which largely rests on the variable incorporation of different rights protection alongside the general commitment to popular sovereignty and collective decision-making.

Procedural democracy

Procedural definitions of democracy draw on the seminal work of Robert Dahl (1971) in *Polyarchy* and include two dimensions of **contestation** and

Table 3.1 Procedural democracy

Contestation (uncertain peaceful competition)		Participation (popular sovereignty)	
Legitimacy of opposition	Right to challenge incumbents	Universal suffrage	Right to vote
Freedom of expression	Free and fair elections		
Freedom of association	Consolidated party system		

participation. Contestation captures the **uncertain peaceful competition** necessary for democratic rule; a principle which presumes the legitimacy of a significant and organized opposition, the right to challenge incumbents, protection of the twin freedoms of expression and association, the existence of free and fair elections and a consolidated political party system. In reference to some of the discussions in the previous chapter, this idea alone has motivated much foreign and aid policy in ways that have led to the 'electoral fallacy', or the over-enthusiasm among certain policymakers for the existence of successive elections as a key indicator for the existence of stable democracy. **Participation,** on the other hand, captures the idea of **popular sovereignty,** which presumes the protection of the right to vote as well as the existence of universal suffrage, or that principle that enshrines the right of participation in the democratic process to all within a country's jurisdiction regardless of social categories, such as race, religion, ethnicity, gender, sexual orientation, etc.[3] The history of suffrage suggests that this is a right that has been the result of long and widespread **social struggle** as mentioned above, at least among Western democracies, while new democracies have enshrined, at least formally, universal suffrage in their new (or resurrected) constitutions during their own moments of transition.[4] Table 3.1 summarizes this definition and its components. Such a procedural definition of democracy can be considered a baseline set of conditions and lower threshold that can be used to assess and enumerate democracy in the world. Indeed, the figure depicting the growth of democracy in the Chapter 1 (see Figure 1.1) is based on this more narrow conception of democracy for determining the scores used to count the number and percentage of democracies in the world.

Liberal democracy

Liberal definitions of democracy preserve the notions of contestation and participation found in procedural definitions, but add more explicit references to the protection of certain human rights. As outlined above, these rights were traditionally understood as citizenship rights, but with the advent of the contemporary international law and practice they have become largely understood as *human rights* (see below). Definitions of liberal democracy thus contain an **institutional** dimension and a **rights** dimension (see Foweraker and Krznaric 2000). The institutional dimension captures the idea of popular sovereignty and includes notions of accountability, constraint of leaders, representation of citizens and universal participation in ways that are consistent with Dahl's 'polyarchy' model outlined above. The rights dimension is upheld by the **rule of law** and includes civil, political, property and minority rights. The protection of these rights provides a particular set of guarantees that guard against the threat of a 'tyranny of the majority' and have their provenance in the 1776 American Declaration of Independence and the 1789 French Declaration of the Rights of Man and the Citizen. Table 3.2 summarizes this definition of democracy. Such a definition is arguably richer (or thicker) as it includes legal constraints on the exercise of power to complement the popular elements in the derivation of and accountability for power. For liberal definitions, popular sovereignty and collective decision-making are simply not enough as outcomes under such a system can undermine the rights of individuals and groups. And we shall see later on in this chapter that many new democracies have been relatively successful in establishing procedural democracy, but have struggled to guarantee the kinds of rights that constitute the liberal definition.

Scholars such as Larry Diamond (1999) and Fareed Zakaria (2007) have written extensively about this 'gap' between the institutional and rights dimensions that characterize the new democracies that have emerged since the late 1970s. Indeed, Zakaria calls such a state of affairs 'illiberal democracy', but what is interesting is that if one looks closely at the collection of so-called 'advanced democracies', especially since the advent of the 2001 'war on terror', there are also evident gaps between the institutional and rights dimension in these democracies as well. Across a wide selection of these democracies, we have seen the passage of anti-terror legislation that undermines many historic rights commitments relating to arbitrary detention, privacy and freedom of movement (see, e.g. Brysk and Shafir 2007), while the prosecutors of the war on terror have sought ways to reinterpret legal protections relating to such human rights as the

Table 3.2 Liberal democracy

Institutional dimension (popular sovereignty)		Rights dimension (rule of law)	
Accountability	Restraint	Civil rights	Property rights
Representation	Participation	Political rights	Minority rights

Adapted from Foweraker and Krznaric (2000).

right not be tortured, or other forms of cruel, degrading and inhumane treatment (see, e.g. Sands 2006).

Social democracy

Social definitions of democracy maintain the institutional and rights dimensions found in liberal models of democracy but expand the types of rights that ought to be protected, including social, economic and cultural rights (although some of these are included in minority rights protection seen in liberal definitions). Such an expanded form of democracy, as summarized in Table 3.3, includes the provision of social and economic welfare and the progressive realization of economic and social rights. It also includes the protection of cultural rights, which are concerned with such issues as mother tongue language, ceremonial land rights and intellectual property rights relating to cultural practices (e.g. indigenous healing practices and remedies that may be of interest to multinational companies). Conceptually, those advocating a pure liberal model of democracy argue that including such social dimensions mixes **intrinsic** and **extrinsic** features of democratic performance, since it is possible for non-democratic regimes to provide social and economic welfare as well as the realization of their associated rights. This has long been the argument of socialist regimes, particularly those of the former Soviet Union, the Communist countries of Eastern Europe and Cuba, as well as in the case of Venezuela under the Bolivarian Revolution of President Hugo Chavez. Proponents of human rights, on the other hand, argue that the sharp distinction between categories of rights is false, since the exercise of one category of rights is related to the other category of rights, and both sets are required for full experience of democratic rule. For example, access to health, education and welfare will have an impact on an individual's ability to participate in the democratic process through voting, acquiring and understanding political information and having the personal capacity and capabilities for critical engagement in the political system. Thus for a full experience of democracy, both sets of rights are required.

Beyond these conceptual and theoretical debates, which see social democracy as a 'type' that **ought** to include this fuller selection of rights protection and provision of social programmes and policy, we saw in the

Table 3.3 Social democracy

Institutional dimension (popular sovereignty)		Rights dimension (rule of law)	
Accountability	Restraint	Civil rights	Property rights
Representation	Participation	Political rights	Minority rights
		Economic rights	Social rights

previous chapter that empirical research on the benefits of democracy includes growth rates that are not worse than under non-democratic rule and patterns of human development that are much better. Moreover, Donnelly (1999) argues that in the relationship between development, democracy and human rights, European welfare states have come closest to the normative ideal of 'rights-protective' regimes, since the welfare system acts to alleviate the worst effects of market capitalism by providing a social safety net. Such an understanding of course has been significantly challenged in Europe since the 2007 financial crisis, as governments across the region have had to cut back on public expenditure in ways that have caused great pain for those most in need of the services expected from the welfare state. Cuts in such countries as Spain, Greece, Portugal, Ireland and the United Kingdom have affected public service workers, those in receipt of housing benefit, educational grants, child benefit and other services typically provided by the state.

The different models of democracy are summarized in Figure 3.1 as a series of concentric circles that capture the notion of ever-thickening definitions of democracy. A version of this figure has been used by the International Institute for Democracy and Electoral Assistance (IDEA), a 29-member state inter-governmental organization based in Sweden that helps build democracy

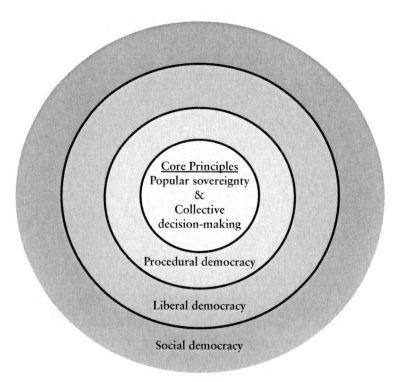

FIGURE 3.1 *Thin and thick definitions of democracy.*

around the world.[5] The figure should not be misunderstood as representing a causal ordering or chronology of democratic development. Rather, it should be seen as a way to represent the core features of democracy (popular sovereignty and collective decision-making) and the increasing overlap with various rights protections. The North American tradition of democracy tends to concentrate on the liberal model, while European and African countries tend to concentrate on the social model. Indeed, in Africa, and in particular, the African Union political discourse, there is great attention to the basket of economic, social and cultural rights as essential for democracy in the region. As we shall see below, the main human rights instrument in Africa is entitled the African Charter on Human and People's Rights, which signals this normative commitment to collective rights found within the social democratic model. Overall, it is important in any discussion of democracy to take account of these various definitions, which should serve as a general guide to the different ways in which democracy has been understood and how it will be understood in new democracies.

Human rights: Evolution and protection

While there is empirical support for the normative definition of social democracy, the previous section made it quite clear that there are still lines of demarcation between these different definitions of democracy that are a function of the **rights protection** that they include (see also Beetham 1999). But thus far, we have not defined human rights explicitly nor have we examined the expansion of human rights, the systems for their promotion and protection and the discourses that have diffused the idea of human rights around the world since the 1948 Universal Declaration of Human Rights. In their modern manifestation, human rights have become an accepted legal and normative standard through which to judge the quality of **human dignity** as it is experienced by over 7 billion people around the world in a multitude of very different social, economic and political contexts. This standard has arisen through the concerted efforts of thousands of people over many years inspired by a simple set of ideas that have become codified through the mechanism of public international law and realized through the domestic legal frameworks and governmental institutions of states around the world.

Human rights are **moral** claims accorded legal recognition and states are legally obliged to ensure that they **respect, protect** and **fulfil** these claims. Respecting human rights requires the state to refrain from violating them. Protecting human rights requires the state to prevent the violation of human rights by 'third' parties, such as private companies, non-governmental organizations, paramilitary and insurgency groups and 'uncivil' or undemocratic movements (see Payne 2000). Fulfilling human rights requires the states to invest in and implement policies for the progressive realization of human rights. As expressed in international law, they are 'specific norms that emerged from a political project' that commenced in the aftermath of World War I and gained traction as an immediate consequence of World War II (Nickel 2007: 7). The 1945 Charter of the United Nations endorsed the existence and necessity of human rights, and the international human rights regime that has emerged since is a 'deliberately constructed, partial international order' that consists primarily of states that establishes a set of norms prescribing the behaviour of those states that become its members (Hasenclever et al. 2000: 3). The regime focuses on holding governments accountable for their policies and practices that affect their citizens. The regime is wholly centred on ensuring the protection of human dignity and the prevention of its violation by states.

In order to realize these aims, the international human rights regime comprises formal institutions (UN and regional bodies) and informal ones (non-governmental organizations), which are involved in the processes of standard setting, monitoring and enforcement (Beetham 1999; Nowak 2003; Landman 2006a). Beginning with the Universal Declaration of Human Rights in 1948, the UN has developed the majority of international human rights standards that exist today and created a system of institutions to implement these standards and monitor their implementation. These institutions include bodies that have responsibility for each of the human rights treaties (known as 'treaty bodies'), 'charter' bodies who derive their authority directly from the UN Charter and specialized agencies, all of which are engaged in standard setting, monitoring and enforcement.

Regions have been involved in the development and implementation of human rights treaties that in many ways reflect their own historical and cultural contexts. Three regions of the world – Europe, the Americas and Africa – have set up human rights regimes with human rights standards and associated institutions. Europe has three regional mechanisms – the Council of Europe (COE), the European Union (EU) and the Organization for Security and Cooperation in Europe (OSCE) – which together forms an intricate, elaborate and expanding system of human rights protection in the region. The European Convention on Human Rights adopted in 1950 under the aegis of the Council of Europe provides individuals the right to appeal to the European Court of Human Rights once legal remedies are exhausted in their domestic jurisdiction. The OSCE has additional institutions that monitor different dimensions of human rights in Europe, while the European Union has a variety of policy instruments for the promotion of human rights, the most important of which include the Copenhagen criteria for membership of the European Union. The Inter-American system created by the Organization of American States (OAS) stands second only to the European system in terms of its spread and effectiveness with a body of law made by and applicable to those states that are party to the 1969 American Convention on Human Rights. It is the only system that allows for **in situ** visits by personnel from the regime to investigate human rights conditions.

The third regional human rights system is in Africa under the auspices of the African Union. Established by the African Charter on Human and Peoples' Rights in 1979, its recent developments include the establishment of an African Court of Human and People's Rights in 2006 to address individual complaints on violations of the Charter. While efforts to develop a regional human rights system in Asia are in their infancy, the League of Arab States has made considerable progress with the adoption of the 2004 Arab Charter on Human Rights, which came into force in 2008.

Human rights: Definition and content

The content of human rights as established in international law is dependent on the creation and adoption of legal standards by states, which allow the human rights community to hold states accountable for those actions that violate the dignity of individuals residing within their jurisdictions. The International Bill of Rights – the 1948 Universal Declaration of Human Rights (UDHR), the 1966 International Covenant on Civil and Political Rights (ICCPR) and the 1966 International Covenant on Economic, Social and Cultural Rights (ICESCR) – and the 1984 Convention against Torture (CAT) highlight the legal protections that individuals can claim from the state. The two Covenants also reflect the most commonly accepted categorization of human rights: (a) civil and political rights, (b) economic, social and cultural rights and (c) solidarity rights.

As we saw above, the first two categories form part of the different definitions democracy. But what do these different categories of rights mean? Civil and political rights protect the 'personhood' of individuals and their ability to participate in the public activities of their countries. Economic, social and cultural rights provide individuals with access to economic resources, social opportunities for growth and the enjoyment of their distinct ways of life, as well as protection from the arbitrary loss of these rights. Solidarity rights seek to guarantee for individuals access to public goods like development and the environment, and some have begun to argue, the benefits of global economic development (Freeman 2002; Landman 2006a). This categorization loosely follows a temporal frame; since we saw earlier that human rights can be seen as the consequence of struggles of peoples against oppression and injustice, successive generations of people have fought for distinct 'generations of rights' with civil and political rights comprising the first generation, economic, social and cultural rights making up the second generation, and solidarity rights, the third. While such a history in the struggle for rights has been well documented, the division of rights in this way is no longer part of the international discourse on human rights. Rather, the international community speaks of human rights as equal, indivisible, interrelated and interdependent, where the enjoyment and implementation of one set of rights are inextricably linked to the fulfilment of the other rights (Boyle 1995; Alfredsson and Eide 1999; Donnelly 1999; Freeman 2002).

Beyond the International Bill of Rights and the Convention against Torture, a second set of treaties protects the rights of individuals who by virtue of being members of a particular group or possessing certain characteristics may be particularly vulnerable to rights violations. The 1966 International Convention on the Elimination of all Forms of Racial Discrimination (CERD) addresses all forms of racial discrimination, the 1989 Convention on the Rights of the Child (CRC) specifies the legal protections to be given to the rights of children and the obligations accrued to the state to uphold these rights and the 1979 Convention on the Elimination of Discrimination against Women (CEDAW) highlights the rights of women and ensures them protection from discrimination on arbitrary or unjustified grounds. Other rights protections have been provided to individuals with disabilities, who belong to an indigenous or ethnic population, and migrant workers.

Taken together, there are now a large number of human rights that have been formally codified (see Table 3.4) which can be enumerated from the different treaties. As definitions and assumptions vary, the total number of rights that ought to be protected also varies, but the list in the table comprises

Table 3.4 List of human rights protected under international law

1.	Non-discrimination
2.	Life
3.	Liberty and security of the person
4.	Protection against slavery and servitude
5.	Protection against torture
6.	Legal personality
7.	Equal protection of the law
8.	Legal remedy
9.	Protection against arbitrary arrest, detention or exile
10.	Access to independent and impartial tribunal
11.	Presumption of innocence
12.	Protection against *ex post facto* laws
13.	Privacy, family, home and correspondence
14.	Freedom of movement and residence

15.	Nationality
16.	Marry and found a family
17.	Protection and assistance of families
18.	Marriage only with free consent of spouses
19.	Equal rights of men and women in marriage
20.	Freedom of thought, conscience and religion
21.	Freedom of opinion and expression
22.	Freedom of the press
23.	Freedom of assembly
24.	Freedom of association
25.	Participation in government
26.	Social security
27.	Work
28.	No compulsory or forced labour
29.	Just and favourable conditions of work
30.	Trade unions
31.	Rest, leisure and paid holidays
32.	Adequate standard of living
33.	Education
34.	Participation in cultural life
35.	Self-determination
36.	Protection of and assistance to children
37.	Freedom from hunger
38.	Health
39.	Asylum
40.	Property
41.	Compulsory primary education
42.	Humane treatment when deprived of liberty

43.	Protection against imprisonment for debt
44.	Expulsion of aliens only by law
45.	Prohibition of war propaganda and incitement to discrimination
46.	Minority culture
47.	No imprisonment for breach of civil obligations
48.	Protection of children
49.	Access to public service
50.	Democracy
51.	Participation in cultural and scientific life
52.	Protection of intellectual property rights
53.	International and social order for realizing rights
54.	Political self-determination
55.	Economic self-determination
56.	Women's rights
57.	Prohibition of the death penalty
58.	Prohibition of apartheid

Sources: Davidson 1993: Appendix 1; Gibson 1996: 37–38; Green 2001: 1069;
             Donnelly 2003: 24.
             Reproduced from Landman, 2006a: 16; and Landman and Carvalho, 2009.

58 rights about which there is reasonable consensus across commentators and analysts. For some, this list constitutes a celebration and achievement of the human rights movement since the 1948 Universal Declaration has a total of 30 articles delineating sets of rights and the subsequent standard setting has led to a greater number of issues being given the status to be recognized as human rights. For others, the list in Table 3.1 may be an illustration of the problem of human rights 'inflation' where too many issues are afforded the status of human rights and therefore lead to a dilution of the power of the concept and the moral weight behind it. For example, protection against arbitrary arrest, detention or exile receives unassailable support, while the right to rest, leisure and paid holidays may raise an eyebrow or two from many quarters, especially during times of economic downturn.

Whether too many or too little, the list of human rights is a function of those rights that have been codified in international law, and nation states around the world have chosen to participate in the international regime of

Table 3.5 Main international human rights treaties

Name of Human Rights Treaty	Parties (N)	Parties (%)
1966 International Covenant on Civil and Political Rights (ICCPR)	167	86
1966 International Covenant on Economic, Social, and Cultural Rights (ICESCR)	160	82
1966 Convention on the Elimination of All Forms of Racial Discrimination (CERD)	174	89
1979 Convention on the Elimination of all forms of Discrimination Against Women (CEDAW)	187	96
1984 Convention against Torture and Other Cruel, Inhuman or Degrading Treatment or Punishment (CAT)	149	76
1989 Convention on the Rights of the Child (CRC)	193	99
1990 Convention on Migrant Workers	45	23
2006 Convention on the Rights of People with Disabilities	104	53

Source: http://www.bayefsky.com, accessed on 14 December 2011.

human rights through signing and ratifying the various treaties for their protection. Table 3.5 shows a list of the main international human rights instruments, along with the number and percentage of countries that are a party to these treaties. This means that they have signed and ratified the treaties and are therefore obliged to uphold the protection of human rights contained within them. It is clear from the table that the 1989 Convention on the Rights of the Child enjoys most international support from countries (99 per cent participation) and that the 1984 Convention against Torture the least support (76 per cent participation). There are political and pragmatic explanations for the variations in participation observed in the table, where some treaties have sets of obligations that compromise or undermine fundamental national interests or practices of some states. For example, many states in the United States have the death penalty for individuals under the age of 16, which would be considered a violation of the rights outlined in the 1989 Convention on the Rights of the Child.

Across the Tables 3.4 and 3.5, however, it seems very clear that the international regime has grown both in **breadth** and in **depth** such that a larger number of rights protections have been formally codified and an increasing number of countries have formally committed themselves to the protection of human rights. Canadian MP and political theorist Michael Ignatieff (2001) describes these developments as nothing less than a 'juridical revolution' in the area of human rights. As we shall see in the next chapter, this juridical revolution has not necessarily been met by a steady increase in the **actual protection** of human rights; a gap that lies at the heart of this book's argument about the precarious nature of this particular set of ideals. Indeed, in 1999, in an article in the New York Times, David Reif reflected precisely on the 'precarious triumph' of human rights. On the one hand, it is a triumph, since even the most optimistic of observers at the time of the 1948 Universal Declaration of Human Rights could have imagined the subsequent growth and influence of human rights discourse and doctrine. It is precarious since these very same achievements can be reversed as many countries witnessed in the first decade of the twentieth century as governments responded to the threat of terrorism. But small legal victories against rescinding rights commitments and the ways in which popular actors have embraced the discourse of rights in the 'Arab Spring' of 2011 demonstrate the power and resilience of these ideals.

Democracy and human rights

The parallel stories of democracy and human rights are certainly intriguing on their own, but this book is also concerned with the degree to which the two concepts exhibit overlaps and inter-relationships. We saw in the beginning of this chapter that there is a 'Venn diagram' of increasing overlap between democracy and human rights depending on the definition of democracy that one adopts. Procedural definitions have the least overlap while social definitions have the most. It is fairly straightforward and intuitive to see the fundamental links between democracy and human rights. But are these connections that are made theoretically upheld empirically? Are democracies better at protecting **all** human rights? Or just **some** human rights? Can authoritarian regimes use the power of the state apparatus and coercive institutions to bring about radical social change that provides most advantage for the least well off and thus offer better protections for social and economic rights? The Cuban regime has long been praised for its socialized medicine and the Chinese regime has significant progress in achieving many of the Millennium Development Goals (MDGs), especially in the reduction of poverty in the rural areas of the country.

The large-scale quantitative analysis of human rights protection conducted since the late 1980s has shown consistent and significant positive effects of democracy on civil and political rights. Using data collected in increasingly large samples of countries across space and time, the empirical political science of human rights has shown that democracies are better at protecting civil and political rights (see, e.g. Mitchell and McCormick 1988; Poe and Tate 1994; Poe et al. 1999; Landman 2005a) and that improvements in the protection of such rights occurs even within a year after a transition to democracy (Zanger 2000). But such a general finding for democracy's impact on human rights has been qualified by other research, which shows that processes of democratization take time to become embedded and that for those regimes somewhere between authoritarianism and democracy may experience greater violations of civil and political rights, the so-called more murder in the middle thesis (Fein 1995). And other research has shown that the crucial institutional arrangement within democracy that has the greatest probability of reducing civil and political rights violations is a significant set of constraints on the authority of the executive (Buena de Mesquita et al. 2005). Elected executives without constraint from the legislative assembly through control over cabinet selection and the use of veto powers may well abuse their power of office and use the state to violate civil and political rights. As we shall see in the next chapter, there have many instances of so-called delegative democracies (O'Donnell 1994; Foweraker et al. 2003) in which executives have made too much of their electoral mandate to rule and have engaged in 'extra-constitutional' behaviour that carries with it less respect for civil and political rights.

These findings suggest that the relationship between democracy and civil and political rights is far from perfect despite having an overall positive and significant relationship. Figure 3.2 shows a scatter diagram of measures of procedural democracy and measures of 'personal integrity rights', which

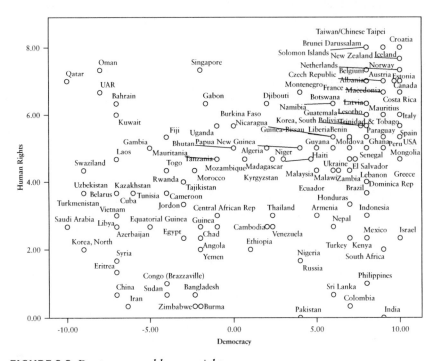

FIGURE 3.2 *Democracy and human rights.*

Sources: Mean combined democracy score from Polity IV data for 2007–2009; mean Cingranelli and Richards (CIRI) score for the Physical Integrity Rights, 2007–2009.

includes the protection of rights relating to freedom from arbitrary detention, torture, assassination, disappearance and exile. The figure shows many things at once. First, it shows the overall positive and significant relationship between democracy and human rights popular in the research literature on this topic. The scatter of data points exhibits a pattern that spreads from the lower left quadrant (low democracy-low rights protection) to the upper right quadrant (high democracy-high rights protection) suggesting that on balance, countries that are more democratic are better at protecting personal integrity rights. Second, the figure shows a wide range of significant 'outliers' where in the upper left quadrant there are countries that despite not having high levels of democracy nevertheless do not engage significantly in the violation of personal integrity rights. It is interesting to note, however, that Bahrain features in this group of countries but that during the Arab Spring of 2011 the regime has resorted to the abuse of these rights when facing a popular challenge to its continued rule. In the lower right quadrant is a collection of countries that despite having relatively high levels of democracy, nonetheless have significant problems with the violation of personal integrity rights. These are the countries that scholars, such as Larry Diamond and Fareed Zakaria mentioned above, find highly problematic and indicative of a democratic failure among certain democracies. The notable cases are those that have made relatively recent transitions to democracy (e.g. Mexico), that have had significant difficulties in consolidating democracy since transition (South Africa), that face internal conflict (Colombia) or that face a mix of internal and external conflict (Israel).

Beyond these somewhat crude empirical observations, there is a final tension or contradiction worth discussing before drawing our conclusions for this chapter. Democracy is founded on the set of principles and ideas that have been outlined here but it is often the product of political accommodation at key moments in a country's history and associated with notions of balance, possibility and working towards agreeable and peaceful solutions to conflicts of interest. The American Founding, for example, was based on a compromise between the interests of large and small states, concerns over the power of the executive (e.g. Hamilton wanted a king), balance of power between the federal and state governments, among many issues debated at the 1787 Constitutional Convention in Philadelphia. The 'path dependencies' related to the decisions made at the Convention still affect American democratic politics today on key issues such as the death penalty, abortion, immigration, taxes, commerce, sentencing, among many other issues. More recent democratic transitions in Portugal, Spain, Chile, Brazil, Mongolia and Mexico, among others, are also characterized by this notion of political accommodation of difference.

Human rights, on the other hand, are based on notions of a 'moral compass', adjudication or judgement and a certain absolutism in reference to the international law of human rights that can close down options and moments of political accommodation. As we shall see in Chapter 7, many countries included different kinds of 'truth' processes as part of their democratic transitions, which sought to uncover the true nature and extent of 'past wrongs' and atrocities committed during periods of Apartheid (in the case of South Africa), authoritarian rule (e.g. Argentina and Chile), civil war (e.g. Guatemala, El Salvador and Sierra Leone) and foreign occupation (e.g. East Timor). Modelled after the International Military Tribunal and the Nuremberg Trials used in post-war Germany, these 'truth commissions' as they became known often have been quite good at uncovering truth. Large sections of the human rights community have adopted a position critical of any use of 'amnesty for truth' (as in South Africa) and have called for prosecution and retributive justice for the victims of these regimes and experiences. While such a position has great moral authority, political realities in many countries have meant that there has been less justice for the victims than the human rights community would have wanted, but this suboptimal achievement of justice is then balanced against future stability and sustainable democracy.

Such an outcome illustrates the tension between the kind of political 'accommodation' that accompanies moments of democratic transition and the absolutist position adopted by much of the human rights community. Many countries have made successful transitions to democracy, but there remain serious questions about a large number of perpetrators responsible for carrying out arbitrary detention, torture, assassination, disappearance and exile who have escaped prosecution for their past deeds. Moreover, there are countries that have undergone democratic transitions that have either not engaged with an official truth process, only recently adopted a truth process (e.g. only in 2012 has Brazil established a truth commission for to investigate its 25 years of military rule between 1964 and 1989) or are still considering which options are politically possible (e.g. Spain and Northern Ireland[6]). But as we shall see in Chapter 6, it has often been the struggle for human rights that has challenged status quo power relations and existing regimes; regimes which then make concessions and in many cases undergo processes of democratic transition. In this way, there is both complementarity and contradiction between democracy and human rights.

Summary and implications

This chapter has provided an overview of definitions of democracy and specification of the growth and proliferation of human rights in the latter half of the twentieth century. It argued that democracy is based on the core principles of popular sovereignty and collective decision-making and that different definitions of democracy – procedural, liberal and social – are derived from the degree to which they incorporate sets of human rights, including civil, political, economic, social, cultural and minority rights. We saw that human rights have grown in breadth and depth since the 1948

Universal Declaration of Human Rights, such that today there are as many as 58 different rights delineated in the various international treaties for the protection of human rights and there are varying degrees of participation from countries in the international human rights regime. Moreover, Europe, the Americas and Africa have established regional systems for the protection of human rights, while the Arab league is in early stages of doing the same. Asia, which itself covers a diverse set of countries in South Asia, East Asia and Southeast Asia, has yet to embark on this path. We have seen that the complementarity between democracy and human rights that exists in theory is born out empirically, at least with respect to the protection of political integrity rights, while the findings for democracy's impact on human development bode well for a demonstration of complementarity for social and economic rights (see, e.g. Landman and Larizza 2009). But the complementarity is not perfect, where many outliers are present and many contradictions between the two remain, especially with respect to democracy's capacity for political accommodation and the 'adjudicative' nature of human rights.

It is important to note, however, that the Arab Spring of 2011 once again reminds us of the power of the language of rights and its possibility for bringing about democratic change. Critiques of authoritarian regimes in the Middle East and North Africa have in part adopted a language of rights that includes economic as well as civil and political demands. To illustrate the power of these ideas, consider the words of Yemeni journalist and human rights activist Tawakkol Karman, who writes with respect to the Saleh regime,

> Saleh's regime carried out 33 years of rule through blood and corruption. We have brought it to its knees through our determination, and through the steadfastness of young people who have confronted the bullets of the regime with bared chests. With politicians and members of the army standing beside us, our success will go further.[7]

Strong words indeed and indicative of the passion for change in the region, as well as the longstanding appeal of two powerful ideas: democracy and human rights.

SUGGESTIONS FOR FURTHER READING

Beetham, David (1999) *Democracy and Human Rights*. Cambridge: Polity Press.

Donnelly, Jack (2002) *Universal Human Rights in Theory and Practice*. Ithaca: Cornell University Press.

Forsythe, David P. (2012) *Human Rights in International Relations*, 3rd edition. Cambridge: Cambridge University Press.

Freeman, Michael (2011) *Human Rights*, 2nd edition. Cambridge: Polity Press.

Landman, Todd (2009) *Human Rights*, Volumes I–IV. London: Sage Publications.

Notes

1 In a number of public gatherings where I have shared the podium with political theorist David Beetham, he has always qualified this claim about democracy by saying that the term may well be 'essentially contested' but democracy is **not** 'essentially contestable'. This is an important clarification since although human communities may disagree on the definition of democracy, they can nonetheless agree on its desirability as a form of rule.

2 For Aristotle, 'democracy' was the corrupt form of rule by the many and was seen as 'mob rule'. Modern understandings of democracy, however, use democracy in similar ways to his use of the term 'polity'.

3 The only remaining justifiable restrictions on participation are age and mental ability, but there is little consensus on threshold conditions for these two categories. There is the additional debate surrounding suffrage for prisoners, as in many states across the United States, convicted felons lose their right to vote forever, and in Europe, the United Kingdom is challenging the right to vote for prisoners.

4 There is an interesting historical case in which the military regime in Brazil (1964–89) extended the right to vote to illiterates in the hope of gaining electoral support for the pro-military political party in the Brazilian Congress, but when this new group of enfranchised individualized exercised their right to vote, the opposition party was to gain. The regime thus retracted the right until the democratic transition many years later (see Skidmore 1993).

5 The figure originated in a lecture I delivered to the staff at IDEA in 2005 as part of its 10-year anniversary celebrations and has since been worked into many of its work programmes and publications, the last of which was a global consultation project that examined the degree to which the European Union was working in the areas of democracy building across its foreign policies. See IDEA (2009).

6 The case of Northern Ireland is an interesting one, since as part of the United Kingdom it has always been considered a democracy, but over 30 years of violence limited the degree to which citizens could express their democratic will, and restrictions put in place and tactics used to combat terrorism compromised certain freedoms and resulted in the United Kingdom being taken to the European Court of Human Rights for the ways in which the government treated terror suspects in prison. The post-Good Friday period has seen a national debate on whether Northern Ireland should engage in a 'truth' process, while the Saville Inquiry set up to investigate the Bloody Sunday killings took 12 years to issue its report, which was published on 15 June 2010. I took part in a Chatham House event that brought together experts and representatives from Northern Ireland and Peru to explore the advantages and disadvantages of establishing a truth commission for Northern Ireland. A Truth and Reconciliation Commission for Britain and Ireland (TRCBI) has been proposed, but to date has not made much progress.

7 Tawakkol Karman, 'Our revolutions doing what Saleh Can't – uniting Yemen,' *The Guardian*, 9 April 2011, p. 34.

CHAPTER FOUR

Waves and setbacks

Introduction

In 1991, Samuel Huntington published a book entitled *The Third Wave*, which described the development of democracy since the nineteenth century as a series of 'waves' that were characterized by the 'ebb' and 'flow' of democracy over time. A wave is defined as a group of transitions from non-democratic regimes to democratic regimes that occur within a specified period of time and that significantly outnumber transitions in the opposite direction during the same period. History has indeed shown that democracy has come and gone in many countries, but with the advent of Huntington's 'third wave' in 1974, it appears that democracy has become more 'sticky', with fewer democratic setbacks and new opportunities for democratic transformation. The developments in the Middle East and North Africa in 2011 show that at least the appeal of democracy and the promise of greater rights protection have been a powerful force for change in the region. The prognosis for the successful installation of democratic regimes across the region, however, remains highly uncertain, as even in the early stages of transformation, great variation across the different countries is evident even though the impulse for change within them has been largely similar.

For Huntington, the first wave began with the advent of 'Jacksonian Democracy' in the United States when suffrage was extended to the majority of white males (clearly an issue that was subsequently challenged by the suffragette movement and the civil rights movement) and continued until 1922 when Mussolini took power in Italy. During this period, the total number of democracies peaked at 29 and then dropped to 12 by the end. The second wave began just after World War II and extended until 1962, with 36 democracies that then dropped to just 30 by 1972. The third wave began with the Portuguese transition to democracy in 1974, which was then quickly followed by Spain and Greece and many countries in Latin America beginning with the 1978 transition in Peru and ending with the Chilean transition in 1989 (see Foweraker et al. 2003). In Asia, South Korea and Thailand joined these other countries in the third wave. Some have argued that the period that followed the 1989 collapse of the Soviet Union and Communist countries of Eastern Europe constitutes a 'fourth wave' of democracy (Doorenspleet 2005), which according to Larry Diamond (2011) has seen signs of reversal across 18 countries ranging from Pakistan in 1999 through to Mozambique in 2009. Yet, at the time that Diamond's list appeared in print, the popular uprisings in the Middle East and North Africa and the top-down reforms taking place in Burma have provided renewed signs of democracy's resilience after this period of alleged decline.

This chapter puts these overall trends into perspective with respect to the arguments being advanced in this book. First, the chapter examines the spread of democracy through the various waves to illustrate the ebb and flow over time in the number and percentage of democracies. It also considers two international efforts to support democracy – the Community of Democracies and the six United Nations International Conferences on New or Restored Democracies (ICNRD1–ICNRD6). Second, the chapter examines the growing gap between **procedural** democracy and **liberal** democracy, where it appears that many new democracies (and a few old democracies) have had difficulty protecting certain sets of human rights, despite an overall positive relationship between democracy and human rights. Third, the chapter discusses the relationship between the timing of democratization and the protection of human **rights in principle** and **rights in practice** (Foweraker and Landman 1997; Landman 2005b; Landman and Carvalho 2009). As outlined in the previous chapter, human rights have been codified through international law and states ratify the various treaties, which commit the state to the protection of human rights **in principle**. But states are also obliged to respect, protect and fulfil human rights such that citizens and residents within the jurisdiction may exercise their rights **in practice**. We will see that the timing of democracy has an impact on both these understandings of human rights in significant ways that are worth our attention. Fourth, the chapter examines significant cases of democratic reversal (Ecuador, São Tome, Fiji, Cote d'Ivoire), attempted reversal (Guatemala) and democratic erosion (Venezuela, Russia, Central Asia) as an illustration of the precariousness of democracy of the kind with which Diamond has become concerned. The chapter concludes with an assessment of these trends as a means to consider the democratic prospects for the countries in the Middle East and North Africa.

Democracy's journey

The journey that democracy has taken from the nineteenth century until today has shown great variation across geographical space, over time, and within democracies as the quality of democracy has changed and continues to change. Figure 4.1 takes the data used in Figure 1.1 and adds markers for Huntington's 'waves' to show the ebb and flow of democracy over time. Both the number of democracies and the number of countries vary over time and thus the **percentage** of democracies is a better indicator for the growth in democracy. Huntington's waves are quite clear from these data where the peaks and troughs roughly map onto his different time periods for the waves. Table 4.1 breaks down these waves into the regions and countries from them that comprise the wave. As is clear from the table, the first wave

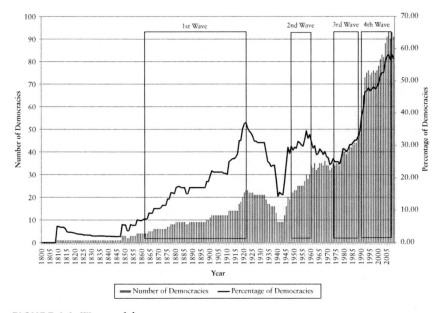

FIGURE 4.1 *Waves of democracy.*

Source: Polity IV.

Table 4.1 Waves of democracy: regions and countries

Wave	Europe	Regions
1828–1926	Western Europe	North America: United States and Canada
1934–1962	Western Europe	Latin America: Costa Rica, Venezuela, Colombia South Asia: India
1974–1989	Southern Europe	Latin America: Peru, Ecuador, Argentina, Uruguay, Brazil, Guatemala
1990 onwards	Eastern Europe	Latin America: Chile, Nicaragua, Panama, Mexico Africa: Benin, Mali, Lesotho, Niger, South Africa, Malawi Asia: Taiwan, Mongolia, Cambodia

was largely confined to Western Europe and the United States. The second wave also featured countries in Western Europe, but added countries in Latin America, as well as India. In the late 1940s and 1950s, Costa Rica, Venezuela and Colombia crafted elite agreements to end periods of violence and promulgate democratic regimes that were a key feature of second-wave democratization. After partition in 1947, India went on to become the world's most populous democracy and is now an emerging power owing to its high rates of economic growth. The third wave involved countries in Southern Europe and Latin America, with democratic transitions in Portugal, Greece and Spain, followed by Peru, Ecuador, Argentina, Uruguay, Brazil and Guatemala. The fourth wave was more geographically diverse with its origins in Eastern Europe, and then Latin America (Chile, Nicaragua, Panama and Mexico), Africa (Benin, Mali, Lesotho, Niger, Malawi and South Africa) and Asia (Taiwan, Mongolia, Thailand and Cambodia). As we shall see in greater depth in the next chapter, one of the popular explanations for the development of democracy focuses on what is called geographical or 'spatial' diffusion, and certainly the regional trends depicted in this table illustrate that many processes of democratization have taken place among adjacent countries. The diversity of the fourth wave challenges this notion of adjacent diffusion, but the events in the Middle East and North Africa once again lend support to this idea, which has featured in many policy discussions.[1]

It is important to observe that throughout the four waves, there has been a distinctive European influence as the first two waves featured Western Europe, the Third Wave featured Southern Europe and the Fourth Wave featured Eastern Europe. It is of course well known that democracy was first conceived in Ancient Greece, but it did not start to flourish until the nineteenth century in the United States and Western Europe. The two world wars interrupted the growth of democracy but also convinced many states that democracy was the best form of government for avoiding violence and inter-state war. The rebuilding of Europe after World War II had an underlying democratic logic, as countries embraced democracy and constructed supernational institutions to 'lock in' future generations of leaders in ways that have sought to avoid democratic breakdown (see Moravcsik 2000). The Council of Europe (COE) was the first set of supranational institutions and was in part fortified by the European Convention on Human Rights (see the Chapter 3), but the evolution of the European Union, originally established to build and protect Europe's energy markets, has in many ways superseded the COE and now has political criteria relating to democracy and human rights for those states wishing to become members. It also has its own monitoring agency in the form of the EU Agency for Fundamental Rights (FRA) based in Vienna.

The story of democracy in Europe is often underappreciated and in many ways has not yet been told. Interestingly, the social history of democracy in the region involves a long and somewhat bloody transformation from feudal states to nation states to empires and wars to democratization and enlargement. And this political transformation was accompanied by an economic transformation from agrarian production to industrialization to post-industrial welfarism to economic integration. These twin processes of transformation have indeed created a strong union of relatively stable and peaceful democracies. Such a story of democracy in Europe does set an example for what can be achieved in the short space of time, particularly if one focuses on that period of time since the mass atrocities and casualties committed during World War II. But to see Europe as the centre of gravity for democracy would be mistaken, as democratic traditions have developed elsewhere such that any talk of democratic diffusion ought to consider the lessons of democracy flowing to as much as from Europe. Indeed, in *Mobilizing for Human Rights*, Edward Cleary (2007) makes a very strong case of a long history of rights traditions in Latin America that have had a profound impact on democratic and authoritarian periods of rule. Many third- and fourth-wave democracies in Europe and the European neighbourhood looked to Latin America for suitable institutional arrangements and variously adopted presidential and semi-presidential systems that are distinctly non-European in character. Experiences with 'truth commissions' in Latin America in the 1980s served as early models for transitional justice and 'lustration' that then featured in such processes of transition seen in South Africa, Eastern Europe, East Timor and Sierra Leone (see Chapter 7 in this volume and Hayner 2010).

Any consideration of the international dimensions of democracy must also address the large role that the United States has played in shaping the course of democracy since the end of World War II. The Marshall Plan itself was a large economic and political intervention from the United States into Europe that helped rebuild countries, strengthen nascent democratic institutions and encourage democracy across continental Europe. The Portuguese, Spanish and Greek transitions during the Third Wave fit within larger logics of the Cold War initially and then European enlargement, while post-Cold War democratization has been accompanied by significant economic, military and technical assistance from the United States through such agencies as the National Endowment for Democracy and USAID to support the development of political parties, media, non-governmental organizations and militaries. In security terms, the United States has maintained significant military bases throughout Europe and NATO has been a mainstay feature of Cold War politics and is now engaged in new interventions such as the one in Libya as a result of United Nations Security Council Resolution 1973.

Any attempt to map the growth of democracy worldwide, however, necessarily relies on definitions of democracy and ways of turning such definitions into threshold conditions for counting democracies. For example, in order to count the number of democracies in the nineteenth century, one has to adopt a fairly narrow definition of democracy that does not include universal suffrage. Many countries had established competitive elections and had reasonably well-developed political parties, but the parties were dominated by elites, and votes were limited to property-owning white men, effectively disenfranchising large segments of the population. Indeed, in *Capitalist Development and Democracy*, Rueschemeyer, Stephens and Stephens (1992) argue that the United States was not really democratic until the 1964 voting rights act, which gave African Americans the right to vote. Moreover, the struggle led by women's movements around the world has achieved at different periods suffrage for women. As women make up more than 50 per cent of the population in most countries, since women tend to have higher rates of longevity than men, denial of this fundamental right undermines the notion of democracy. Most people find it surprising that Switzerland, a so-called old democracy (i.e. one that achieved democracy before the third wave) did not extend the right to vote to women until as late as 1971.

It is thus clear that any discussion of the growth of democracy must include a consideration of human rights in the ways that were outlined in Chapter 3. From the trends in democratization discussed in this chapter thus far, we have seen a number of countries where basic democratic thresholds have been achieved, but closer examination of rights protections suggests that many democracies still have a gap between the procedural-institutional dimensions of democracy and the fuller rights dimensions. There are some clear trends in the data on different measures of rights and their relationship to democracy. Analysis of the ratification of human rights treaties has shown two major trends. First, older democracies tend to ratify fewer human rights treaties than newer democracies. Second, when ratifying these treaties, older democracies file more 'reservations' to these treaties than newer democracies (see Landman 2005a). Reservations are formal exceptions to the content of a treaty to which a state may have a particular objection, given its own legal culture or legal system. For example, the United States lodged a reservation about the death penalty when it signed the International Covenant on Civil and Political Rights, since under the US Constitution, the jurisdiction over the use of the death penalty is left to the individual states in the US Federal system. While reservations do not necessarily invalidate treaties, there are degrees to which such reservations undermine a treaty's true 'object and purpose'. What is interesting here is that well-established democracies ratify fewer treaties with more reservations than newer democracies. One popular explanation argues that older democracies have more established legal systems and constitutional protections in place and that they take their treaty obligations more seriously than newer democracies. Another popular explanation argues that many new democracies ratified all the human rights treaties with little to no reservations because they wanted to attract international economic and technical assistance.

But what about the actual protection of human rights? Figure 3.2 in the previous chapter showed the general positive relationship between the level of democracy and a combined measure of civil and political rights. The overall relationship is not perfect as is evident from the scatter of countries in the figure, and there are many democracies on the right hand

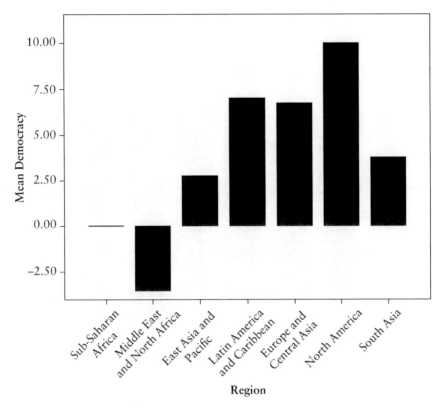

FIGURE 4.2 *Mean democracy scores by region.*

Source: Polity IV 2010.

bottom area of the figure that have high levels of democracy, but relatively low levels of human rights protection (and compare the regional charts in Figure 4.2 and 4.3). For the purposes of our discussion here, these lower levels of rights protection are among the newer democracies. We can thus conclude that older democracies are better at protecting civil and political rights than newer democracies, even though these democracies ratify fewer treaties with more reservations. The higher ratification rates from the new democracies with the associated poorer performance in rights protection have led some to argue that many new democracies made 'insincere commitments' to the international law of human rights (see Smith-Cannoy 2012).

Democratic setbacks

Beyond these general trends in democratization and the relationship between democracy and human rights, both in principle and in practice, there have been a significant number of democratic 'setbacks' that are worth

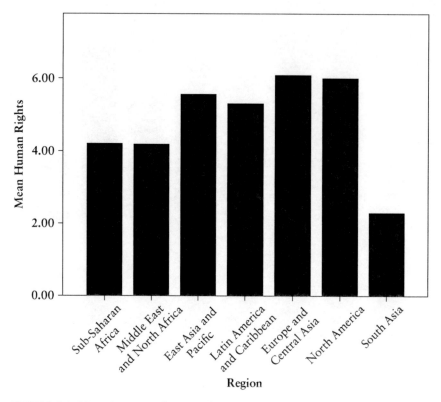

FIGURE 4.3 *Mean human rights score by region.*

Source: Cingranelli and Richards (CIRI), 2010, physical integrity rights index.

considering in any overall assessment of democratization in the world. In the preceding sections, we have seen a fairly positive story about the growth and proliferation of democracy in the world, which in many ways accelerated from 1974 onwards with the advent of the third wave. This process means that more countries in the world are democratic than non-democratic and that the final region in the world that has seemed impervious to democratic transformation has begun to experience cracks in the edifice of authoritarianism. The world was surprised at the fall of the Berlin Wall and the Eastern European transitions, the release of Mandela and the South African transition and has once again been taken by surprise by the rapid set of transformations in the Middle East and North Africa. But to focus only on these positive developments ignores the notion of precariousness developed throughout this book. There are stories of democratic setback, but like the stories of democratic advance, they exhibit great variation in the nature and extent to which they have come about in individual countries. We will now consider notable examples of **failed democratic reversal** in Spain (1981), Argentina (1986, 1987, 1988 and 1990) and Guatemala (1993); **successful**

democratic reversal in Peru (1992), Pakistan (1999), Ecuador (2000), São Tome (2003), Fiji (2006), Honduras (2009) and the Ivory Coast (2011); and **democratic rollback** in Venezuela, Russia and Central Asia.

On 23 February 1981, Antonio Tejero led a group of 200 armed officers from the Guardia Civil in an attempted coup in the Spanish Congress during the elections for the Prime Minister Leopoldo Calvo Sotelo. The group held the congress hostage for 18 hours, but the King of Spain Juan Carlos I broadcast a televised address in which he denounced the coup and asked for the maintenance of law and order and the continuance of the democratically elected government. Even the coup attempt had been preceded by a period of increasing political tension and popular disaffection with the government, democracy prevailed and Spain has not experienced any further such attempts since. In similar fashion, a band of army mutineers known as the 'carapintadas' (painted faces) staged a series of uprisings against Argentina's new democratic government of Raúl Alfonsín between 1986 and 1988 and against the successor government of Carlos Menem in 1990. These uprisings were carried largely in response to the continued investigations into military atrocities committed during the now infamous 'dirty war', which was reputedly responsible for the death and disappearance of approximately 30,000 people. Like in Spain and Argentina, disgruntled military personnel made two coup attempts during the Cerezo Presidency in 1988 and 1989, but on 25 May 1993, successor President Serrano dissolved congress in an attempted '**autogolpe**' (or self-coup). A combination of popular protests and the denunciation from the Court of Constitutionality with the support of the military meant that Serrano did not have the necessary political support to succeed.

Across these three examples, democratic institutions, though weak and popular support for democracy, though young, led to the failure of such coup attempts in these countries. The figure of the King in Spain, Presidents Alfonsín and Menem in Argentina and the court in Guatemala were such that these attempted coups simply did not garner enough popular support to succeed. The resilience of nascent democratic institutions and popular support for democracy in these cases led to the failed reversals. But in other cases, coup attempts have been successful and ushered in periods of authoritarianism even though the countries had just recently undergone prolonged processes of democratic transition. In 1992, just 2 years after being elected on a broad populist platform for reform, President Alberto Fujimori of Peru succeeded in bringing about an **autogolpe**, dissolved congress and oversaw a period of authoritarianism that would last until his infamous exile from the country in 2000 (see Chapter 7 in this volume). On 21 January 2000, a coalition of an indigenous people's organization and junior military officers fomented a coup against President Jamil Mahuad in Ecuador and sought to establish a populist democracy based on the ideas of Hugo Chavez in Venezuela (see below). While the president was exiled and the coup enjoyed a certain amount of popular support, it was soon reversed by senior military officers and a new President was installed. The final and most notable case of a coup against democracy took place in Pakistan on 12 October 1999 when the Chief of the Army Staff General Pervez Musharraf overthrew Prime Minister Nawaz Sharif. In this case, the judiciary held that the coup was legal and justified, and after a period of emergency rule, Musharraf won a popular referendum in 2002 and stayed in power for another five years.

Less-well-known cases include those of São Tome in 2003, Fiji in 2006, Honduras in 2009 and the Ivory Coast in 2010. The 16 July 2003 coup São Tome was short-lived and another attempt in 2009 was thwarted. Both insurrections led by the military were ostensibly driven by concerns over economic inequality and corruption and in particular, the relationship of these two issues to the promise of billions from auctioning rights to the country's oil supply. Fiji has long been subjected to military coups, with four such events during the 1980s and 1990s. The 2006 coup took place in early December after a period of rising tensions between the military and civilian leaders over the 2000 coup, while the coup itself received endorsements from courts and the Fiji Human Rights Commission, and the new military government of Frank Bainimarama positioned itself as 'clean-up' operation, effectively ridding the system of corruption, electoral irregularities and over-dependence on ethnic divisions. Bainimarama restored the presidency to Josefa Iloilo in 2007, and after a court ruling that the government was not legitimate, Epeli Nailatikau was put in power and new elections scheduled for 2014. As a consequence of these developments, Fiji has been suspended from the Commonwealth.

The cases of Honduras and Ivory Coast involved constitutional and electoral issues. In 2009, a dispute over proposed constitutional reforms in Honduras culminated in a coup against President Manuel Zelaya. Instigated by the Supreme Court, which saw Zelaya's proposed reforms as a veiled attempt to bring a Chavez style government to Honduras[2], the military removed him from office and exiled him to Costa Rica. International reaction from the United Nations, the Organization of American States, the European Union and the United States[3] objected to this ousting, and a final resolution of the crisis involved the installation of a new president Profirio Lobo with elections on 27 January 2010. Ivory Coast has had many tensions and disputes relating to its democracy, and it has had a history of military intervention since its independence in 1960, while the most recent events involved a post-election dispute over the results. On 2 December 2010, Mr Alassane Outtara was declared the winner of the presidential elections with 54.1 per cent of the popular vote compared to 45.9 per cent for the incumbent President Laurent Gbagbo. A standoff with increasing violence from both sides ensued, ushering in a foreign intervention from UN and French military forces (i.e. the former colonial power) and threats of an intervention from the Economic Community of West African States (ECOWAS) forces was made. By April 2011, Ggagbo had surrendered and power was restored to Mr Outtara.

In this case, the integrity of an electoral result was contested by the sitting president but defended by external forces and power was restored to the winner of the election.

These cases were all examples of overt challenges to democratic rule, where the sitting president is ousted, the congress is sidelined or the incoming president is prevented from assuming power. But there are cases in which democratically elected leaders use the office of the executive to concentrate their base of personal power, marginalize opposition forces and undermine the quality of democracy itself. In such cases, democracy is not overthrown but eroded, and so-called strong men (and it really is men) seek to remain in office indefinitely through the manipulation of popular opinion and concentration of power. The most notable cases in which this has occurred are Venezuela under Hugo Chavez, Russia under Vladimir Putin and The Central Asian republics of Tajikistan, Uzbekistan and Kirgizstan.[4]

Venezuela has been a democracy for over 50 years when in 1958 a new 'elite settlement' ended a prolonged period of conflict and ushered in democracy. The Pact of Punto Fijo provided a framework for democracy that included a power-sharing arrangement between the forces on the left (represented by the Democratic Action party, Acción Democrática or AD) and the on the right (represented by the COPEI – Social Christian Party of Venezuela. Comité de Organización Política Electoral Independiente – Partido Social Cristiano de Venezuela).[5]

Democracy in Venezuela from this settlement until the late 1980s proceeded along a path of 'taking it in turns' where power would alternate between these two parties; however, the confined nature of the system led to calls for reform and popular unrest in the early 1990s, and an unsuccessful coup attempt in 1992 led by Hugo Chavez, a career military officer who had founded Revolutionary Bolivarian Movement. After his release from prison, he founded the Fifth Republic Movement and was elected president in 1998. Upon assuming the presidency, Chavez steadily increased power into the office of the executive and ruled over Venezuela in highly personalistic fashion, while at the same time holding periodic elections for his continued rule across three consecutive terms (1999–2000, 2000–06, 2006 to the present) and surviving a popular referendum for his removal in 2004. Long-time scholar of Venzuelan politics Daniel Levine argues that throughout his time in office, Chavez had been 'chipping away' at democracy, and that more recently his use of emergency powers and 'enabling laws' gave him unprecedented power over Venezuela that has transformed his 'erosion' of democracy into an 'avalanche' (see Levine 2011). These powers included more state control over the media and the internet, more constraints on civil society and NGOs, blocking international funding for organizations that promote political rights, undermining judicial independence and constraining opposition parties in the National Assembly. Coupled with this erosion of democratic institutions, the Chavez regime was accused of having one of the worst records for corruption in the whole region of Latin America, according to research conducted by the NGO Transparency International.

Commentators have made comparisons between Venezuela and Russia, where similar moves to concentrate executive power have taken place. Indeed 20 years after newly democratized Russia survived a coup attempt to reverse Gorbachev's reforms and oust newly elected President Boris Yeltsin, the world has watched as Prime Minister (and Former President) Vladimir Putin continues to undermine democratic institutions. The end of the Cold War and the collapse of the Soviet Union were some of the most momentous occasions of the twentieth century, and many previously authoritarian countries in Eastern Europe embraced democracy. Hopes were high for Russia as Gorbachev initiated reforms that led to new democratic elections in 1991, but Russia has in many ways followed a political course that marked it out as significantly different from other post-Communist states, many of which have now become EU member states (e.g. Bulgaria, Czech Republic, Estonia, Hungary, Latvia, Lithuania, Romania, Slovakia and Slovenia). Russia and, as we shall see, the post-Soviet republics in Central Asia, have consolidated power in the executive and limited the power of other political institutions, undermined the protection of human rights (most notably in the conflict with Chechnya) and stalled democratic progress to the degree that now commentators see Russia as increasingly authoritarian (see Hassner 2008; Shvetsova 2010).

Across Russia and Central Asia, we have seen an increasing concentration of executive power and a deepening suspicion and consequent repression of civil society and many civil and political rights. The war in Chechnya and the Russian 'war on terror' have led to widespread abuse of human rights (FIDH 2002), including arbitrary detention, disappearances and extra-judicial killings. Vladimir Putin has for the medium term and despite widespread demonstrations, consolidated power in Russia, while the presidents in the Central Asian republics have proved resistant to regular democratic alternation of power, despite the optimism with which their countries were greeted after the collapse of the Soviet Union. In 2012, Russia passed a new law that requires internationally funded domestic NGOs to register with the government as 'foreign agents', which in effect limits their ability to provide a basis for political dissent (failure to comply with the law carries fines and possible imprisonment).[6] Alongside this new law, the drama of the 'Pussy Riot' trial, sentencing and release of one musician have raised significant concerns about the protection of freedom of expression in Russia. The Central Asian republics showed a remarkable formal commitment to the human rights agenda through ratification of all the major international human rights instruments in the early 1990s and yet have had dismal records in the actual protection of human rights across the region (Landman 2005a; Smith-Cannoy 2012).

Summary: The fifth wave?

The waves and setbacks documented here should demonstrate why any assessment of the prospects for democracy in the world should remain cautiously optimistic. On the one hand, the world has seen a proliferation of democracies from 1974 onwards that has really exhibited a 'wave like' pattern. The rapid pace in and spread of democratization in the world has been truly unprecedented and has been a remarkable historical development that should not be under appreciated. The appeal of democracy has stretched across the world and now includes struggles in the final region long thought to be impervious to such change. On the other hand, many of the newest of these democracies have struggled with a large number of challenges. In the case of the former Communist countries, governments have had to oversee the dual transition from a command economy to a market economy alongside the development of democratic institutions, the holding of elections and the open competition of nascent and transformed political party organizations. In capitalist countries, governments have had to grapple with transitions from long periods of authoritarian rule, and in the case of Latin America, economic contractions relating to dependent capitalist development and the debt crisis of the 1980s. African countries that have embraced democracy have had similar challenges relating to patterns of dependent development and the persistence of patrimonial politics (Bratton and van der Walle 1997; Lindberg 2006), while those in Asia have had to democratize powerful state structures responsible for successful export-led growth strategies. Throughout the second, third and fourth waves of democratization, countries such as Colombia, Venezuela and India have struggled to maintain democracy in the face of income inequalities and heightened levels of violence.

In addition to the economic and political challenges associated with transitions to democracy, the new democracies have also had to contend with a growing gap between the formal institutional dimensions of democracy and the human rights dimensions (see Diamond 1999; Zakaria 2003). Cases such as Brazil and Mexico, which are now economically successful, have had a series of relatively free and fair elections with healthy competition between political parties and yet, have worrying records with respect to the violation of civil and political rights and a general struggle to fulfil economic and social rights despite such high rates of economic growth. During the presidential term of Felipe Calderón (2006–12), the Mexican government has been struggling against organized criminal organizations associated with trade in illegal drugs, which has been characterized by an unprecedented increase in extra-judicial killings (Philip and Berruecos 2012). During this period, there have been 48,000 reported killings that are associated with the struggle against organized crime, while it remains unclear about the unreported killings and the main perpetrators responsible for the killings.

Moreover, efforts by the Mexican state have brought allegations of serious violation of human rights (see Landman 2012).

Against this backdrop of cautious optimism, the Arab Spring presents an analogous set of questions about the prospects for democracy in the region, including the geographical proximity of the countries undergoing transitions, their relative levels of economic development, their 'prior regime' types and the variation in political outcomes that have thus far been obtained. Arguably the most dramatic set of changes took place in Tunisia and Egypt, which, according to World Bank development indicators, have lower average per capita incomes than Libya. Change thus was initiated in countries that were not necessarily the wealthiest in the region (see Chapter 2 and Chapter 5 in this volume on modernization and democracy) and which have had underlying economic discontent behind much of their initial mobilizations. The leaders in Tunisian and Egypt were toppled relatively quickly, but there are serious questions as to whether the rest of the state apparatus is being transformed more towards democracy. In the run-up to the new elections, the Egyptians opted to put former president Hosni Mubarak on trial, much like was done in Iraq with Saddam Hussein. But it is not at all clear that the trial and elections and new government of Morsi provide a meaningful opening for the establishment of long-term democracy in the country. The uprisings in Libya and Syria (and to some degree in Bahrain and Yemen) have been met with a fierce response from the incumbent regimes, while the international community responded to the situation in Libya with NATO air strikes and some support for the rebels, who ultimately overthrew Gaddafi. Despite the horrific reports of violent repression of dissidents and deadly conflict in Syria, there has not been a similar intervention.

It is tempting for commentators and policy analysts to compare the Arab Spring to earlier waves of democratization and 'project' a particular model of democratization with a particular set of 'sequences' on the region. Such a view is both optimistic and inappropriate. It is **optimistic** since it assumes that regime change in the region necessarily converts into democratization, it is **inappropriate** since it assumes that there is a standard sequence through which transitional countries proceed. It is clear from the developments in the region that protest mobilization was largely initiated as an economic critique based on rising expectations primarily among young people coupled with a real decline in economic opportunity. When met with government repression, efforts at mobilization focused on regime change framed politically as the primary objective to address the economic crisis. It is not clear that democracy and democratization were central in the framing of the protests. Rather, much mobilization focused on the incumbent regime and regime change itself. The protests in Tunisia began in rural areas that are remote from the capital Tunis and became nationalized and generalized over time in the face of repression and an unyielding incumbent regime, which in the end was overthrown (see Anderson 2011; Breuer et al. 2012). The protesters in Egypt were more based in Cairo initially, while in Libya, the rebels were more organized along tribal lines (Anderson 2011: 2). Out of three cases that have undergone regime change, Tunisia and Egypt have had elections, but while elections are an important feature of democracy, they do not mean that democracy has been achieved. Moreover, the countries in the region need to reconcile over issues around Islam, secular law, legal frameworks for democracy and the competition between political parties, some of which are not popular and may not share value orientations that resonate favourably with Western governments.

SUGGESTIONS FOR FURTHER READING

Diamond, Larry (2011) *The Spirit of Democracy: The Struggle to Build Free Societies Throughout the World.* Henry Holt and Company.
Huntington, Samuel (1991) *The Third Wave: Democratization in the Late Twentieth Century.* Norman, UK: University of Oklahoma Press.
Keane, John (2009) *The Life and Death of Democracy.* New York: Simon and Schuster.

Notes

1 On 27 September 2012, the representation to the European Union of the State of North Rhine Westphalia along with the German Development Institute hosted a policy event in Brussels on democratic diffusion, the Arab Spring and EU democracy promotion, where precisely these kinds of issues were raised with the respect the dramatic development across the Middle East and North Africa.

2 Such a characterization refers to Venezuelan President Hugo Chavez, who sought to bring about his Bolivarian Revolution through populist means.

3 President Obama condemned Zelaya's removal as 'illegal'; see http://news.bbc.co.uk/1/hi/8125292.stm; last accessed 22 July 2011.

4 I exclude Turkmenistan, since after the collapse of the Soviet Union, it never engaged in what could be described as an electoral process and the death of its leader President Saparmurat Niyazov (the Turkmenbashi) in December 2006 led to his successor Kurbanguly Berdymuhamedov maintaining the authoritarian regime, who has reduced the more cultish aspects for which Niyazov was famous.

5 For thorough analyses of this period, see Levine (1989) and Peeler (1992).

6 The law was passed in July 2012 and threatens the work of such NGOs as Amnesty International and Transparency International. See http://www.bbc.co.uk/news/world-europe-18938165; last accessed 24 October 2012.

CHAPTER FIVE

Evidence and explanations

Introduction

We saw in the previous chapter that the experience of democracy, democratization and the advancement of human rights are both vast and highly variegated. Many countries and regions have made great progress in establishing democracy and protecting human rights during the course of the twentieth century and early years of the twenty-first century, while other countries have seen setbacks or continued forms of authoritarian rule where democracy continues to be elusive and human rights continue be violated. For analysts of global politics, these trends across time and space are referred to as 'variation', and as we shall see in this chapter, such **variation** is in need of **explanation**. The social sciences have developed and continue to develop theories and methods that help us understand how, why and under what conditions are the advance of democracy and human rights possible. This combination of theories and methods seeks to reduce the complexity of what we observe in the world and look for common sets of factors that account for the kinds of changes that were discussed in the previous chapter.

The different theories involve concentrating either separately or an in integrated fashion on (1) broad sets of **social and economic conditions**; (2) different kinds of **choices and strategies** made by leaders, followers and opposition groups; and (3) a host of **international factors** that both hinder and help the advance of democracy and human rights. Methods for testing these theories and providing explanations for the variation in democracy and human rights that is observed involve **statistical analysis of a large number of countries** over time and space; **comparative historical analysis** of a smaller subset of countries within and between regions; and **case studies** that map out the processes and pathways that particular countries have taken on the road to greater democracy and a fuller protection of human rights. Throughout these analyses, the focus is on identifying a series of generalizations that can be made about why and under what conditions democracy comes about and how the protection of human rights can be improved.

This chapter thus discusses these different sets of explanations to show how analysts have sought to explain the trends in democracy and human rights. The discussion examines the underlying assumptions of the explanations, the factors upon which they focus and the methods that they have used to support their arguments. There are many debates surrounding these different explanations since they have significant implications for the ways in which we understand the current state of global politics and what we think we can do to make a positive difference. You will see how different explanations have had an influence on policymakers and practitioners that are working to bring about and support the advance of democracy and human rights. The explanations considered here include (1) the so-called modernization perspective (both in its original and revised forms); (2) comparative history and 'macro-historical' change; (3) rational choice and 'games of transition'; (4) democratic transformation and transnational advocacy; and (5) international dimensions and diffusion. The chapter does not settle on any one of these explanations as superior, but examines their strengths and weaknesses while identifying in what ways they can be (or have been) linked to international policy and practice.

Modernization

As we saw in Chapter 2, attention to the trade-offs between 'abundance' and 'freedom' is based on a basic assumption that high levels of economic development are related to higher levels of democracy and, by extension, better protection of human rights. This assumption has been a bedrock of the 'modernization' perspective, which posits that as countries undergo large processes of socio-economic development, they experience a series of changes that also encourage the development of democratic institutions. This theory began in part with a book entitled *Political Man* published by Seymour Martin Lipset in 1960 and in part with a book entitled *The Stages of Economic Growth* published in 1961 by Dankwart Rustow, which both see a (a) direct link between economy and politics and (b) a natural process of development through 'stages' that are increasingly progressive. Modernization theory claims that as countries save and invest at appropriate levels (usually 20% of gross domestic product is taken as a good proportion of national savings) that help enhance their infrastructure and social institutions, liberal democratic institutions will flourish. The stages of development lead to higher levels of education, improve social and spatial mobility and promote the political culture that supports liberal democratic institutions. In this way, the theory assumes that the process of socio-economic development is 'a progressive accumulation of changes that ready a society to its culmination, democratization' (Przeworski and Limongi 1997).

The theory has been hugely popular and hugely influential and in many ways 'rediscovered' or given a new impetus with the end of the Cold War, where the defeat of Communist ideologies led to a certain triumphalism for Western ideals relating to democracy and human rights. Indeed in *The End of History and the Last Man*, Francis Fukuyama (1992) argues that the Western model was not only successful, but the only possible set of ideas for the world, and that it was only a matter of time, that the rest of the world would arrive at state of well-developed capitalist democracy. In an article in 1997, Max Singer summarized the optimism of the modernization perspective as follows:

> Because some societies learned to increase productivity, presently about 1/7th of the world's population lives in wealthy, democratic, and peaceful countries – unlike anything seen in history. The process that changed them is still continuing, probably accelerating, and there is every reason to believe that it will continue until by the end of the coming century, or the one after, essentially all the world will be wealthy, democratic, and peaceful as North America and Western Europe are now (Singer 1997: 28).

The appeal of and the arguments that sustain the modernization perspective have been supported primarily by large-scale statistical analyses across many countries at different periods of time. The original analysis conducted by Seymour Martin Lipset used multiple indicators for economic modernization and categories of countries that included stable and unstable democracies and stable and unstable dictatorships. He found that, on average, stable democracies had higher values for his measures of economic modernization than any of the other categories of countries. He concluded from this that the 'more well to do a nation, the more likely it is to sustain democracy'; a claim that has then been subjected to increasingly sophisticated statistical analysis that continues to this day. Analyses have added more sophisticated measures of democracy and economic development, a greater coverage of time, and have controlled for a number of factors related to modernization. The result of these analyses, as outlined already in Chapter 2, is that there is a positive and significant relationship between economic development and democracy.

The assumptions of the modernization perspective and the methods for supporting it have also influenced analysis of the variation in the protection of human rights. Studies from the 1980s compared indicators on the protection of different kinds of civil and political rights and correlated them with measures of economic development. More sophisticated analyses that followed, as in the research on democracy, added different measures of human rights and more time to their analysis, as well as additional sets of factors that help explain the variation in human rights protection. The results of these studies are very similar to the work on democracy: wealthy countries have better records at protecting these sets of human rights than poor countries, even after controlling for other key factors like democracy, war and the size of the population (see, e.g. Poe and Tate 1994; Landman 2005b). Additional measures on the quality of economic development also show that wealthy countries with better distributions of income have better records of protecting civil and political rights (Landman and Larizza 1999). The theorizing and discussion of these results make less of a straightforward appeal to modernization per se, but the assumptions and impulse behind such studies are very much in line with the modernization perspective. In this case, it is assumed that wealthy countries have more resources necessary to protect human rights, but the direct connection between economic **change** and **transformation** is not seen as such a critical factor as in the work on democracy. Indeed, one study found no relationship between economic change and the protection of human rights (see Poe and Tate 1994).

Despite the political interest and robust statistical support for the modernization perspective, there are continued worries about its limitations. It places too much emphasis on economic modernization and economic progress, effectively making a highly material and deterministic argument for political change. It tends to ignore historical processes, which are often highly contingent and where change occurs in less than uniform ways across different countries. It ignores the individuals either at the elite or popular level who have had a stake in the creation of democracy and the struggle for human rights. It ignores the timing of economic modernization, since the global powers of the today modernized in some cases more than 100 years before other countries, which has given them a 'head start' as well as a dominant position in the global political economy that may well prevent other countries from modernizing in the same way, or at all. Indeed, some studies have shown that the relative position of a country in the global political economy conditions the relationship between economic development and democracy (see Burkhart and Lewis-Beck 1994; Foweraker and Landman 2004).

Finally, from within the perspective itself there have been revisions to its basic premise. For example, in *Political Order in Changing Societies*, Samuel Huntington (1968) has argued that economic modernization leads to raised expectations within different social groups and that in the absence of proper institutions for channelling and representing these expectations, a country undergoing rapid modernization may actually become less politically stable. This view is of course is a direct challenge to the optimism of the modernization perspective. It does not undermine it completely but adds these further dimensions of **institutions** and **order** that need to be taken into account. The main differences between modernization and

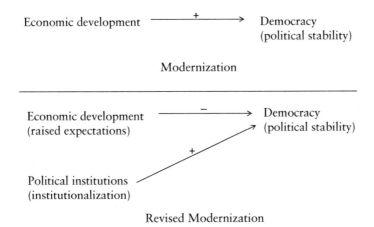

FIGURE 5.1 *Modernization and revised modernization.*

revised modernization are captured in Figure 5.1, where the automatic association between economic development and democracy is modified so that economic development could have a negative impact on political stability (read democracy) which can be tempered by the degree of political institutionalization.

Interestingly, many years later in the *Clash of Civilizations*, in addressing global challenges after the Cold War, Huntington (1996: 192) argues that 'economic development is the major underlying factor' generating democratic transitions, which shows that his position is more or less in line with the modernization perspective broadly understood. The attraction of the modernization perspective continues until today, and as Chapter 2 argued, many of its assumptions formed the basis for the neo-conservative view that political change could be accelerated through force (see Fukuyama 2006). And no doubt there will be a connection made between the relative wealth of the Middle East and China (or at least its rapid economic advance) and the process of political mobilization and liberalization that is apparent. There is a strong impulse for policymakers and practitioners to take the modernization perspective and its statistical findings as a basis for foreign and aid policy, which privileges economic development as a means to democratization, and it assumes that democratization itself is a sequential affair that necessarily moves from one stage to the next in linear fashion.

My own cautious optimism in this book about the appeal of democracy and human rights is not necessarily linked to economic development per se (although wealth in a country does provide more flexibility for governments), as many of the cases discussed in this book have achieved democracy and increased protection of human rights in the absence of large-scale economic modernization. And the Arab Spring does renew my optimism for political progress and transformation away from tyranny and authoritarianism. It may be that Fukuyama's argument in *The End of History* is correct in his claim that democracy and human rights represent a set of ideas that are unrivalled in their appeal to and respect for human dignity and that such appeal motivates individuals and groups to push for change. But this motivation is not necessarily borne of their economic circumstances. Rather, the values associated with democracy and human rights have a natural appeal to those living under oppressive regimes. The Reith lectures from Burmese dissident Aung San Suu Kyi on **liberty**[1] and **dissent**[2] illustrate the power of these ideas, particularly for those to whom they have been denied. A few excerpts from her lecture are apt for our consideration here:

> The freedom to make contact with other human beings with whom you may wish to share your thoughts, your hopes, your laughter, and at times even your anger and indignation is a right that should never be violated.
>
> . . .
>
> If pressed to explain what the word means to them, they would most likely reel off a list of the concerns nearest to their hearts such as there won't be any more political prisoners, or there will be freedom of speech and information and association, or we can choose the kind of government we want, or simply, and sweepingly, we will be able to do what we want to do.
>
> This may all sound naïve, perhaps dangerously naïve, but such statements reflect the sense of freedom as something concrete that has to be gained through practical work, not just as a concept to be captured through philosophical argument.

Macro-historical change

While the appeal of the modernization perspective is strong, much doubt remains about the 'mechanisms' that connect economic development to higher levels of democracy and/or better protection of human rights. For many, it is precisely the **unevenness** of economic development and the great variation of that process across countries in terms of factor endowments (i.e. land, labour and capital), timing of development (e.g. before or after the industrial revolution; before or after decolonization), the role of the state (command economy, state-led development, **laissez faire** modes of development), and the different models of development and the degree to which a country pursues so-called import-substitution (as in Latin America between the 1930s and 1960s) or export promotion (as in case of the East Asian 'tiger' economies in the 1970s and 1980s). This great variation, many have argued, will condition the probability that democracy will flourish and whether the country embraces a 'rights-protective' culture in its legal framework and state institutions (see Donnelly 1999). Over-reliance on particular factor endowments (oil for example) can concentrate wealth and power in the hands of those who have no interest in democracy or rights. Rapid state-led development may encourage a mindset that thinks the repression of labour is essential in the short term for economic advance (see Geddes 1990). Market protections for primary exports may skew the distribution of wealth and power to landed elites who block any moves towards democracy.

Common to all these kinds of arguments about the establishment of democracy and rights, is a focus on groups of countries that are compared across periods of economic transformation as instances of macro-historical change and typically do not involve the use of statistical analysis. Rather, these arguments and explanations focus on broad sets of economic change, large social variables such as social classes and the alliances that form between them; state power at the domestic and international levels; the distribution of land, labour and capital; and models of development followed by particular sets of state elites. Countries are not seen as all on the same linear trajectory, but as discrete units that follow pathways of development that take them the traditional to the modern world. The key message from this kind of work is that democracy is not the inevitable outcome of economic modernization, that different routes to modernity might actually involve significant violence and conflict and non-democratic solutions to maintaining order such as communism and fascism and that routes followed by some countries (such as the United States and some European countries) are not available to those that undergo subsequent processes of economic development.

Three particularly notable studies are Barrington Moore (1966) *The Social Origins of Dictatorship and Democracy*, Rueschemeyer, Stephens and Stephens (1992) *Capitalist Development and Democracy* and Acemoglu and Robinson (2006) *The Economic Origins of Dictatorship and Democracy*. All three studies are motivated by a connection between economic development and democracy, but none of them see a necessary or direct connection between the two. Rather, they argue that processes of economic development unleash different sources of power for different groups of people in society, each of which will have different motivations to bring about (or not) democratization. The first two studies engage in various sets of comparisons across countries with similar pathways or routes to the modern world, while the latter study provides historical case examples that confirm more formal economic models of the incentive structures that are conducive to democratic and non-democratic systems.

The comparison of routes to modernity reveals that **democracy is but one outcome** alongside fascism (a so-called revolution from above) and communism (a revolution from below). Barrington Moore's (1966) comparisons of the so-called liberal route include a focus on the violent

nature of 'bourgeois revolutions' that are necessary for democracy, since
they allow a country to break from its feudal past and pave the way for
democratization. In comparing a larger number of countries than Moore
(1966), Rueschemeyer, Stephens and Stephens (1992) show that such
violence may not be necessary and that the true agents of democratization
are the **working classes**, whose success in obtaining political inclusion is
tempered by the dominance of particular sets of elites. Thus, the type of
economic modernization and who benefits from it, along with the ways
in which subordinate groups such as the working class are included in the
political system, determine whether a country achieves democratization.
In both cases, the comparison of **pathways** and **processes**, and not simple
measures of statistical association, provides a richer and more nuanced
understanding of how democracy does or does not come about as a result
of economic development.

In many ways, the Acemoglu and Robinson (2006) study is a natural
outgrowth of these two earlier studies. They too are intrigued with the
empirical reality that many countries in history underwent profound
economic development, but did not achieve democracy. They too focus
on the mixed set of incentives that occur whenever a country undergoes
economic development. But they model these incentives using the tools of
modern economics, and they focus on the allocation of political power
and resources and how that allocation links to public preferences for
democracy. They examine the costs and benefits associated with the use of

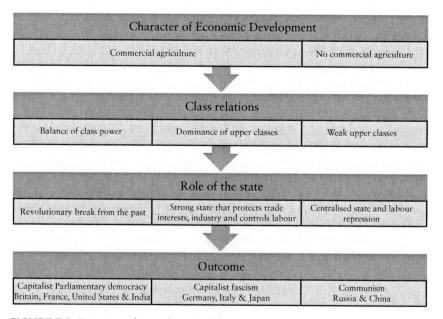

FIGURE 5.2 *Routes to the modern world.*

Source: Moore 1966 adapted from Landman 2008: 117.

	Uruguay, Argentina	Colombia, Ecuador	Brazil	Bolivia, Venezuela	Chile, Peru	Mexico	Paraguay
Development	Export expansion Agriculture Non-labour intensive	Export expansion Agriculture Non-labour intensive	Export expansion Agriculture Non-labour intensive	Export expansion Agriculture Mineral	Export expansion Agriculture Mineral	Export expansion Agriculture Mineral	No Export expansion Agriculture Non-labour intensive
Mobilizing agent	Clientelistic parties	Clientelistic parties	State	Radical mass parties	Radical mass parties	Revolution	State
Industrialization	Before 1930	After 1945	1930–1945	After 1945	After 1945	Before 1930	After 1945
Initial democracy	Before 1930	1930–1945 Ecuador after 1945	1945–1965	1930–1945 Bolivia after 1945	1930; 1930–1945 for Peru	Before 1930	After 1945
Outcome	Full stable democracy > 12 years	Restricted stable democracy > 12 years	Restricted stable democracy > 12 years	Full unstable democracy < 12 years	Restricted unstable democracy < 12 years	Authoritarianism	Authoritarianism

FIGURE 5.3 *Pathways to initial democratization.*

Source: Ruschemeyer, Stephens and Stephens 1992 and Landman 2008.

repression and show how the consolidation of democracy is the function of many different factors, including the strength of civil society (stronger civil society is good for democracy), the structure of political institutions (aggregating different interests is good for democracy), the nature of political and economic crises (severe crises are bad for democracy), the structure of the economy (over-reliance on a few industries is bad for democracy) and the level of economic inequality (high concentrations of wealth are bad for democracy).

These historical and somewhat 'longer-term' studies are helpful for us to understand the contingent nature of the establishment and maintenance of democracy and certainly shed light on such processes taking place today. It is clear that democracy is not an automatic outcome of economic development but one that relies on a set of **necessary** and **sufficient** conditions falling into place. Lower-class mobilization for inclusion that is met with some form of accommodation and balance of power and institutionalized through political party organizations that can compete under a system in which victory is possible provides a good set of conditions for the successful installation of democracy. Such an institutionalized system carries with it the need for basic rights protections, such as the right to vote, the right to exercise free speech and the rights to association and assembly. The contestation for power needs systems in which independent associations such as political parties can form, aggregate their interests, express their demands and grievances and seek political power through the electoral process. But as we saw in Chapter 3, democracy also requires the guarantee of social and economic rights as well as the protection of minority and cultural rights. The former set of rights provide avenues for the least well-off to participate in democracy, while the latter set of rights protect individuals from undue discrimination on the basis of race, gender, ethnicity, religious affiliation and other social categories.

Games of transition

The broad attention to the economic 'preconditions' of democracy, whether seen as having necessary or contributing influences on the establishment of democracy, does not have much to say about the actual **individuals** involved in bringing about democracy. The economic accounts focus on large 'macro' variables such as classes, class relations and alliances, state power and underlying processes of economic change. These accounts do not give the actors that make democracy possible their full attention, and it is this dearth of attention to individuals that has spurred a lot of analysis that focuses precisely on 'who did what, when, how, and why'. General Franco decided to legalize the Spanish Community party, Mikhail Gorbachev decided to pursue a policy of **glasnost** and **perestroika**, Augusto Pinochet decided to have a plebiscite for his continued rule, F. W. De Klerk decided to release Nelson Mandela from prison, the Generals of Burma Myanmar decided to release Aung San Suu Kyi and the Egyptian military elite decided not to support Hosni Mubarak (and have proved reluctant to leave power). These and other intentional choices have had profound implications for democratization and the advance of human rights. But these choices can also be subjected to systematic and stylized analysis that moves beyond the narratives and delves into the motivations of leaders, the different calculations they make about preserving their power and their interactions with others at the moment of decision.

Any analysis that focuses on such choices typically uses the power of 'game theory' to explain the trade-offs leaders face in making such profound decisions, the likely response from their opponents and the structure of different outcomes that result from their strategic interaction with others. Based on the modelling of choice behaviour from the so-called prisoners dilemma' in which two criminal suspects are held in separate cells and presented with different choice scenarios, game theory applications in democratization focus on the choices that elites make and how such choices either lead to democracy or maintain authoritarianism. Such analyses assume that authoritarian leaders in power (government) want to remain in power and leaders out of power (opposition) want to win control over power. But each set of leaders – either in government or in opposition – can choose different strategies for obtaining power. So-called hardliners in government will want to use repression to hold onto their power and resist moves towards liberalization, such as the release of celebrated political dissidents. So-called softliners in government see partial liberalization (e.g. eliminating restrictions on the press, freeing political dissidents, allowing independent associations to form) as a way to appease the opposition and maintain their hold on power. In the opposition, two groups are also present who hold different views on their strategy for engaging with the authoritarian government. On the one hand, 'radicals' have no desire to negotiate with the regime and seek its overthrow, even if that requires violence to do so. On the other hand, 'moderates' are willing to negotiate with the government to move a reform agenda forward in the eventual hope of establishing democracy.

The crucial aspect of this kind of explanation for democracy is what the softliners in the government choose to do and what the moderates in the opposition choose to do. These two groups of leaders represent the 'democratic potential' for a country about to undergo a transition. If the softliners truly have more power vis a vis the hardliners, then it is in their interest to liberalize the authoritarian regime and seek a deal with the moderates in the opposition. If the moderates in the opposition truly have more power than the radicals, then it is in their interest to seek some kind of negotiated settlement with the softliners in government. However, such

		'Softliners' in the authoritarian regime: Break from authoritarian regime and liberalize (Cooperate)	'Softliners' in the authoritarian regime: Do not break from authoritarian regime (Defects)
Moderates in the opposition	Break from their radicals (Cooperate)	R, R Democracy with guarantees, elite pact in the centre	S, T Authoritarian regime remains with some concessions
	Do not break from their radicals (Defects)	T, S Democracy, but with no guarantees, always a threat from the radicals	P, P Authoritarian regime survives, polarization continues

Note: T = temptation to defect, R = reward, P = punishment, S = sucker's payoff; these are listed in order of preference such that T>R>P>S

FIGURE 5.4 *Democratic transformation: A revised 'Dynamic Model'.*

Source: Adapted from Przeworski (1991: 69); Cohen (1994: 67–68); Landman (2006: 42).

a formulation leaves open the possibility that the softliners do not seek to liberalize and that moderates do not seek a settlement. Such a state of affairs means that the strategic interaction between softliners and moderates can lead to four different outcomes in which democracy is but one possible outcome. Figure 5.4 summarizes the game theoretic approach to democratization where it is clear that softliners in government can liberalize (i.e. 'cooperate' with the moderates) or maintain the authoritarian regime (i.e. 'defect' from the moderates), and where moderates can negotiate (i.e. 'cooperate' with the softliners) or reject any negotiation and seek violent overthrow of the regime (i.e. 'defect' from the softliners). The figure also shows that there are four ordered 'payoffs' associated with these different choices:

1 The temptation to defect (T) is the most preferred
2 Reward for cooperation (R) is the next preferred
3 Punishment for defecting (P) is the next preferred
4 The so-called sucker's payoff for choosing the losing strategy (S) is least preferred

Only when the softliners and the moderates cooperate with each other is democracy possible and both sets of actors are rewarded (R, R). Otherwise, the three other outcomes are obtained, which include maintenance of the authoritarian regime with some concessions (e.g. release of prisoners and relaxation of press censorship), democracy with no real guarantees (highly unstable) and survival of the authoritarian regime.

Such an approach reveals the precariousness of democracy and its reliance, at least in the early years, on deal making, assurances and the balance of power within the previous authoritarian regime and within the new democracy. On this view, democracy is not the automatic outcome of social processes, but the **contingent outcome** of political choices. For example, in Poland, game theory can explain both the continued authoritarianism of the Jaruzelski government during the period of martial law in the 1980s and the transition to democracy in 1989. In the early 1980s, several 'moves' in the game between the Solidarity Movement and the government resulted in stalemate, open confrontation and the declaration of martial law. The changing political environment in Moscow under Gorbachev led the Polish government to change its preferences and issue a series of reforms that included the legalization of Solidarity and at least nominal representation in the Polish Parliament (see Colomer and Pascual 1994). A similar analysis can explain democratic transition in Chile. In a very careful analysis of over 40,000 internal documents of the Chilean military, Darren Hawkins (2002) shows that a 'rule-oriented' faction within the military regime of Augusto Pinochet had become increasingly worried about international criticism of the regime for its violation of human rights. This faction gained influence within the regime and was behind many of the concessions that were made and that culminated in holding a plebiscite on Pinochet's continued rule in 1988. In the event, Pinochet lost the plebiscite and Chile underwent a transition to democracy during 1989 and 1990. In both cases, the changing calculations of softliners in the government led to different outcomes from their interactions with moderates in the opposition and to transitions to democracy.

For the contemporary period during the Arab Spring, hardliners in the Ben Ali regime in Tunisia were not strong enough to counter the rise of popular protest, and the regime fell relatively quickly. New elections were held in October 2011, just 10 months after the uprising. In Egypt, the military opted not to repress the opponents of Mubarak (although some exceptions did occur) and it became increasingly clear that his resignation was imminent. Like Tunisia, Egypt held elections in a relatively short period after the fall of the regime given how long it had been in power. In Libya, the situation was different. Mohamar Gaddafi had strong support from loyal followers and calculated that he could survive the rebel advances. The changing external environment from the NATO intervention gave more advantage to the rebels who ultimately captured and then killed Gaddafi in October 2011. Across these three cases, it is possible to focus on the decisions and calculations made by elites in the regime and in the opposition to compare and contrast the different outcomes that were obtained. As in the theoretical range of possibilities, these cases show variation in outcomes that differ in terms of the timing of regime change and the potential for democratic transition. Tunisia and Egypt have embarked on the first steps to democracy with their elections, but the subsequent period of consolidation will require tolerance of and accommodation between different political forces in these countries.

The making of democracy

The game theoretic approaches have value in moving the explanation of democratization beyond the focus on structural conditions such as economic modernization and showing the array of different political outcomes that can be obtained from the strategic interaction of elites. But both the structural and rational explanations for democratization tend to leave out any sense of other forms of agency, such as those from popular protest, social movements and civil society organizations. In popular accounts of democratic transition during the third wave of democratization (e.g. O'Donnell et al. 1986), there is a passing reference to the 'resurrection of civil society' that coincides with elite pact making, where some role for social mobilization is acknowledged. However, history has shown that the making of democracy is also about mobilization from below, and it is clear that the fall of the Berlin Wall and the Arab Spring have had a large role for popular forces for change. Ordinary people gathered together in public spaces to contest the power of incumbent regimes. It is here that the idea of human rights has a significant role to play. The history of the struggle for rights is one in which popular groups mobilize for the extension of rights protections from the state, and if such protections are not forthcoming, continued struggle can lead to regime change, followed by a process of democratization that carries with it an improvement in rights protections (Foweraker and Landman 1997). Cross-national and quantitative research has shown that even during the first year after a democratic transition, rights conditions can improve dramatically (Zanger 2000). But the differences across categories of human rights matter as well. Popular mobilization can often take the form of a critique of the absence of protection of social and economic rights. Such mobilization and organization of protest can in turn provoke a repressive reaction from the state. If the crackdown and limitation on freedom are significant, then the demands and language of rights articulated by popular movements can shift to demands for the protection of civil and political rights, as well as a call for regime change.

In a study on social mobilization and citizenship rights in Brazil, Chile, Mexico and Spain, popular movements arose initially through a critique of the socio-economic problems of authoritarian regimes and their impact on the lower classes of society. Group formation and mobilization, however, led to crackdowns and a shift in demand to civil and political rights, which over time led to regime change and transitions to democracy in three of the four cases (Brazil, Chile and Spain) (Foweraker and Landman 1997). The transition in Mexico arguably took place in 2000 with the victory of the National Action Party over the PRI (see the Introduction in this volume) and has been seen by many as the culmination of long and multiple waves of social mobilization (see Haber et al. 2008). More recently, the so-called occupy movements that have sprung up in cities in the United States, United Kingdom and Spain, for example, much of the critique and demands have been articulated in terms of economic problems. The construction of '1% versus 99%' is a direct critique of income inequality, corporate greed and dysfunctional systems of governance and regulation. Repressive responses from city police forces, for example, in Oakland, California, in November 2011, can expand the critique beyond economics to one of civil and political rights and the proportionality of state response. In similar fashion, many of the initial demands from the protests in the Arab Spring focused on the inability for the authoritarian regimes in the region to deliver economic prosperity to those that are less well-off. The critique quickly shifted to a broader call for regime change that involved demands for civil and political rights. In addition, the alternative use of new technology and social media has illustrated the ability for common people to find new avenues for expressing their voice. Thus freedom of speech and assembly become topics of contention as these various movements have sought to have their message heard.

The emphasis on the struggle for rights from below and variations in state response from above suggests that democratic transformation involves what Dankwart Rustow (1970) called a 'long period of inclusive struggle'. Social mobilization around rights helps build the popular foundations for democracy, but as in some of the explanatory frameworks outlined in this chapter, there are no guarantees that such mobilization will lead to democracy. Rather, at a crucial 'decision phase', states can make concessions and maintain the bulk of their authoritarian institutions. States may crack down and seek to quash an emerging movement (as in Tiananmen Square in 1989 or the Monk's protest in Burma in 2007), but such a move always brings with it the memory of the event and a long-term desire within the populace for regime change and justice (see Chapter 7 in this volume). This interaction between society and the state suggests a much longer view on political change that involves both the macro-variables of economic modernization and the micro-variables of choice and strategy. Democratic transformation (see Figure 5.5) takes place through several key phases, none of which are inevitable and none of which are irreversible.

International dimensions

The final set of explanations focus on what can be broadly understood as the international dimensions. Countries are not isolated units in 'autarky' but part of a larger system of interaction and inter-dependence. What goes on in one part of the world can have an impact on what happens in another part of the world, but how this happens can vary across different international dimensions. The dimensions of most interest that help us understand the advance of democracy and human rights include direct state-to-state (i.e. bilateral) interactions, multilateral interactions involving institutions such as the United Nations or the World Bank, transnational engagement from international non-governmental organizations and 'agentless' processes of diffusion brought about by the increase in the flow of information and value sets from one part of the world to another. Variously described as 'contagion', 'diffusion' and 'globalization', these processes that spread democracy and human rights through both intentional and unintentional means, and it often difficult to disentangle the two when seeking to explain the international dimensions of democracy and human rights.

The idea of contagion refers mostly to the influence of processes among a set of contiguous or nearly contiguous countries. Thus, the democratic transitions in Southern Europe all happened in the space of a few years between 1974 and 1977, while in Eastern Europe, the fall of the Berlin

Authoritarianism	Mobilization and liberalization	Moment of decision	Consolidation	Habituation
Hardline control of state apparatus Restriction on or violation of human rights	'prolonged and inconclusive political struggle'	Strategic interaction between 'softliners' in regime and 'moderates' in opposition	Recurrent elections Alternation of political power Implementation of rights regime	Societal acceptance of new democratic institutions and rules for contesting power
	Demand for social and economic rights shifts to civil and political rights	Democracy is one of four possible outcomes Reversal is possible	End of overt challenges to rule through violent means	May take a generation or more

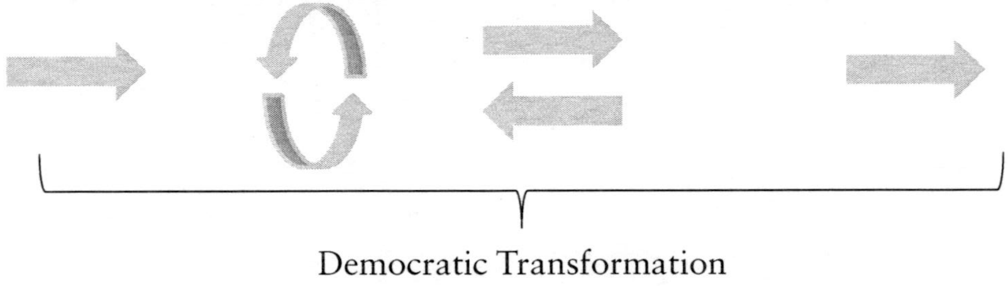

Democratic Transformation

FIGURE 5.5 *Democratic transformation.*

Source: Rustow (1970).

Wall and subsequent transitions in Eastern Europe were geographically and temporally close to one another. In Latin America, contagion processes began in 1978 and were more or less completed at least in South America by 1990 when Chile elected its first democratic president since 1970. One could argue that contagion processes have been at play during the Arab Spring, as events that began in Tunisia quickly spread to Egypt (not entirely contiguous but very close), Yemen, Libya, Syria, Bahrain and beyond. While proximity and time are fascinating to see as the call for democracy and rights spread, the concept of 'contagion' remains largely descriptive in that some sort of change is 'caught' by neighbouring countries, but it begs the question as to why a country is susceptible to catching the new ideas and how groups within the receiving country pick up those ideas and try them in their own systems.

Contagion is part of the idea of diffusion, which is understood both as a process and an outcome of political change. In my own view, diffusion should be seen more as a process than an outcome. Diffusion effects (also called neighbourhood effects, demonstration effects and social 'bandwagonning') manifest themselves in the spread of norms, ideas and practices not only among neighbouring states, but between states that can be quite far away from one another. Indeed, the protesters at the Occupy Wall Street site in New York were selling badges that said 'Fight Like an Egyptian', making direct reference to the occupation of Tahrir square in Cairo. Here, a popular 'repertoire of contention' (see McAdam et al. 1997) was diffused from protests in Egypt to those in New York (and as it happens in other cities). Diffusion as a process means that it is a mechanism through which a set of norms, ideas and practices gets transferred between states. It is time-dependent and exhibits a temporal causal flow in ways that can be tracked and explained using empirical methods. It has both intentional and unintentional dimensions, which is to say, the flow of norms, ideas and practices can proceed in an **uncoordinated fashion,** but equally there are occasions in which certain **intentional behaviours** from state and non-state actors can accelerate the process of diffusion.

Intentional dimensions of diffusion include coercive and non-coercive agencies. Military intervention such as the coalition invasion of Afghanistan in 2001 and Iraq in 2003 to ostensibly bring about democracy are the most salient recent examples of coercive intervention. The NATO operation in Libya is another example of coercive imposition. Even though the intervention was ostensibly to protect civilians who were vulnerable from attack by the Gaddafi regime, it certainly contributed to the efforts of the rebels seeking to overthrow of the regime. The Marshall Plan in Europe and the rebuilding of Japan by the West after World War II are also good examples of intentional intervention that was made possible after the recipient country had been defeated in war. But a lot of diffusion takes place through the exercise of 'soft power' (Nye 2009), diplomacy and transnational advocacy networks

(TANs) comprised of large and influential international non-governmental organizations (see Keck and Sikkink 1998). In the latter case, international non-governmental organizations communicate with domestic NGOs and in conjunction with inter-governmental organizations put pressure on states to bring about political transformation. The most notable examples of these kinds of diffusion have been presented in Risse, Ropp and Sikkink's (1999) *Power of Human Rights*, which shows that pressure and activity from transnational advocacy networks on authoritarian states in many case led to regime change and the development of an institutionalized human rights culture. Activism from the international arena complements and supports the mobilization phase of democratic transformation outlined above (see Figure 5.5). But again, such activism from above does not guarantee such a transformation if intransigent elites seek to hold onto to power, as was the case in Libya under Gaddafi, or as is the case in China with respect to Tibet, or Cuba under Fidel Castro.

The spread of ideas is not just some ephemeral phenomenon, but also has a material base that is important to understand. Increased levels of trade, labour mobility and technology transfers (i.e. material processes and exchanges) bring with them associated values, norms and practices and thus act as a social 'transmission belt' for diffusion. The economics of trade and comparative advantage shows that as countries specialize in economic activity for which they have comparative advantage (i.e. capital intensive or labour intensive production), the increased exchange of goods and services bring countries and their cultures closer together. The search for new markets (including cheap labour markets) brings not only a transfer of technology but also ideas and tastes, which in the long run can have an impact on the demand for democracy and human rights. These material and non-material bases for diffusion are clearly different but not mutually exclusive. Moreover, with the spread of information and communications technology (ICTs) along with the democratization of that technology, ideas and practices in one part of the world can easily be captured and assimilated into another part of the world. Diffusion thus has intentional and unintentional as well as material and non-material dimensions, which complement one another in ways that help explain an increase in demand for democracy and human rights.

Finally, it is important to point out that the process of diffusion for democracy may be different than for human rights. The discourse and advocacy for human rights since the Universal Declaration in 1948 have increasingly become reliant on the international law of human rights and its associated institutions and agencies at the international and regional level. The international law of human rights provides a certain amount of jurisprudence about the content of human rights and establishes state obligations to respect, protect and fulfil human rights. These obligations carry with them the obligations to report to the various bodies that monitor compliance with UN human rights treaties. While deeply flawed and seen by many as nothing more than a paper tiger, the process of filing reports and receiving comments from the treaty bodies places human rights discussions firmly in the public domain and as such provides international and national non-governmental organizations with significant leverage to call states to account over serious human rights abuses; leverage which may well serve to bring about regime change in the long run. Treaty ratification has been shown to have a positive and significant influence on state practice, but an influence that is conditioned by other factors, such as levels of economic development, domestic mobilization and international linkages (see Landman 2005; Simmons 2009).

The international architecture for human rights has grown in depth and breadth, as more and more rights become enumerated for protection, more states ratify international treaties and more regions establish their own mechanisms for the promotion and protection of human rights. In contrast, no such equivalent mechanisms, jurisprudence or content (at least derived from an international set of legal standards) exists for democracy. On the one hand, this means that there is no standard against which to make appeals and no set of institutions with which to engage such as the Human Rights Council, the Office of the High Commissioner for Human Rights or the Treaty Bodies. On the other hand, the absence of such institutions for the promotion of democracy means that it is less well-defined and democracy advocates can remain flexible in how they define it, how they establish it and how they build it over time. As I argued in Chapter 3, democracy is less contentious and 'absolutist' in discursive terms and thus offers more room for manoeuvre for those seeking to bring it about.

Summary

This chapter has considered a variety of explanations and the kind of evidence used to support them for the spread of democracy and human rights. It has shown how earlier attention focused on the so-called structural conditions or the macro-social variables relating to the large-scale processes of economic modernization. Studies since the 1950s have shown a positive and significant relationship between levels of economic development and democracy, but the precise relationship between the two is still open to debate, even though there is a general consensus that development is certainly good for democracy. From a purely economically rational perspective, a wider economic base allows a democratic government to deliver benefits to key constituents and thus 'buy' loyalty to democracy itself. But when attention is focused on the changes unleashed by socio-economic modernization, the direct association with democracy is thrown into question, as the nature of development, classes, class alliances and state power all have contingent effects on the probability of democracy taking root and surviving in the long run. And even if the macro-conditions are favourable, analysis of the micro-conditions suggests that strategic interactions at the 'moment of decision' can lead to outcomes that are not democratic, while subsequent 'games of transition' may eventually lead to democracy.

The 'transformational' perspective advanced in this chapter recognizes the starting conditions for democracy, as well as the contingent nature of its arrival, but it also focuses on the role for popular agency in the struggle for democracy and how that struggle can be both long and inconclusive. This perspective challenges the patience of policymakers, particularly those working in the business of 'democracy promotion' who are often dependent themselves on the electoral cycle at home to 'deliver' on their foreign policy objectives. The chapter has shown that any attention to democratic transformation must take into account the international dimension in terms of contagion and diffusion and the (un)intentional aspects of democratization. It has also argued that in many ways the struggle for rights and the 'right to have rights' has been an important catalyst for processes of democratic transformation, where demands for economic and social rights shift to demands for civil and political rights. This struggle for rights has had further support with the advent and subsequent development of the international human rights regime that began formally with the 1948 Universal Declaration of Human Rights. Indeed, the 'architecture' for human rights makes their international diffusion easier in many ways as popular groups can use the language of rights as leverage for regime change within their own countries.

While it is difficult to present an entirely coherent assessment of the different findings from the different kinds of explanations available that account for the growth in democracy and human rights, there are some common lines of agreement and perhaps even a consensus. The installation of democracy and the development of institutions that guarantee the protection of human rights are precarious. The interaction between and among regime strength, power, individual and collective rationality and the incentives that structure that rationality all have an impact in the degree to which democracy and human rights can develop in any one country. Democracy is one outcome of many, which is contingent on a variety of different factors falling into place, but history has shown that it is an outcome that continues to be obtained.

SUGGESTIONS FOR FURTHER READING

Boix, Carles (2003) *Democracy and Redistribution*. Cambridge: Cambridge University Press.

Coppedge, Michael (2012) *Democratization and Research Methods*. Cambridge: Cambridge University Press.

Landman, Todd (2008) *Issues and Methods of Comparative Politics: An Introduction*. Oxford and London: Routledge.

(Continued)

Moore, Barrington (1966) *Social Origins of Dictatorship and Democracy*. Boston: Beacon Press.

Ruschemeyer, Dietrich, Stephens, Evelyne Huber and Stephens, John D. (1992) *Capitalist Development and Democracy*. Cambridge: Cambridge University Press.

Simmons, Beth (2009) *Mobilizing for Human Rights: International Law in Domestic Politics*. Cambridge: Cambridge University Press.

Notes

1   See http://downloads.bbc.co.uk/rmhttp/radio4/transcripts/2011_reith1.pdf

2   http://downloads.bbc.co.uk/rmhttp/radio4/transcripts/2011_reith2.pdf

CHAPTER SIX

Agents and advocates

Introduction

The 'transformational' approach to understanding the development of democracy and human rights advanced in the previous chapter is seen as a series of phases that are not necessarily automatic or inevitable and that certainly contain a high probability of regression or reversal. These phases include the coming together of necessary and sufficient conditions for at least the **decision** to embrace democracy, but that decision is subject to a wide range of strategic calculations from elites who in turn are conditioned by popular mobilization and demand making from groups in civil society. Historical developments in the latter half of the twentieth century and beginning of the twenty-first century, however, suggest that the notion of popular 'agency' and the proliferation of 'advocates' for democracy and human rights have changed in ways that are important to consider here. Domestic struggles for rights and regime change have particular modalities and pathways that are of significant importance for us to understand political change. But these domestic struggles do not take place in isolation. Rather, they are joined by advocates at the international or 'transnational' level in ways that place additional pressure on states to **at least** make concessions to opposition movements and **at most** contribute to all out regime change and democratization. The connections between and among these actors have become enhanced and in many ways made more complex through the recent 'democratisation of technology' and the direct forms of voice that the democratization of technology encourages (see Crook 2011). This chapter considers the domestic and international agents and advocates responsible for bringing about democracy and the promotion of human rights. It examines the domestic dynamics of social movements and their relationship with regime concession and change. It then looks at how such efforts of domestic change can be 'transnationalized', which is to say, how domestic groups seek assistance from international non-governmental and international governmental organizations to put pressure on regimes to bring about reforms. It concludes with a consideration of how the democratization of technology has contributed to these processes of change, particularly with the advent of the Arab Spring.

Domestic mobilization

Any analysis of the mobilization of domestic agents for change is predicated on a number of assumptions about why and how individuals either form or join protest movements. Early theories of social protest concentrated on the idea of 'grievance' that is shared among a large group of individuals who engage in collective action against the incumbent regime. In this view, grievance has been seen as a sociopsychological phenomenon that was related to perceptions of 'relative deprivation' (e.g. see Ted Robert Gurr's seminal book, *Why Men Rebel*) or mass action based on the psychology of the crowd (e.g. see Elias Canetti's classic book, *Crowds and Power*). Subsequent theories questioned the grievance models, which failed to explain how equally aggrieved people come together to form groups and manage to coordinate collective action in ways that could challenge the power of existing regimes. These critiques argued that 'grievance is everywhere', but it is not clear how such grievance can be converted into sustained collective action in ways that can overturn unpopular regimes (see Foweraker 1995).

Theories based on the 'rationality' assumption from economics questioned how it was possible to keep individuals motivated to remain in a protest group and to sustain collective action over time. The 'problem of collective action', as it became known, pointed out that as group size got large, the benefits for any one person to remain committed to the movement decreased dramatically (see Olson 1965). The problem is also known as the 'free rider' problem, since in areas of mobilization involving so-called public goods, it is irrational for someone to participate in a movement if the benefits would accrue to that person even if they did not participate. Interestingly, at the time the *Logic of Collective Action* (Olson 1965) was published, many countries experienced widespread social protests in the forms of anti-war movements, student movements and women's movements among others. There is thus a paradox between the theory of the free rider and the actual outbreak of social unrest. The struggles for democracy and human rights **are** struggles for the extension of public goods and thus fall within the paradox. Freedom is indivisible even if our understanding of human rights is based on protection of the individual person. If a group is successful in toppling a regime and bringing about democratic change, benefits of life under the new regime would be extended to the whole society not simply to those who were involved in the struggle. By this reasoning, it would be **irrational** for any one person to join the protest movement, particularly if it means a risk to life as we have seen in President Bashar al-Assad's repressive response to political dissidents in Syria since 2011.

The classic solution to the free-rider problem has been for analysts and commentators to identify what kinds of 'private' or 'selective' incentives there are for those individuals who participate in social protest and popular mobilization against incumbent regimes. Such selective incentives can include **material gains** and the **promise to hold power** once the regime has been removed. Throughout history, individuals that have participated in collective action and protest across many different groups in society have received income for their participation, such as money or goods (landowners' livestock, silverware, etc.) that result from successful mobilization (see, e.g. Mark Lichbach's *The Rebel's Dilemma*). But this history also includes multiple examples of social struggles for democracy and human rights. For example, the struggle for citizenship rights in Europe and North America across the eighteenth, nineteenth and twentieth centuries has been characterized by groups that have mobilized for reasons other than for strict material gain (see, Marshall 1963; Barbalet 1988; Foweraker and Landman 1997). Thus, the less 'economic' explanations tend to focus on different kinds of incentives that may include factors such as pride, moral victory, being involved in something that is 'right' and being motivated by values that underpin a commitment to democracy and human rights (Risse et al. 1999).

Many struggles against authoritarianism have a strong economic component, but this is much different than social mobilization being motivated by strict individual material gain. Rather, economic critique forms part of an overall critique of regime ineffectiveness or corruption, which helps galvanize an opposition movement to seek overthrow of the regime. Economic failure or predatory forms of economic development in which the proceeds of economic expansion are not distributed fairly or when government elites are perceived to have misused funds, hoarded national income and exhibited opulent lifestyles can motivate popular mobilization through an appeal to an economic argument. Indeed, the Mubarak regime in Egypt, Gaddafi regime in Libya and Ben Ali regime in Tunisia (not to mention regimes such as those of Baby 'Doc' Duvalier in Haiti, Charles Taylor in Liberia, Idi Amin in Uganda and Saddam Hussein in Iraq) were all guilty of hoarding a significant proportion of national income and engaging in extremely opulent lifestyles. In the case of Tunisia, dissident groups used websites that track airplanes by enthusiasts to show that Ben Ali's presidential airplane was being used for leisure activity; a fact that contributed to the mobilization against him.[1] In Egypt, the discourse of the protestors who occupied Tahrir Square had significant elements of economic critique about the regime. In these cases and many others, however, it is important to stress that initial economic critiques become joined by larger political critiques that, depending on regime responses, can lead to the call for an overthrow of the incumbent regime and the installation of democracy.

Within the broader economic theories of social protest is an attention to the resources that movements have and the constraints under which they operate. Resources include money, membership, skills, communication networks, organizational coherence and strategic alliances between different groups with a common interest in regime change. The nature and extent of such alliances and the degree of organizational coherence are quite dynamic and subject to change, but across a 'cycle of protest' (Tarrow 1994), groups come together and can produce quite large public manifestations. Both the **timing** and **shape** of such cycles of protest are contingent further on the opportunities available for mobilization. Within democratic societies, such opportunities can include significant shifts in political alignments among elites and or political parties, 'critical elections' (Key 1955), government inquiries, economic crisis, declaration of war, among other major events. Political opportunities also include the relative **openness** and **responsiveness** of government to the demands of social movements, where countries vary from closed and unresponsive systems to open and responsive systems (see Kitschelt 1986). In non-democratic societies, political opportunities include key decisions from leaders, (e.g. F. W. De Klerk releasing Nelson Mandela from prison in South Africa or the Generals in Burma/Myanmar releasing Aung San Suu Kyi from house arrest), death of a leader (e.g. the death of Kim Jong Il in North Korea), defeat in war (e.g. the British defeat of Argentina in the Falklands/Malvinas War) and severe economic crises or economic critique. They may also include events that attract widespread international attention, such as the April 2012 Grand Prix in Bahrain, in which opposition groups stepped up their activities in the run up to the event, called for the event to be cancelled and increased their protests on the streets of the capital.

Beyond these considerations of motivation and the formation of successful challenging groups, theories of domestic mobilization also assume the existence of some form of 'civil society' in which independent groups are able to become established and mobilize for change. Civil society has been variously describes as the 'private realm' (Foley and Edwards 1996) of voluntary associations, clubs, guilds, interest groups and other non-profit organizations that are distinctly different from private households on the one hand and the state on the other (see also Rueschemeyer et al. 1992; Cohen and Arato 1992).[2] While they are part of a private realm, civil society groups occupy the 'public sphere' and are seen to be a crucial component or 'arena' for democracy (see Linz and Stepan 1996). Within civil society, like-minded groups come together and form larger social movements and challenge the state in ways that seek change within particular issue areas (e.g. women's rights legislation, nuclear power station construction, or student fees) or seek fundamental change of the political system. It has been argued that civil society is a necessary precondition for social protest movements, and the work on transitions from authoritarian rule suggests that civil society must at least be 'resurrected' before challenges to rule can begin in earnest (O'Donnell et al. 1986).

Such a precondition, however, is problematic if one is to explain how collective action leads to democracy and a greater protection of human rights. Indeed, comparative research has shown that social mobilization is entirely possible under authoritarian conditions with virtually no presence of civil society as it is popularly understood. This research shows further that networks for mobilization exist in latent form that are then the basis upon which social movement activity develops. For example, comparisons of social mobilization in authoritarian Brazil, Chile, Mexico and Spain showed that protest from labour movements and other social movements was not only possible but actually contributed to regime transformation (see Foweraker and Landman 1997). Other studies have shown similar patterns of social mobilization for human rights have been possible across a wide range of country cases in Africa, Latin America and Eastern Europe (see Risse et al. 1999; Hawkins 2002).

Whether civil society is present or not, however, the key to any successful pattern of mobilization is the formation and aggregation of groups. Some groups can be unrelated to political questions initially but can become politicized over time as they engage with the state for prolonged periods. The classic example from the United States is the fundamental role played by Baptist Churches and religious networks in the civil rights movement (see Chong 1991). In Latin America, particular kinds of self-help groups such as women's organizations, soup kitchens, neighbourhood associations and religious 'base communities,' most notably associated with the Catholic Church, became politicized during prolonged periods of authoritarian rule and served as the foundation for challenges to incumbent rulers (see Foweraker 1995; Foweraker et al. 2003; Cleary 2007; Philip and Panizza 2011). Other groups, however, are intentionally political in their advocacy for particular causes, such as women's liberation groups, gay rights groups, anti-war groups, green groups, among many others. Such advocacy groups have been crucial for the kinds of large-scale patterns of domestic mobilization that have led to significant political transformation of the kind relevant to our discussion here. Their day-to-day activities include fund raising, awareness raising, education, research and report writing and documentation of problems within their own issue area. But in times of crisis, networks of advocacy groups form an important social movement 'infrastructure' that can help mobilize large numbers of people.

Differences between these groups tend to be minimized during the build-up to large protests, but continued tensions can have an impact on the longevity of protest and coherence of a mass movement itself. Indeed, a cycle of protest typically peaks at the time of a major event (regime change or massive repression) and during the decline of the wave after such an event old divisions reappear, movement cohesiveness disappears and numbers of people mobilized decrease significantly. Moreover, groups that obtain power after regime change may not be in line with the expectations of those who took part in the cycle of protest. For example, the emergence of the Muslim Brotherhood as a significant contender for political power in Egypt after the fall of Mubarak has not sat comfortably with many who were involved in the protests against him.

Any optimism about the potential for civil society actors to become mobilized under authoritarian conditions needs to be tempered, since it is very important to understand that there are no guarantees that such mobilization will lead to positive change. The comparative study of protest movements under conditions of authoritarian rule has shown a great variety of outcomes around the world. Cycles of protest and regime response unfold over long, contested and inconclusive periods, which may or may not result in regime transformation towards democracy and a greater protection of human rights. Rather, protest can be met with increased repression and further consolidation of authoritarian rule. Key factors for change that are outside the process of social mobilization include new external factors that provide different signals and opportunities for regime opponents, and/or a change in the calculus of authoritarian leaders themselves as they seek to maintain their power. The interaction between these different factors means that regime transformation may well be partial, halting and regressive even though there is widespread popular support for change.

For example, analysis has shown that attempts by the Solidarity movement led by Lech Walesa in Poland in the early 1980s failed to bring about regime change, as the Jaruzelski regime was able to rely on external backing from the Soviet Union. Martial law was imposed between 1981 and 1983, where political opponents of the regime were interned or killed, and those in prison not released under an amnesty until 1986. Real regime change did not occur until the Gorbachev administration in the Soviet Union initiated the glasnost and perestroika reforms (see Colomer and Pascual 1994). In similar fashion, increased social mobilization in the early 1980s during the Pinochet regime in Chile was met by a harsh state of siege that lasted for nearly 2 years in which political opponents were routinely detained and tortured (Hawkins 2002). It was only when Pinochet made a bid to prolong his stay in power in an calculated decision to hold a popular referendum (or plebiscite) did a new possibility for regime change become possible. The 'No Campaign' mobilized supporters to vote against Pinochet, whose ultimate defeat led to a relatively rapid period of regime change that ushered in democracy.

In both the Polish and Chilean cases, it was not inevitable that social mobilization, though possible under conditions of authoritarian rule, would lead to regime change. Rather, initial mobilization was met with a harsh repressive response and prolonged period of continued authoritarianism. Changes in external signals and internal decision-making provided new opportunities for mobilization, which in both cases ultimately saw the ousting of dictators and regime transformation. These cases are not unique, as across the world, there are numerous instances in which mobilization is shut down, authoritarianism prevails and supporters of democracy and defenders of human rights struggle on until conditions open up for new rounds of mobilization. The period of regime transformation in Burma/Myanmar, for example, has been very long indeed, with many fits and starts; however, it has now emerged as a 'least likely case' of democratization (see Landman 2008; also Howarth 1998: 182). The military has been in power since 1962 and pro-democracy activist Aung San Suu Kyi has been repeatedly placed under house arrest, while successive anti-government protests (e.g. in 1988 and 2007) have been met with harsh repression. Beginning with the 2008 referendum, however, Burma has seen a gradual and halting liberalization, with the release and 2012 electoral victory of Aung San Suu Kyi, who gained a parliamentary seat. In 2001, an article published in *The Journal of Democracy* argued that at best, Burma had been engaging in **liberalization** but not democratization, since many of its small reforms were rescinded in the face of increased social mobilization (Reyolds et al. 2001). The election of Aung San Suu Kyi, however, signals that the regime accepts the legitimacy of the opposition (a key criteria for democracy) and now reforms will need to continue with respect to constitutional issues (federalism, agreements with minority communities and systems of representation), dismantling a predatory state (particularly the military complicity in the drug trade) and the professionalization of the armed forces subject to civilian rule (Reynolds et al. 2001).

International mobilization

There are a number of agents and advocates at the international level that also form part of my understanding of democratic transformation. The communities of practitioners for democracy and those for human rights are markedly different in many ways; however, they share a number of similar goals: (1) provide assistance to those seeking to bring about political change at the domestic level, (2) establish and work with international legal standards and standards of best practice and (3) provide a normative 'transmission belt' that helps diffuse the ideas, values and practices associated with democracy and human rights. These individuals work for inter-governmental organizations (IGOs) and international non-governmental organizations (INGOs). The different status of these organizations often means that they have different mandates (and therefore work across different terrains of engagement) and different styles of carrying out their work, but there are many areas of complementarity and in my view, they represent an important set of actors for the advance of democracy and human rights. Typical inter-governmental organizations include the United Nations, European Union, the Organization of American States, the African Union, the Community of Democracies, the Inter-Parliamentary Union and the International Institute for Democracy and Electoral Assistance. Typical international non-governmental organizations include Amnesty International, Human Rights Watch, the International Federation of Human Rights Leagues (FIDH), Minority Rights Group International, Article 19, the International Service for Human Rights and the World Organisation Against Torture (OMCT).

Human rights and transnational advocacy

In many of the country examples described in the last section on domestic mobilization, there have been moments during a cycle of protest and campaigns for political reform during which an appeal is made to international groups for assistance. This may come in the form of such groups already having a presence in the country or domestic groups appealing to groups outside the country. Across a number of studies (e.g. Keck and Sikkink 1998; Risse et al. 1999; Bob 2005; Tarrow 2005; Sikkink 2011), it has become clear that networks form between domestic groups struggling for human rights and international advocacy organizations of the kind listed above. Since the network forms between groups on the ground and these international organizations, analysts have described this kind of phenomenon as a 'transnational advocacy network'. The network transcends the traditional boundary of the state and makes possible coordinated forms of mobilization that join together domestic and international activists.

The basic cycle of events within this understanding of advocacy proceeds in a number of phases. First, the domestic-based groups mobilize for particular human rights issues in their own country. Second, the government of that country denies there is a problem and may well repress the group. Third, the group makes an appeal to international advocacy groups who in turn raise awareness through their networks of like-minded organizations and engage in advocacy work with inter-governmental organizations. Fourth, the transnational network puts pressure on the government in question to initiate reforms and redress the claims by the domestic-based group. This cycle of events has become known as the 'boomerang model' since as the name implies, the appeal outwards to the transnational network comes back to the original country from which a human rights challenge has been made (see Risse et al. 1999). The resulting process of reform is not necessarily a linear progression that sees dramatic improvement in the protection of human rights, but a halting process of reform that may well include periods of regression and stagnation. Nevertheless, the domestic struggle for rights is buttressed by the efforts of the transnational advocacy network, where the country in question may be raised as an issue for consideration by such bodies as the United Nations General Assembly, Security Council, Human Rights Council or Office of the High Commissioner for Human

Rights. These bodies, however, would not consider such issues without the coordinated efforts of the non-governmental organizations who raise awareness, campaign for change and advocate for new standards and responses from the inter-governmental organizations.

Other research has shown that how domestic groups frame their struggle can have an impact on the degree to which their issue is taken up but international organizations. For example, in a systematic comparison of social mobilization in Nigeria and Mexico, Clifford Bob (2005) finds that how a group 'markets' its 'rebellion' affects its ability to garner international support. The Movement for the Survival of the Ogoni Poeple (MOSOP) in Nigeria mobilized around the oil exploration activities of Shell in the Niger Delta, but until the movement changed its frame from one of 'environmental damage' to a struggle for 'human rights', it did not receive significant international attention. The charisma, leadership and subsequent assassination of its leader Ken Saro-Wiwa certainly raised global awareness of the issue, but international advocacy on behalf of the Ogoni was enhanced significantly with the human rights reframing. Analyses such as this suggest that there may well be 'surplus demand' in groups seeking international attention combined with 'limited supply' of support from the international community. Transnational advocacy is thus not a simple process of mobilization, but one that is subject to politics, contingent combinations of factors and skilled framing of human rights struggles to win over groups that comprise the transnational network. Indeed, Bob's (2005) analysis shows that international human rights NGOs can act as 'gatekeepers' for those issues and causes that receive attention and support.

Exporting, importing and supporting democracy

The advance of democracy and human rights is not always a 'bottom-up' process initiated by domestically based groups who then capture the attention of international organizations. There are official policies of governments and inter-governmental organizations that seek to promote democracy and human rights through a variety of tools and instruments. The motivations and goals of the policies, the combination of emphasis on democracy and human rights and the instruments at their disposal for pursuing the policies vary greatly across different governmental and inter-governmental organizations. The motivations range from idealistic and value-based concerns over human well-being to the material national interests of the 'promoting' state. Emphases on democracy and human rights vary and are often elided in formal policy documents that pronounce support for democracy, good governance and human rights across a range of different instruments. The tools and instruments include coercion and the use of force (Whitehead 1996), financial inducements through aid conditionality, budget support for democratic reform projects, electoral observation and monitoring, financial support for civil society groups or political party organizations, among many others.

From Wilsonian interventionism in the early years of the twentieth century to the American-led invasion of Iraq in 2003, coercion has often been used in the name of democracy to rid countries of unsavoury leaders and try to induce domestic political transformations that result in long-term democracy. Such interventions are part of the 'liberal international' tradition and have been motivated by a variety of interests, many of which are not related to democracy or human rights, but may create a network of allied states for the state that is promoting democracy in this way. Beyond direct coercion and intervention, they are many avenues through which democratic states and inter-governmental organizations seek to promote democracy and human rights. Indeed, the unintended consequences of overt interventionism have created reticence and criticism among many states to engage in large 'nation-building' projects, such as NATO in Afghanistan since 2001. Democratic states and inter-governmental organizations typically have different financial means to pursue policies that promote democracy and human rights. Budget support and programme funding can range from large-scale reform of state institutions to specific projects that build capacity and bring about incremental change in line with larger objectives to promote democracy and human rights. Such forms of 'aid conditionality' tie financial assistance to demonstrable improvements in democracy and human rights. Some programmes like the US Millennium Challenge Account match aid to achievement across specific assessment criteria. Other programmes look for areas of reform where assistance is likely to make a difference, such as the development programming carried out by the United Nations Development Programme and the United Kingdom's Department for International Development.

In addition to these differences in policy motivations and means for realizing different outcomes, often the 'verb' that is used to describe policies matters significantly for the ways in which they are implemented and perceived. During the early 1990s, for example, the verb 'export' was used to describe US approaches to promoting democracy around the world, where it was argued that 'advancing the democratic cause can be America's most effective foreign policy in terms of not merely good deeds but of self-interest as well' (Muravchik 1992: 6). Here, democracy is conceived as a product that can be exported abroad and that it brings benefits to the country that imports it as well as the one that exports it. Perhaps an extreme form of the exportation approach was seen in the neo-conservative policy objectives of taking initial interventions in Afghanistan and Iraq and turning them into longer-term commitments to bring about democracy through force. The Obama Administration has been described as having a more pragmatic than ideological approach to promoting democracy and like his predecessors; Obama has had to maintain close relations with less than democratic countries. Indeed, Obama has pursued a mixed strategy that combines democratization 'where it appears to be occurring with a willingness to continue to close ties with seemingly stable authoritarian governments' (Carothers 2012: 6).

The verb 'promote' has been used by the European Union whose European Instrument for Democracy and Human Rights 'provides support for the promotion of democracy and human rights in non-EU countries' (Landman 2012). The instrument includes efforts to enhance respect for human rights, strengthen the role of civil society, support and strengthen international and regional frameworks and build confidence in electoral processes.[3] Through its process of enlargement, the European Union has been able to move beyond the logic of economic integration to one of political integration, where its most well-known Copenhagen criteria for membership include achievements in democracy and human rights. This internal logic to EU enlargement, however, has also influenced its external relations, such that the European Union fully recognizes that as an '[a]s an economic and political player with global and diplomatic reach, and with a substantial budget for external assistance, [it] has both influence and leverage, which it can deploy on behalf of democratization and human rights' (European Commission Communication 2001). There is now a combined interest within the European Union in promoting democracy, good governance and human rights in ways that are linked with questions of security, enlargement, technical cooperation, poverty reduction and the Millennium Development Goals, as well as conflict-prevention, crisis-management and conflict resolution.

In contrast to the verbs 'export', 'import' and 'promote', the International Institute for Democracy and Electoral Assistance (IDEA), a 27-member inter-governmental organization founded in Sweden in 1995 intentionally uses the verbs 'build' and 'support' for its work on democracy (IDEA 2005, 2008). IDEA's choice of verbs reflects its overall understanding of democratization as a **process** that is **built within societies** by **people who live in them,** and not by an external model that imposed from without. Since its founding, IDEA has worked on providing expert comparative knowledge across many different issue areas relating to democracy building and now has a range of programmes on electoral processes; constitution-building processes; political parties, participation and representation; and democracy and development. IDEA is thus a significant global 'knowledge broker' for individuals and organizations seeking to bring about democracy or to improve the quality of democracy worldwide.

New technology and the 'norms cascade'

The end of the twentieth century and the beginning of the twenty-first century have shown an exponential growth in new technology that has become increasingly faster, more powerful, less expensive and more widespread than ever before. The integration of smart phone technology with the power of the internet has led to an explosion of communication and a democratization of voice that has been possible hitherto. A single video captured on a smart phone can transform criminal investigations, accountability for multinational companies and responsiveness of governments. Increasingly, information of consequence can be obtained and disseminated rapidly in ways that challenge 'official' versions of events. In the United Kingdom, for example, video footage captured during the G20 riots in London have changed the nature of a case against the Metropolitan Police and its rough handling of newspaper salesman Ian Tomlinson, who was caught up in the protests and died as a result of his encounter with the police. In the absence of the public-produced video footage, there would not have been enough evidence to find the police responsible for his death.

The use of social media such as Twitter and Facebook has made the kind of mobilization discussed in this chapter even more possible, where key multimedia messages can be shared in seconds contribute to social mobilization in two important ways. First, it is possible to see the new technologies as a 'resource' like money or membership that can be used by a movement to encourage its growth and coordinate its activity. Shared on-line spaces can be used for mobilizing groups and coordinating activities. Indeed, during the student protests in London in November 2011, a group of students from an organization called Sukey made a phone application freely available that allowed individual students to provide real-time updates of police activity and protest dynamics, which were then aggregated, mapped and sent back to individual smart phones (see www.sukey.org). The organization FrontlineSMS has devised cost-effective ways for groups to aggregate text-based information to monitor events ranging from electoral violence to sexual harassment of women (see www.frontlinesms.com). Second, through iteration across networks, messages from social mobilization have become more 'modular' and easier to apply to multiple settings with localized modifications. Charles Tilly, the seminal analyst of 'contentious politics', argued that social movements utilize different 'repertoires of contention' which become modular and 'transportable' between contexts. The new technologies accelerate this modularity and flexibility as new repertoires of contention are shared around the world. Indeed, it is telling that the imagery and messages coming out of the Arab Spring have been replicated through the 'Occupy' movement in countries such as the United States and United Kingdom.

It would be an exaggeration to say that this new technology is the cause of such momentous change, but it has been a remarkable means through which the messages of change can be communicated rapidly. In Tunisia, for example, local protest activities and state response caught on mobile phones and posted in local dialects were picked up by the Tunisian diaspora community, translated into Arabic and then fed back into Tunisia through mainstream media organizations such as Al Jazeera. In this way, new technology allowed protest groups to 'leapfrog' the state, communicate their message to a larger audience that was then fed back into their country and helped mobilize national protests against their government. In this case, grievance was present, communicated, expanded and nationalized through new technology. In an on-line survey of approximately 400 Tunisians, 97 per cent of the sample kept up to date with developments during the revolution during December 2010 and January 2011 on Facebook, 55.3 per cent on YouTube and 22.9 per cent on Twitter. Between 45 per cent and 59 per cent of the sample felt that social media was more informative, safer way to communicate about the developments during the revolution, and both made them angry about the regime and hopeful for the future. More importantly, more than 75 per cent of the sample learnt through social media about local protests and friends and acquaintances who were going to take part (Brauer et al. 2012).

Summary

It is clear from the discussion in this chapter that democracy is 'made' and human rights are 'won' through social struggle. This struggle has a large domestic component as locally based individuals, groups and organizations come together at critical junctures and seek change 'from below' in ways that transcend differences and coalesce around the common cause of political transformation. Where local mobilization is blocked through state retrenchment, groups have the possibility of taking their struggle to the transnational level, where their cause becomes part of a large advocacy network comprised of international non-governmental organizations which interact with states and inter-governmental organizations. These international agents in turn can put pressure on recalcitrant states to implement political reforms and accommodate the demands of local groups. The appeal from below can be in line with the foreign policy interests of states and inter-governmental organizations in ways that bring about political transformation; however, this chapter has made clear that there are many factors that come together in contingent ways that limit the probability of successful transformation. The recent changes in the Arab Spring have many of these different features and offer a stark set of contrasting examples of that illustrate the variety of outcomes possible during significant moments of political transformation. Some domestic mobilizations have been successful in toppling their non-democratic leaders (e.g. Egypt, Tunisia), others have been embraced internationally and supported through military intervention (e.g. Libya), while still others have been met with international paralysis and national resistance (e.g. Syria). The making of democracy and the struggle for human rights are not easily achieved, but as this chapter has shown, they are nonetheless well worth the effort.

SUGGESTIONS FOR FURTHER READING

Foweraker, J. and Landman, T. (1997) *Citizenship Rights and Social Movements: A Comparative and Statistical Analysis.* Oxford: Oxford University Press.

Risse, T., Ropp, S. C. and Sikkink, K. (eds) (1999) *The Power of Human Rights: International Norms and Domestic Change.* Cambridge: Cambridge University Press.

Smith-Cannoy, Heather (2012) *Insincere Commitments: Human Rights Treaties, Abusive States and Citizen Activism.* Washington, DC: Georgetown University Press.

Notes

1   Dr Anita Brauer from the German Development Institute in Bonn presented evidence for the case of Tunisia at an event in London on 'New Technology and Human Rights' on 15 December 2011.

2   A more formal definition is offered by Rueschemeyer et al. (1992: 6) 'the totality of social institutions and associations, both informal and formal, that are not strictly production-related nor governmental or familial in character'.

3   See http://ec.europa.eu/europeaid/how/finance/eidhr_en.htm

CHAPTER SEVEN

Truth and justice

Introduction

On 26 April 2012, the Special Court for Sierra Leone convicted Charles Taylor, former president of Liberia, on 11 counts across a range of crimes against humanity and other offences. These included murder, rape, sexual slavery, enslavement, terrorism, violence to life, health, physical or mental well-being of persons, outrages upon personal dignity, cruel treatment, pillage, inhumane acts and, most notably, enlisting and conscripting or using children younger than 15 to participate actively in hostilities. This is a long list of offences and is quite particular to a number of laws that comprise the body of what is described as international humanitarian law and the international law of armed conflict (ILAC). The court found that these crimes were committed alongside Mr Taylor's aiding and abetting of the Revolutionary United Front (RUF) and the Armed Forces Revolutionary Council (AFRC). The case is significant since he is the first head of state to be indicted, tried and convicted by an international tribunal since the Nuremburg trials in 1945–46. Between Nuremburg and the Special Court for Sierra Leone, the international community has constructed an ever-increasing and elaborate legal framework that can be used to hold people to account for crimes against humanity. Special tribunals such as those for the Former Yugoslavia (ICTY) and Rwanda (ICTR) have been joined by the International Criminal Court in The Hague, The Netherlands, which was established by the Rome Statute and came into force on 1 July 2002. This development of international law and its culmination in the establishment of the ICC have been described as the international 'institutionalization of criminal liability' (Falk 2000: 4).

Such developments, however, have not only occurred at the international level, as throughout the latter half of the twentieth century, more than 100 countries have embraced legal and quasi-legal processes to address 'past wrongs' of some kind, which typically include large-scale human rights violations and crimes against humanity committed during periods of civil war, authoritarian rule and foreign occupation (see Hayner 2002; Olsen et al. 2010, 2012; Sikkink 2011). Popular processes include trials, amnesties, truth commissions, commissions of inquiry, reconciliation forums, human rights commissions and 'lustration' processes which seek to provide a public accounting of what has happened, who is responsible, who the main victims of the crimes against humanity are (or were) and what should be done about the truth that is discovered. Between 1970 and 2007, there have been 848 of these different processes, where the most popular have been amnesties (424 or 50% of the total), followed by trials (267 or 32% of the total), truth commissions (68 or 8% of the total), lustration policies (54 or 6% of the total) and reparations (35 or 4% of the total (Olsen et al. 2010: 39). Between 1979 and 2009, there have been more than 425 cumulative years of prosecution for human rights violations (Sikkink 2011: 21). The use of trials has increased dramatically over this period, while the use of truth commissions has declined dramatically since 2000 (Olsen et al. 2010: 100, 2012: 208). Despite the overall decline in the use of truth commissions, however, Brazil, after many years of delay and alternative approaches, launched its own truth commission on 16 May 2012 to investigate the human rights abuses committed during the period of military rule between 1964 and 1985. It is telling that Brazilian President Dilma Roussef, herself a political prisoner during the military regime, personally launched the truth commission.

This proliferation of international law and development of domestic processes of accountability for the past since World War II – what Sikkink (2011: 96–7) calls the 'two streams of justice cascade' – demonstrate a very real and very strong human desire to 'never forget' what has happened and to ensure that such atrocities occur 'never again' (**nunca mas** in Spanish and **nunca mais** in Portuguese). Embracing the truth in this way, however, is not automatic or an inevitable part of political transition in the ways that have been outlined in this book. Indeed, whether and what kind of process is embraced is a function of possible routes to political accommodation after periods of conflict, authoritarian rule or other periods during which large-scale human rights violations have taken place. For example, both Northern Ireland and Spain are still debating whether and what kind of truth processes to undertake. In Northern Ireland, there has been the Saville Inquiry into the Bloody Sunday incident, but there has not yet been a truth commission of the kind seen in countries such as South Africa (1996–98), Peru (2001–03) or Sierra Leone (2002–04). In Spain, there are continuing debates about having a truth commission for the Spanish Civil War and for the authoritarian period under General Franco.

These examples are broadly understood as fitting into the idea of 'transitional justice', where some accounting of the past becomes a feature of political transition from one regime type (typically but not always authoritarian) to another (typically but not always democracy). The international and domestic examples have both temporary and permanent features to them. At the international level, there are specific legal bodies that have been established to deal with specific cases (i.e. Rwanda, the Former Yugoslavia and Sierra Leone) and there are permanent bodies that deal with emerging, ongoing and past cases such as the International Criminal Court (ICC). At the domestic level, there are temporary truth and justice mechanisms (e.g. trials and truth commissions) that deal with specific time periods and there are permanent National Human Rights Institutions (NHRIs) that have oversight for all matters relating to human rights within a domestic jurisdiction. As of August 2011, there are 70 such NHRIs that have been accredited by the ICC across the globe from Afghanistan to Zambia.[1]

This chapter focuses on four key questions for the domestic level. First, it considers the choices that countries make at the time of transition (or many years later) about whether and what kind of truth and justice process to undertake. Second, it discusses the legal mandate and scope of any formal body that is established and how that is linked to the type of truth and justice made possible. Third, it outlines the different methods that have been used for discovering the 'truth' through these processes and how these methods are important for the kinds of truths that are produced. Fourth, it examines the different kinds of justice that are made possible by them. These four elements – choice, mandate, methods and justice – are both inter-related often highly contested. They also shape the kind of politics that are possible during and after a period of transition.

Choice of truth mechanism

The two previous chapters showed that democratic transformation in any country involves highly contingent processes of challenge, contestation, mobilization, compromise, negotiation and deliberation. One key aspect of this transformation concerns the question as to whether a country should embark on some sort of truth process or truth mechanism. The arguments for having a truth process are numerous: in order for a country to move forward, it must address the problems of the past; give people voice over what has happened; restore the dignity of those who were victimized under the previous regime; provide an opportunity for perpetrators to acknowledge their actions; and to pursue some form of justice against those who committed offences and offer redress to those who suffered. The moment of reckoning made possible by a truth process can provide significant catharsis for society and be a period of public acknowledgement that provides the basis on which to build a new democratic society. The arguments against having a truth process are equally numerous: any uncovering of the truth will be biased and partial (and may reflect the values of 'victors'); will run the risk of 're-traumatizing' the victims and their families; will raise the political stakes of the game and risk a return of the authoritarian forces to prevent a public process of acknowledgement; will incur huge expenses for very little tangible benefit; and will prevent rather than facilitate a country's process of democratic transformation.

The question **to have or not to have** a truth process is a critical one and is often a function of underlying political power and the nature of the forces that have thus far succeeded in moving a country forward. The dynamics of choice can involve the relative power of the forces that are part of a political settlement at the moment of transition. For example, if the military retain some authority or threaten to disrupt democracy then any truth process will be difficult. Indeed, in Argentina, after the defeat of the military regime in the Falklands/Malvinas conflict and its withdrawal from politics, successive democratic governments struggled to bring accountability to past wrongs and suffered repeated and real threats from the military that sought to disrupt democracy. Even though Argentina had a truth commission (The National Commission on the Disappeared, CONADEP) and trials for the key actors in the military junta that conducted the 'Dirty War' between 1976 and 1983, the years that followed the defeat of the military have been marred by the government enacting and rescinding amnesties for the perpetrators of egregious human rights violations. Only in the last few years has Argentina once again become a major protagonist for truth and justice (see Sikkink 2011: 60–83). In Brazil, the relatively peaceful extraction of the military from power between 1974 and 1985 meant that there was less pressure on (or more resistance within) the country to have a truth commission and only in 2012, more than 25 years after the end of authoritarianism has it been able to establish a truth commission. Spain underwent a relatively rapid period of democratic transition between 1975 and 1977 (Foweraker and Landman 1997) and is still deliberating on the relative merits of having a truth process. In contrast, the rapid and 'least likely' transition in South Africa (see Howarth 1998) brought with it one of the most notable (for good and bad reasons) truth commissions in the post-Cold War period.

Once a decision has been taken to have some sort of truth and justice process, there is then the choice over what kind of process to have. Again, this choice is influenced by a number of political and economic factors as each option carries with it different costs and benefits with respect to material, moral and long-term cultural concerns. The evidentiary requirement for trials and full-blown legal proceedings can involve significant costs both in terms of time and money, and the choice of the mechanism is very much related to what kind of justice a country desires (see below). Politically, the strict legal outcomes (guilty, not guilty, no case to answer) associated with trials can be threatening to perpetrators from the previous regime and may not be politically possible for that reason. Truth commissions can have punitive and non-punitive mechanisms attached to them and they may allow 'amnesty for truth' as in South Africa or seek some form of retributive justice once the truth is known. As in the case of trials, the prospect of this kind of justice may well alienate the very powers that are required to participate in the truth mechanism. The process of lustration adopted in many former Communist countries of Eastern Europe involves expunging government institutions of perpetrators of past wrongs. Here, the process involves identifying personnel within state institutions that had a significant role to play in repression and social control of society and then deciding what to do with them. The process can involve exclusion from the new system or some form of inclusion based on confession and truth telling (see Olsen et al. 2010; Roman 2011). Each of these options carries with it significant political risk and the possibility of backlash. If personnel from the former regime are excluded, then reconciliation could be undermined even though trust has been achieved. On the other hand, if these personnel are included in the new regime, reconciliation may be achieved at the expense of trust (see Roman 2011). There are these significant trade-offs associated with these choices.

There are many reasons behind the choices that countries make concerning the kind of truth and justice process that they adopt. A broader comparative view shows that there are some common factors that determine whether and what type of process a country adopts. Across the 848 examples of different mechanisms that have been adopted around the world between 1970 and 2007, there are four common political factors that have been identified that help explain the adoption of at least two or more mechanisms: (1) the level of repression in the society (higher repression increases the probability of adoption); (2) the amount of time that has passed since the height of repression (more time increases the chance of adoption); (3) the democratic history of the country (many cases are countries like Chile where democracy was 'interrupted' by a period of authoritarianism); and (4) the degree of ethnic fractionalization in the country (higher fractionalization lowers the probability of adoption) (see Olsen et al. 2010: 56–8). In addition to these four political factors, analysis also shows that countries with significant economic growth (i.e. change in GDP) have a much higher probability of adopting one or more of these truth and justice mechanisms. Indeed, as the change in GDP increases, the probability of not having a mechanism drops and the probability of having a trial increases (trials are expensive). At comparatively lower rates of change in GDP (0% to 2.5%), the probability of adopting either amnesties or truth commissions increases, but for rates of growth above 2.5 per cent, the probability for these mechanisms drops in favour of trials (Ibid., 73–6).

Beyond the identification of these key factors that account for adoption of these mechanisms, the analysis of these data show that the process of transition itself can have an impact on what mechanisms a country chooses.

Indeed, countries in which the previous authoritarian regime has collapsed tend to choose the combination of amnesty and trials (some with and some without truth commissions), while those countries that have undergone a negotiated transition tend to issue amnesties first and then have trials (some with and some without truth commissions) (Olsen et al. 2010: 153–9). The recent case of Brazil is illustrative, since it underwent a very long period of negotiated transition between 1974 and 1985, the enactment of its Amnesty Law in 1979 and now the establishment of a truth commission. This makes sense from a political point of view, since regime collapse brings with it a more open 'political opportunity structure' (see Chapter 6) for groups in civil society including human rights organizations to mobilize in favour of the adoption of a trial mechanism and/or a truth commission. Negotiated transitions, on the other hand, often involve actors from the previous regime which will reduce the probability that any truth or justice mechanism would be adopted.

Mandate and scope of a truth process

The variation in the adoption of different truth mechanisms identified above is not only a function of the nature of the transition itself but also the legal mandate and scope for each mechanism. The mandate and scope will include what can be investigated, by whom and over which period, as well as the additional powers the mechanism will have in calling witnesses and investigating lines of inquiry to gather evidence. The mandate and scope will also have an impact on the kinds of evidence that are gathered and how they are gathered. For example, the Chilean truth commission was tasked with documenting those cases of human rights abuse that took place under the Pinochet regime **for which a positive identification could be made**. The fact that many individuals 'disappeared' during this period means that any such compilation was necessarily and grossly incomplete. In addition, a truth commission may be tasked with investigating only the most 'egregious' violations that have taken place, which can lead to an undercounting of particular types of crimes. For example, it is entirely possible for a victim to have been detained, tortured and then killed, where a project documenting the 'most egregious' violations will only count the killing. In this case, the detention and torture remain under counted and can lead to biased findings (see Landman 2006; Landman and Carvalho 2009).

Beyond these concerns over enumeration of atrocities (see below), the mandate and scope of a truth and justice processes produce five major types of mechanism: (1) trials, (2) truth commissions, (3) amnesties, (4) reparations and (5) lustration. These different mechanisms are not necessarily mutually exclusive as many truth commissions have also had the use of amnesties (e.g. South Africa) and reparations (e.g. Peru), and it is entirely possible for a county to have a truth commission and trial, as in the case of Argentina (see Sikkink 2011).

Trials typically include those domestic or international legal bodies that try individuals for crimes against humanity and where the country in which the crimes were committed is involved in the trial (see Olsen et al. 2010: 32). Thus, trials can include the tribunals for Rwanda and the former Yugoslavia, as well as the Special Court for Sierra Leone. In addition to these legal bodies, there are some trials conducted under the auspices of 'universal jurisdiction' in which a state uses its own domestic court system to try someone from another state. For example, former Chilean President Augusto Pinochet was detained in the United Kingdom in 1998 as a result of a request from a judge in Spain who sought Pinochet's extradition to stand trial in Spain for crimes against humanity that were committed against Spanish citizens while he was head of state. Even though Spain and the United Kingdom have an extradition treaty which would have allowed for the transfer of Pinochet, there was a long drawn out set of proceedings in the House of Lords in the United Kingdom, which resulted in (a) the Lords agreeing that he should be tried and (b) that he was of ill health and should be allowed to return to Chile. He was then indicted in Chile, but died before any conviction was secured. The principle of universal jurisdiction, however, was bolstered by the case (Sands 2006; Sikkink 2011).

Underlying the use of trials are three simple ideas, neatly summarized by Sikkink (2011: 13):

1 [T]he most basic violations of human rights—summary execution, torture, and disappearance—cannot be legitimate acts of state and thus must be seen as crimes committed by individuals.

2 [I]ndividuals who commit these crimes can be, and should be, prosecuted.

3 [T]he accused are also bearers of rights, and deserve to have those rights protected at a fair trial.

It has taken until the passage of the Rome Statute in 1998, which established the International Criminal Court to realize these three ideas in practice and in ways that can apply to all states. Moreover, the commitment to the idea that perpetrators themselves have rights means that evidentiary standards need to be met and that conditions of a fair trial need to be upheld at all times. These conditions mean that such trials tend to be **prolonged, expensive** and most important for any conception of justice, **highly selective**. The International Criminal Tribunal for the Former Yugoslavia (ICTY) has been in operation since 1993 and the International Criminal Tribunal for Rwanda (ICTR) since 1994. The ICTY has an annual budget of $300 million, while the 2002–03 budget for the ICTR was $208.4 million (Olsen et al. 2010: 66). Both bodies have successfully convicted perpetrators of crimes against humanity, but the convictions are for a selective number of perpetrators. Trials such as the ones conducted by these bodies tend to focus on the main perpetrators and thus do not achieve widespread justice in convicting a large number of individuals involved. In Rwanda, domestic courts became overwhelmed with cases and a community-based process of justice known as the **gacacca** system has been used to provide reconciliation between opposing groups through alternative means that in many ways complement those of the international tribunal and the domestic court system (see Clark 2011).

In contrast to trials, truth commissions are less prolonged, are less selective in their attention to perpetrators and are less expensive. Typically, truth commissions last between 2 and 3 years and their cost can be as high as $20 million as in the case of South Africa, but such costs are nothing near the costs associated with trials. Depending on how one counts them, there have been between 40 (Hayner 2010) and 68 (Olsen et al. 2010: 39; see also Landman 2006) truth commissions so far, where Uganda had the first in 1974 and Brazil is the latest country to establish one in 2012. Their main aims and objectives as well as their composition have varied over these many years and countries, but they share the following common features: (1) they focus on the past, (2) they do not focus on specific events, but seek to discover a broader picture, (3) they are temporary, (4) they have the authority to access all areas to obtain information (see Hayner 1994: 604, 2002: 14) and (5) they have a legal mandate to 'clarify', 'establish the complete picture', 'investigate serious acts of violence', 'establish the truth' and 'create an impartial historical record'. Despite these common features, there has been a lot of controversy over their findings, their funding, the methods they adopt to investigate the truth (see below) and the degree to which they have achieved justice (see below).

Amnesties are seen as a 'practical mechanism to secure democratic transition and rule of law by appeasing potential spoilers' (Olsen et al. 2010: 36). They are an official declaration of the state that protects individuals who have been accused or convicted of human rights violations from prosecution or pardon them and then release them from custody. For example, the 1979 Amnesty law in Brazil and the 1987 Law of Due Obedience in Argentina protected members of the armed forces from prosecution for such crimes as murder, disappearance and torture. In South Africa, amnesties were issued on an individual basis in exchange for evidence from perpetrators. Those that had committed human rights abuses during the period of Apartheid (from either side) were granted immunity from prosecution if they gave statements to the Truth and Reconciliation Commission. It seems odd at first blush to refer to amnesties as part of a truth and justice mechanism, and there are spirited arguments on both sides, but the reality of politics shows that amnesties are used frequently and have constituted 50 per cent of all mechanisms adopted between 1970 and 2007 (see above). The **acceptance** of amnesties whatever their frequency as a viable component for any truth and justice process rests very much on the conception of justice one has, a subject that is discussed further below.

Methods for uncovering the truth

The idea of 'truth' is contested. Even if 'facts' about a case are known and there is detailed forensic evidence of the victim, his or her cause of death, etc. the circumstances around the death, the context of the death and the interpretation of the death can vary greatly across different accounts (see, e.g. Wilson 2001). But truth processes seek to account for many deaths and associated crimes against humanity over many years of the kind detailed in the 2012 conviction of Charles Taylor. To provide some idea of the scale of these crimes, the civil war in El Salvador between 1980 and 1991 claimed more than 70,000 lives; the conflict in Guatemala between 1962 and 1996 claimed between 119,300 and 145,000 lives; the period of the Dirty War in Argentina between 1976 and 1982 is estimated to have taken 30,000 people; while the 100 days of inter-ethnic violence in Rwanda claimed as many as 900,000 people (Landman 2006: 107–25). As we shall see, however, it is crucially important to understand that each of these figures is an **estimate** and not a definitive total. For any period under investigation there are a **circumscribed** but **unknown** number of crimes against humanity that have been committed and there are different methods for counting this unknown population of violations. In other words, the total number of violations is finite, but what that number actually is remains unknown when a truth process begins. Counting large-scale human rights violations and crimes against humanity is thus a huge challenge (see Ball et al. 2000; Landman and Carvalho 2009; Taylor et al. 2012).

Moreover, counting is only one of many methods a truth process will use, as typically, many truth mechanisms include both quantitative and qualitative elements. For example, both the South African Truth and Reconciliation Commission (TRC) and the Peruvian Truth and Reconciliation Commission (CVR) had quantitative and qualitative features. In South Africa, the TRC took 21,296 statements from deponents about the various human rights violations that took place under Apartheid between 1960 and 1994 and from these statements reported 46,696 violations (36,935 were deemed gross violations) that had affected a reported 28,750 victims. In addition to the data project that collected and coded all the statements, the TRC also conducted public hearings around South Africa to hear people's stories and to give voice to the many different communities affected by Apartheid. In Peru, the CVR took 16,917 statements and then through comparison and careful statistical estimation determined that between 61, 007 and 77,500 people had died or disappeared, where the most likely estimate was 69,280 (see Ball et al. 2003). In addition to the data team, the CVR also conducted

30 **estudios en profundidad** (in-depth studies) and conducted public hearings to provide a greater understanding of what it meant to live in conflict and to learn first-hand about the kinds of atrocities that had been committed by state and non-state agents during the 20 years of conflict between the government and the **Sendero Luminoso** ('Shining Path') rebel insurgency (see Landman 2006, 2012b; Landman and Carvalho 2009).

Common across both the quantitative and qualitative methods used during truth mechanisms is the importance of the **narrative** (Landman 2012b). Narratives are at a base level 'stories' that people tell about things that they have experienced directly or indirectly, as well as the evaluative impressions that those experiences carry with them (e.g. the subjective experience and registering of emotions, feelings and insights connected to such experiences). Such stories are often complemented with other items that can form the universe of data and evidence a truth mechanism will use to develop its account, including journals, field notes, letters, conversations, interviews, photos, other artefacts and videos and films (see Clandinin and Connelly 2000: 98–115; Riessman 2008; Sandercock et al. 2012). These stories can be taken in and of themselves, or they can be used to develop a large picture of what has happened to a society during a period of conflict, authoritarianism or occupation. The quantitative projects that form part of truth commissions will collect thousands of narrative statements, deconstruct the 'grammar' of human rights events into databases according to a 'who did what to whom' model, and then analyse the patterns of abuse that occurred according to the legal categories made explicit by the truth commission (see Ball et al. 2000; Landman 2006; Landman and Carvalho 2009). These narratives, however, also contain additional qualitative information about how people were feeling when the events took place; the social, political and cultural context under which they occurred; and the long-term impact that the events had on the victim (if they survived), their families and friends. The narratives provide the **human** element to the tales of atrocity that capture the meaning of inter-personal violence, state-repression and fear of non-state actors such as death squads, paramilitaries, guerrillas and other militants.

In my own view, the quantitative and qualitative approaches are a necessary part of any truth-telling process. Not only can the quantitative approach provide a macro-picture of the pattern of violations that have taken place, but can also, if done using particularly advanced forms of statistical analysis, reveal which groups were more responsible for the violations and which groups were more likely to be victims. For example, analysis conducted across three different samples of narratives in Guatemala showed that indigenous people were six times more likely to have been targeted by government forces (Ball 2000) and in Peru, indigenous people living in the mountainous region of Ayacucho made up nearly half of all the documented deaths (Ball et al. 2003; Landman 2006). Analytical statements such as these could not be made in the absence of quantitative analysis of narrative reports.

Equally, however, the true human element of periods documented by truth commissions also needs to be captured through other means. Qualitative methods of ethnography and in-depth interviewing provide unique insights into the mindset of perpetrators and victims alike and provide the kinds of rich understandings that complement the statistical estimations.

Types of justice and the impact of truth processes

Just as there are 'varieties' of truth that emerge from different methodological approaches, there is much variation in the understanding of justice and the impact that truth processes have on the politics and psyche of a country. The United Nations defines transitional justice as 'the full set of processes and mechanisms associated with a society's attempts to come to terms with a legacy of large-scale past abuse, in order to secure accountability, serve justice and achieve reconciliation' (United Nations 2004: 4). Here, there is a direct link, and in my view, tension between the goals of accountability, justice and reconciliation. A truth process can identify perpetrators, victims and survivors of large-scale violations of human rights, but then a series of question remain. What to do with the perpetrators? If the perpetrators are not tried, convicted and sentenced does that mean that there has not been justice? Does conviction and imprisonment hinder or help the process of reconciliation? Does justice include material redress for survivors and families of victims? What is a fair settlement figure for material redress?

There are many arguments for and against a conception of justice that includes conviction and imprisonment for perpetrators, or what is known as retributive justice. Three strong arguments for this kind of justice have been outlined by Sandoval Villaba (2011: 4)

1 international law obliges states to investigate, prosecute and punish such crimes;
2 reparation under international law includes bringing perpetrators to account
3 accountability for past crimes is crucial to prevent such atrocities in the future

We have seen so far in this chapter that the two streams of the justice cascade have indeed fortified the legal basis for the first two of these arguments. The development of international law between the passage of the UN Charter and the establishment of the Rome Statute and the increasing use of tribunals and trials show that this notion of retributive justice is becoming entrenched and in many ways is an **expected** and **appropriate** response to mass atrocity. Human rights groups such as Human Rights Watch are strongly behind the idea of retributive justice and have been critical of the use of amnesties, for example, since they undermine the basic principle of accountability for past crimes, which here is defined as a perpetrator receiving his or her 'just deserts'. For example, in its report Adding Insult to Injury on the accountability for human rights violations committed in Nepal during its civil war, Human Rights Watch (2011: 3) says,

> The Nepal authorities have argued that transitional justice mechanisms (a truth and reconciliation commission and a commission to investigate enforced disappearances, which are provided for in the CPA but not yet established) trump the normal criminal justice system in relation to widespread human rights abuses committed during the conflict period. This is in contradiction to findings by Nepal's courts and provisions in international law.
>
> Under its international obligations, Nepal is obliged to initiate investigations and criminally prosecute those responsible.[2]

There are strong arguments against the strict application of retributive justice. First, achieving the goals of peace and reconciliation can be seen as coming before justice in its strict sense, where peace brings an end to all out confrontation or repression, and reconciliation involves all sides on a conflict or regime transition to reach some sort of political accommodation that allows a country to move forward. Second, tribunals and trials take time, while countries often want to move forward with a new system quickly. Third, retributive justice, to be effective, must be impartial and not seen as vengeance wrought by those who are now in power. Engaging in vengeance can undermine the credibility of the new power holders as well as the foundations being laid for the new society.

An alternative and in some ways complementary form of justice is **distributive** justice, where some determination of economic costs of violations has been made and a material or financial contribution to the survivors and families of the victims can be offered. It is entirely possible to have conviction and sentencing of perpetrators alongside the payment of reparations. The legal obligation for reparations lies with both the state and the individual (see Sandoval Villalba 2011: 6). Reparations are not only directly financial in nature and can include health programmes, rehabilitation and restitution. It is also possible for external actors, such as wealthy countries to set up programmes for reparations to be carried in third countries. The issue of reparations is highly complex as it is difficult to put a financial figure next to egregious crimes that have been committed. There are also the issues of identifying the victims and the perpetrators with a degree of verification that could yield a payment of reparation. More importantly, working out policies for reparation can exacerbate political tensions and may threaten a political settlement; re-traumatize victims and/or exacerbate harm; lead to the social marginalization or exclusion of victims; and create tensions for development or nation-building processes following a period of conflict or authoritarianism (Llif et al. 2011: 2).

A relatively new form of justice (for transitional countries anyway) is **restorative** justice. Unlike an adversarial or tribunal approach as in retributive justice, processes of restorative justice involve perpetrators and victims coming together and seeking reconciliation and mutual understanding. It is typically practised on a community level and is founded on a different understanding of crime as not only an act against another person, but also the community from which that person comes. It also recognizes the large 'social dimension' of crime and the collective as well as the individual responsibility for crime. The process itself involves dialogue and negotiation, where the outcome is about problem-solving and healing rather than punishment per se. This is a radically different way of addressing the question of truth and justice. Outcomes under such a process may well include some form of punishment for the perpetrator, but it is one that agrees through a process of dialogue and negotiation of all parties affected, rather than a 'case' being made to a tribunal that then reaches a judgement and passes a sentence.

As mentioned above, owing to an overwhelming number of cases in the Rwandan court system, community **gaccaca** courts have engaged in this form of restorative justice to heal the wounds of the large-scale inter-ethnic violence that took place in 1994. In the United Kingdom, Jo Berry, daughter of Conservative MP Sir Anthony Berry, who was killed in an IRA bombing that took place in Brighton in 1984, has worked with IRA bomber Pat Magee. Magee was responsible for the bomb that killed her father and their work together promotes a process of conflict resolution that is very much like the restorative justice model outlined here. At a micro-level, Jo Berry has transcended individual emotions and difference to reach out to Pat Magee as a way of dealing with her own past. She also sees that they are both a product of larger systemic forces and that individual-level blame and discussions of culpability are not particularly helpful for making long-term progress. Such processes of restorative justice are becoming more prevalent in the areas of community crime, schools, care homes, etc. but it is clear that this model of reconciliation is equally applicable for large-scale atrocities committed during times of conflict or authoritarian rule.

Beyond these different notions of justice, what has been the impact of the different truth and justice mechanisms? Since as we have shown already in this volume, transitional processes are highly complex and contingent, where is it difficult to establish direct links between particular mechanism and particular outcomes (see, e.g. Cesarini 2009), but it is possible to explore changes within and across different countries that have variously engaged with truth and justice processes. Large-scale comparative analysis has shown statistically significant and positive benefits for the presence of particular truth and justice mechanisms. For example, for Latin America between 1976 and 2004, Sikkink (2011: 150–3) shows that the average level of human rights violations was much lower for countries that engaged in a long-term process of prosecutions for past crimes. For a global sample, she finds that while the average level of human rights violations has decreased slightly between the 1980s and 2005, the levels of violations were higher than the global average for countries that did not have prosecutions and lower than the global average for countries that did have prosecutions (Sikkink 2011: 183–8, 273–7). These results were obtained for a measure of truth commission experience and the cumulative total of prosecution years over the period of her analysis. In similar fashion, Olsen et al. (2010: 131–51) find that the adoption and implementation of truth and justice mechanisms in general have positive and statistically significant effects on both democracy and human rights, where levels of each are higher for countries that have undergone various combinations of truth and justice mechanisms.

These findings are for aggregate measures of democracy and human rights are of the kind we have already seen in Chapter 3 of this volume, but are their attitudinal and cultural impacts of the truth and justice processes? It is difficult to assess such an impact in the same broadly comparative way since individual level data across such as wide sample of countries have not yet been collected. There has been some systematic research using survey data after the experience of the Truth and Reconciliation Commission in South Africa (see Gibson 2004). This research conceptualizes and measures what is meant by 'truth' and 'reconciliation' for a sample of 3,700 South Africans. The analysis reveals three distinct sets of findings. First, there is a high level of consensus across the sample on the truth that was discovered by the TRC. Second, there was some degree of reconciliation achieved. Third, the truth process itself contributed to that understanding and acceptance of reconciliation (Gibson 2004). The Institute for Justice and Reconciliation in South Africa has carried out a regular 'Reconciliation Barometer' since 2003, which gauges the progress of reconciliation across different issues areas, including human security, political culture and democratic consolidation, national unity and the legacy of Apartheid. Despite mixed results for the degree of progress on many of these issues (e.g. increases in physical security but decreases in economic security; growing confidence in some aspects of governance, but distrust of local government), the barometer, like the study by Gibson (2004), shows that South Africans want to have a unified country and that they agree that Apartheid committed crimes against humanity. But with respect to justice, the barometer shows that South Africans want more to be done to prosecute the perpetrators of those crimes (see IRJ 2010).

Other country studies that do not utilize attitudinal data also find complex feelings and understandings of truth and justice processes alongside other features of transition. Historical analyses of Spain, Germany, Austria, Costa Rica and Nicaragua show remarkably different national experiences with confronting the past. In some cases (Spain), a policy of selective amnesia has prevailed, in others (Germany) direct and 'top-down' confrontation with the past has been fruitful in promoting reconciliation, while in others (Austria) absence of confrontation with the past means that authoritarian tendencies can haunt the present (see

Aguilar 1996; Sa'adah 1998; Cruz 2005; Art 2005 as discussed in Cesarini 2009). Such variation in outcome and impact of transitional justice processes is not surprising given the many different experiences with atrocity that countries have had and the many paths that they have pursued in dealing with the past.

Summary

Truth and justice remain contested and partial concepts. They are partial since the whole truth of what has happened can never be known and every last perpetrator can never be prosecuted. They are contested since that which is uncovered will be differently understood and 'owned' by different segments of society, while the actual judicial outcomes (if they take place) will not satisfy everyone. As we have seen, the decision to adopt a truth and justice mechanism (or mechanisms), the defining mandate and scope for the process and its eventual impact are subject to great variation across the world. Despite this variation, however, the record shows that countries continue to embrace truth and justice mechanisms of some kind as they seek to redress past wrongs. As countries such as those that comprise the Arab Spring (or the notable case of Burma) undergo remarkable and dramatic political change, the ensuing years will involve these societies coming to terms with their past, building a new future that recognizes that past and finding some way to prevent atrocities from ever happening again.

SUGGESTIONS FOR FURTHER READING

Cesarini, Paola (2009) 'Transitional Justice', in Todd Landman and Neil Robinson (eds), *Sage Handbook of Comparative Politics*, pp. 497–521.
Hayner, P. B. (2002) *Unspeakable Truths: Facing the Challenge of Truth Commissions*, London: Routledge.
Olsen, Tricia D., Payne, Leigh A. and Reiter, Andrew G. (2010) *Transitional Justice in the Balance: Comparing Processes*, Weighing Efficacy. Washington, DC: United States Institute for Peace.
Sikkink, Kathrin (2011) *Justice Cascade: How Human Rights Prosecutions are Changing World Politics*. New York: Norton.

Notes

1 See http://www.ohchr.org/Documents/Countries/NHRI/Chart_Status_NIs.pdf, accessed on 25 May 2012.

2 Full report available here: http://www.hrw.org/reports/2011/12/01/adding-insult-injury-0, accessed 28 May 2012.

CHAPTER EIGHT

Threats and pitfalls

Introduction

The previous chapters have mapped out the advance (and setbacks) of democracy and human rights, the reasons (and explanations) for that advance and the attempts across many countries (through mechanisms for transitional justice) to redress the past wrongs that have been committed during periods of authoritarianism, conflict and foreign occupation. These accounts have shown a general positive and encouraging trend in global politics and certainly the regime change and dramatic developments in the Middle East and North Africa are seen as yet another reason to be optimistic about the overall direction of this trend. But as this is a cautiously optimistic book, it must be realistic in also considering the fact that there remain significant threats to the long-term sustainability of both democracy and human rights. These threats involve forces that are **internal** to democracy and the tensions between democracy and human rights. These threats also involve forces that are **external** to democracy that relate to a larger set of global transformations that have and that are taking place. The threats can be grouped as follows:

1 inter-state and intra-state conflict;
2 economic globalization and inequality;
3 global terrorism and its response;
4 environmental degradation and climate change;

Each of these threats is considered in terms of their internal and external impacts on democracy and human rights. We will see that the primary threat to the protection of personal integrity rights is intra-state conflict, which in itself is not too surprising given high levels of violence that are experienced in times of civil war and other internal conflicts (e.g. one need only look at the violence of the conflict in Syria between the Assad regime and the Free Syrian Army in 2012). We will see that structural inequalities **between** countries and that poverty and inequality **within** countries related to processes of economic globalization can undermine the ability for the full exercise of human rights as well as the quality of democracy itself. While global terrorism presents a direct threat to democracy and security around the world (Enders and Sandler 2005), the **response** to the terrorist threat among the world's democracies has undermined the very rights commitments that were the hallmarks of the twentieth century (Sands 2006; Brysk and Shafir 2007). Finally, the Rio +20 United Nations Conference on Sustainable Development in 2012 showed that the challenge of sustainable development is at the forefront of policymakers' minds as the world finds ways in which to increase economic abundance and raise overall levels of welfare without long-term adverse effects on the environment. But the links between consumption, poverty, rights and democracy mean that there are additional political and legal challenges to the quest for sustainability. Let us consider these different threats and pitfalls in turn.

Conflict

Armed conflict of one type or another has been a constant feature of world politics. The twentieth century was a very bloody century indeed, and any kind of armed conflict poses a direct threat to democracy and the enjoyment of human rights (see Keane 2004). Not only do different kinds of armed conflict lead to the deprivation of the fundamental right to life, but countries in conflict have additional problems in the guarantee of 'physical integrity rights' on a day-to-day basis as state and non-state actors commit a variety of atrocities (see Poe and Tate 1994). Civil war has been identified as the most significant explanation for high levels of violation of these rights while other kinds of domestic conflict are also positively related to higher levels of integrity rights violations (see Poe and Tate 1994; Landman 2005b; Landman and Larizza 2009). While states engage in greater repression during times of conflict, which leads to higher levels of human rights abuse, democracies tend to use less repression than authoritarian states (Davenport 2007). Nevertheless, the existence of conflict and the prevalence of human rights abuse can threaten the quality and stability of democracy if conflict remains prolonged and the violations that have taken place are widespread and egregious.

For example, in the case of Peru, successive democratic governments between 1980 and 1992 sought to combat the Maoist insurgency **Sendero Luminoso** while also trying to consolidate democratic rule. The conflict between the government and the rebels led to a large number of killings, estimated between 61,007 and 77,552, where the state was found to be responsible for 30 per cent of the violence overall (see Ball et al. 2003). The conflict led to the breakdown of democracy in 1992, followed by the ousting of President Fujimori in 2000 and process of transitional justice under the auspices of the Peruvian Truth and Reconciliation Commission. In similar fashion, the conflict in Colombia between the state, the rebels, the paramilitaries and the drug cartels has been a constant threat to democratic stability in a country that established democracy in 1959 after a prolonged civil conflict known as **La Violencia** (see Hartlyn 1989; Roldán 2002; Roldán 2010). In contrast to Peru, Colombia has not succumbed to outright authoritarian rule and has had regular elections, the formation of new political movements and rising visibility for previously marginalized groups such as ethnic minorities, gays and lesbians and evangelical Christians (Roldán 2010: 63–4). However, the country has seen an increase in the use of authoritarian and antidemocratic policies in the face of increasing levels of violence, as Roldán (2010: 80) notes:

. . . the existence or threat of violence can very effectively be used to justify the expansion of executive powers, the restriction of civil rights, and the suppression or demonization of dissent, while appearing to do so in defense of democracy and political stability.

Beyond these two examples, what kinds of conflict are there in the world? And is the level of conflict getting better or worse? While definitions vary, there are effectively four different types of armed conflict in the world: (1) inter-state conflict, (2) intra-state conflict, (3) international intra-state conflict and (4) extra-systemic conflict (see Themnér and Wallensteen 2012).[1] Inter-state conflict involves armed conflict between two or more countries, where the primary belligerents are the states themselves. Intra-state conflict involves the government of a country and a non-governmental party (typically rebel group, guerrilla organization, separatist movement, etc.) where the conflict itself remains within the jurisdictional territory of that country. International intrastate conflict involves the government of the country and a non-governmental party, but also involves troop support from a third country for the government, the non-governmental party or both disputants. Finally, extra-systemic conflict involves a state and a non-state group that is outside its own territory, such as in colonial conflicts. It is clear that each of these different types of conflicts represents a threat to democracy and human rights, but each has not been equally prevalent. The most popular form of conflict is intra-state conflict, which between 1946 and 2011 varied between approximately 15 conflicts and over 50, followed by inter-state conflict, extra-systemic (which ceased in 1974 with the fall of the Salazar government in Portugal) and international intra-state. Intra-state conflicts reached a peak of over 50 in the early 1990s and have declined to roughly 30 through the latter 1990s and early years of the twentieth century.

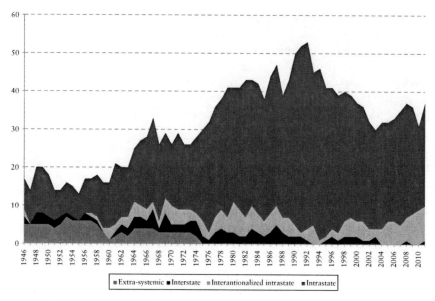

FIGURE 8.1 *Armed conflicts by type, 1946–2011.*
Source: Themnér and Wallensteen (2012).

Inter-state conflicts have declined dramatically, while international intra-state conflicts have become more prevalent (see Figure 8.1).

Terrorism

Domestic and international terrorism has been an enduring feature of politics long before the terrorist attacks on the United States on 11 September 2001. Democracies and non-democracies alike have suffered various forms of terrorist violence from sectarian groups (e.g. Northern Ireland), separatist movements (e.g. the Basque Country in Spain), urban guerrillas (e.g. the Tupamaros in Argentina), leftist groups (e.g. the Red Brigades in Italy), rightist groups and individuals (e.g. Timothy McVeigh in the United States or Anders Behring Breivik in Norway) and various forms of Islamist terrorism such as that which the world has experienced from Al-Qaeda; itself an ill-defined and amorphous network of terror cells operating around the world (see Holmes 2009). While terrorists carry out attacks on many different countries, there have been a large number of analyses that have examined whether democracies are more vulnerable to terrorist attack than non-democracies. Indeed, the logical combination of **lower costs** and **bigger gains** for terrorists makes democracies more likely to be attacked. The idea of lower costs comes from the assumption of the ease of mobility without detection and the sharing of information within open and free societies that makes it easier for terrorists to organize within them. The idea of bigger gains comes from the assumption that democracies need to respond in order to satisfy their publics and thus a targeted terrorist attack can reap the publicity benefits from such democratic response (see Plümper and Neumayer 2009). Comparative and statistical analysis using data on terrorist events and regime type has shown that countries classified as democracies are subjected to more terrorist attacks than those classified as non-democracies (see Pape 2003; Enders and Sandler 2006; Marshall and Gurr 2006; Li 2005). One consequence of this finding has been to think of democracies as having to confront a fundamental dilemma between security and liberty and that to increase security democracies must therefore decrease liberty.

Alternative analysis suggests otherwise. It is not clear that democracy as a **system** is the target for terrorists. Rather it is the national citizen from particular countries with high strategic value that makes particular countries more vulnerable to attack. Thus, in order to assess the relative vulnerability to terrorist attack, analysis needs to examine with whom a country is allied, whether the ally is powerful and whether that ally is also a democracy. Once this is done, it is clear that countries with powerful democratic allies (i.e. friends with United States and the United Kingdom) are more likely to be attacked (see Plümper and Neumayer 2009). Indeed, controlling for the alliance structure shows that if the terrorist's home country is a democracy, the likelihood of attack decreases, and if the target country is a democracy, then the likelihood of attack becomes non-significant (Ibid., 86–90). Taking the alliance structure into account thus undermines the strong case for restricting liberties.

Regardless the assumptions, theories and statistical findings about democracy and terrorism, the attacks on 9/11 fundamentally changed global politics in ways that have threatened the long-term sustainability of democracy and protection of human rights. The 9/11 attacks posed an immediate but not necessarily **existential** threat to the United States or to American democracy per se. The swift response in the United States and many other democracies (e.g. the United Kingdom, Israel, Spain, Canada and Germany), however, was to seek ways in which to enhance executive power and curb individual rights in order to fight terrorism more effectively. Typically, legislation sought to grant governments the power to detain individuals suspected of being engaged in terrorist activity indefinitely and without charge. Arbitrary detention of this kind, however, is prohibited across a wide range of international human rights instruments (e.g. Article 9 of the 1966 International Covenant on Civil and Political Rights); and it is a typical right that receives full protection in national democratic constitutions and historically dates back to the Magna Carta of 1215. While the obligation to uphold this particular right can be suspended during times of emergency if and only if a state is facing an existential threat, other rights, such as the right to life, freedom from slavery or servitude and privacy remain protected (see Landman 2007b: 90).

Despite these constraints, many democracies have restricted liberties in the post-9/11 period and their mass publics initially supported the enactment of legislation that restricted them. With time, however, there has been a quiet 'judicial revolution' among many democracies that has led to a rollback of the more draconian human rights restrictions. In the United Kingdom, for example, various anti-terrorism acts passed during the New Labour Government between 1997 and 2010 sought to empower the government to detain terror suspects indefinitely. The government made permanent all preceding anti-terror legislation through the Terrorism Act 2000, **before** the 9/11 attacks on the United States. In the wake of the 9/11 attacks (and alongside the 2004 Madrid bombing and 2005 London terror attacks), the government argued that Britain was facing an existential threat that should allow it to suspend its rights obligation under Article 5 of the European Convention of Human Rights, which guarantees the right to liberty and security (see Ghandhi 2002: 216). Initially, the Anti-terrorism, Crime and Security Act 2001 gave the government the power to detain foreign terror suspects indefinitely; a power which was expanded to include all terror suspects after the Law Lords deemed the previous power as discriminatory. But even this power was found by the Law Lords to be 'disproportionate' and that the government failed to make the case that the United Kingdom was indeed under an existential threat. Subsequent anti-terror bills sought to empower the government to detain terror suspects for different lengths of time, including 90 days, 42 days and 28 days. The political debates during the passage of this legislation led to the first defeat of the Blair government in the House of Commons (see Landman 2007a: 83–7).

The UK case is not unique in the types of restrictions democracies have sought to bring to fight terrorism. Indeed between 2001 and 2008, 20 established democracies in North America, Europe and the Pacific have enacted laws that have increasingly placed restrictions on different categories of liberties, including privacy rights, procedural rights and rights for immigrants and foreigners (Epifanio 2011). The total number of restrictions varies between 1 and 28 with an average number of approximately 13 restrictions across the sample of democracies, where countries such as the United States and United Kingdom have enacted the most number of restrictions and the Scandinavian countries, Canada and Switzerland the least (see Epifanio 2011; Epifanio et al. 2012). In some cases, however, the separation of powers as well as supranational legal authorities such as the European Court of Human Rights has meant that national and international judiciaries have been able to scrutinize the rights restrictions put in place by governments after 9/11. The initial impulse to curb liberties as the solution to fighting terrorism has been tempered by legal analysis and judgements which have found the key arguments for rights restrictions on the basis of threats to security wanting. In US domestic anti-terror policy, represented must notably by the Patriot Acts of 2001 and 2004, lower court challenges to provisions on material support to terrorist organizations (even if such support is training in non-violence) have been overturned by the US Supreme Court (see **Holder v Humanitarian Law Project** 2009); however, in **US v Jones** (2012), the court held that secret deployment of a GPS tracking device on a suspect's car violated the 4th Amendment protection to privacy found in the US Constitution. While not a direct challenge to the Patriot Act itself, the court's ruling addresses an underlying desire among law enforcement agencies to use new technological means to pursue potential criminals and terrorists on US soil. The ruling curbs the use of these technologies on the grounds the right to privacy.

The more significant challenges to US anti-terror policy have come from the US Supreme cases regarding the detainees at the Guantanamo Bay facility. In its pursuit of terrorism after the 2001 invasion of the Afghanistan, the United States redefined individuals as 'enemy combatants' in order to circumvent the international law of armed conflict most notably found in the various Geneva Conventions. Rights guarantees normally enjoyed by prisoners of war were suspended for enemy combatants, many of whom were taken to third countries to be interrogated with the use of torture (i.e. 'extraordinary rendition') and/or ended up in the detention facility in Guantanamo Bay, where they stayed without judicial proceedings for many years. Across four separate cases – **Hamdi v. Rumsfeld** (2004), **Rasul v. Bush** (2004) **Hamdan v. Rumsfeld** (2006) and **Boumediene v Bush** (2008) – the US Supreme Court challenged the Bush administration's denial of detainees' right to challenge their detention, the use of military tribunals and the denial of **habeas corpus**. All but 169 detainees have now been released, and in May 2009, President Obama ordered that the facility be closed:

For over seven years, we have detained hundreds of people at Guantánamo. During that time, the system of Military Commissions at Guantánamo succeeded in convicting a grand total of three suspected terrorists. Let me repeat that: three convictions in over seven years. Instead of bringing terrorists to justice, efforts at prosecution met setbacks, cases lingered on, and in 2006 the Supreme Court invalidated the entire system. Meanwhile, over five hundred and twenty-five detainees were released from Guantánamo under the Bush Administration. Let me repeat that: two-thirds of the detainees were released before I took office and ordered the closure of Guantánamo.

There is also no question that Guantánamo set back the moral authority that is America's strongest currency in the world. Instead of building a durable framework for the struggle against al Qaeda that drew upon our deeply held values and traditions, our government was defending positions that undermined the rule of law. Indeed, part of the rationale for establishing Guantánamo in the first place was the misplaced notion that a prison there would be beyond the law – a proposition that the Supreme Court soundly rejected. Meanwhile, instead of serving as a tool to counter terrorism, Guantánamo became a symbol that helped al Qaeda recruit terrorists to its cause. Indeed, the existence of Guantánamo likely created more terrorists around the world than it ever detained.

So the record is clear: rather than keep us safer, the prison at Guantánamo has weakened American national security. It is a rallying cry for our enemies. It sets back the willingness of our allies to work with us in fighting an enemy that operates in scores of countries. By any measure, the costs of keeping it open far exceed the complications involved in closing it. That is why I argued that it should be closed throughout my campaign. And that is why I ordered it closed within one year.

In the time that has passed since that speech, the facility has not been closed, as it would appear that the 'costs of keeping it open' have not exceeded the 'complications involved in closing it'; and it is not clear if, when or how the remaining detainees will be tried and or released. Alongside the redefinition of individuals that led to the creation of Guantánamo, officials in the US justice department sought to redefine particular forms of interrogation techniques, such as 'waterboarding' as not constituting torture, and this perception and the attitudes that accompanied it created an environment in which the scandal at the Abu Ghraib facility in Iraq was made possible (see Greenberg and Dratel 2005). Again, in his May 2009 speech, President Obama declared that such practices were to be banned and stated 'We must leave these methods where they belong – in the past. They are not who we are. They are not America'.

Obama's speech does raise a number of significant points concerning how the anti-terror foreign policy of the United States has undermined the values and principles of democracy that it has sought to promote in the world (see Chapter 6 this volume). But he also defends the necessary balance that is required between and among accountability, transparency and security:

> I ran for President promising transparency, and I meant what I said. And that's why, whenever possible, my administration will make all information available to the American people so that they can make informed judgments and hold us accountable. But I have never argued – and I never will – that our most sensitive national security matters should simply be an open book. I will never abandon – and will vigorously defend – the necessity of classification to defend our troops at war, to protect sources and methods, and to safeguard confidential actions that keep the American people safe. Here's the difference though: Whenever we cannot release certain information to the public for valid national security reasons, I will insist that there is oversight of my actions – by Congress or by the courts.

It would appear that with respect to the Obama Administration's use of unmanned aerial vehicles (UAVs) or 'drones' to attack suspected terrorist strongholds in places such as Pakistan, Yemen and Somalia, the balance has been towards security rather than transparency. Indeed, between 2008 and 2012, the United States has carried out over 300 drone attacks in Pakistan, more than 40 attacks in Yemen (although there are many more unconfirmed attacks) and fewer than 10 attacks in Somalia (Bureau of Investigative Journalism http://www.thebureauinvestigates.com/; see also Becker and Shane 2012). The death toll varies depending on the use of different sources, where it is estimated that between 2,545 and 3,285 people killed have been in Pakistan, 339 to 977 people have been killed in Yemen and 58 to 169 people have been killed in Somalia. The contrast between the stated principles in the May 2009 speech and the reality of the use of drone attacks is stark. While President Obama oversees and approves each decision to attack using drones, there are an increasing number of concerns being raised about the utility of the policy and the potential moral and ethical dilemmas it raises (see Becker and Shane 2012).

Domestic and international terrorism poses a huge threat to democracy and human rights, where attacks on democracies have and can cause great loss of life and can create an extreme climate of fear, where levels of trust in fellow citizens decline, suspicion of 'the other' rises and an overall sense of insecurity prevails. The negative consequences of the persistent threat of terrorism, brought home in high relief since the 9/11 attacks, undermines the safety and security promised by democracy (see Chapters 9 and 10 this volume). The response to terrorism from the world's most established democracies has undermined fundamental principles of the rule of law, accountability and protection of human rights. When established democracies curb liberties in the name of security and cooperate with non-democratic and rights-abusive states in the name of the 'war on terror', strong signals are sent about the devaluing of fundamental rights commitments that have been the outcome of centuries of struggle (see Ishay 2008 and Sands 2006). When larger geo-strategic interests related to the 'war on terror' prevail, the true victims are the norms, morals, values and rights upon which modern democracies are meant to be based.

Economic globalization

The world has been changing in an increasingly inter-connected fashion since the middle of the twentieth century. While inter-connectedness has always been a feature of the world of states (see Held et al. 1999), the pace of economic and technological advance in the latter half of the last century until now has meant that states are now more than ever affected by developments in other states. The volume and flow of information, capital, tastes, fashions, ideas and people between and among countries means that domestic political systems (of whatever kind) have become increasingly subject to outside influence. Economic globalization forms a large part of these dramatic developments and involves the flow of capital, labour and tastes in ways that have implications for domestic politics and domestic regime dynamics. There has been much debate about the possible impact of economic globalization on democracy, with arguments for overall positive effects, negative effects and neutral (or no) effects (Li and Reuveny 2003). Drawing on the discussion in Chapter 5 in this volume, positive arguments make an indirect link between globalization and democracy through the idea that globalization promotes economic development, which in turn promotes democracy. Alongside such positive economic factors are additional factors relating to penetration of international business, lower information costs and the diffusion of democratic values, decentralization and the reduction of incentives for authoritarian leaders to remain in power (Li and Reuveny 2003: 33). Arguments for no effect suggest that states are simply less vulnerable to global changes than suggested and that globalization itself has been exaggerated (Ibid., 38). The arguments for a negative impact of globalization include a reduction in state autonomy, internal inequalities and ethnic conflicts, destabilization of domestic balance of payments and a widening gap between rich and poor countries (Ibid., 35.).

This latter category of critique is worth closer examination for our present purposes on the threats and pitfalls that confront contemporary democracies and their ability to promote and protect human rights. There is a general consensus that global distribution of income is highly unequal, where various estimates suggest that the top 20 per cent of the richest countries in the world have roughly 80 per cent of global income; however, there is much debate and disagreement over (a) why this state of affairs has come about, (b) whether and how this is a problem and (c) whether trends are getting better or worse. The theory of free markets suggests that some inequality is natural but that through the free flow of economic resources, market competition will reach an equilibrium in which in the long run, inequality between states will decrease. Counter-arguments suggest that the assumption of a 'free flow' of goods and information is flawed and that powerful states have controlled market advantage through the General Agreement on Tariffs and Trade (GATT) between 1946 and 1986 and now the World Trade Organization (WTO), which was created as part of the 1986 Uruguay round. Such control has yielded a continuing dominance of wealthy countries over the share of overall global income. The overall trends in income distribution have changed. In his now famous book, *The Bottom Billion*, Paul Collier (2008) argues that 1 billion rich people face a world of five billion poor people, but that even more importantly, the 'bottom' billion people (i.e. the poorest billion people in the world) are indeed getting poorer, even though overall global wealth has risen.

This structure of the global economy suggests that opportunities vary greatly for people around the world and that this difference in opportunity will have an impact on political stability, political institutions and for the topic of this volume, democracy and human rights. In the 1960s, 'dependency' theory made the same observation about the structure of the world economy and argued that it would be harder for developing countries to make progress in the face of this persistent structure. While this idea was largely dismissed by neo-liberal economic theory and analysis through the 1980s and early 1990s (see, e.g. Brohman 1996; Cammack 1997; Meier and Stiglitz 2001; Stiglitz 2002, 2012), a focus on the links between structure of the global economy and the politics of development persisted. In the 1990s, analyses showed that the overall economic benefits of development for democracy were different for countries that occupied different positions within the global economic system (see, e.g. Burkhart and Lewis-Beck 1994; Foweraker and Landman 2004). The positive relationship between development and democracy of the kind discussed in Chapter 5 in this volume appears to be strongest for countries in the 'core' of the global economic system (i.e. the world's richest countries), followed by those on the 'semi-periphery' (i.e. middle income countries) and 'periphery' (i.e. the least developed countries). In practice, this means that democracies that do form in these peripheral economies may well have greater challenges to overcome and may well need more time to consolidate democratic rule. Since these studies, Collier (2008) has shown that the peripheral countries that largely comprise the 'bottom billion' have actually become poorer, which makes their probability of either establishing or maintaining democracy lower than before.

Global comparative analysis has also shown that poorer countries have higher levels of human rights violations (see, e.g. Mitchell and McCormick 1988; Poe and Tate 1994; Landman 2004; Davenport 2007). While the exact causal mechanism that explains this relationship has not been fully specified, it is reasonable to argue that poor countries lack the necessary resources for the kinds of institutions and infrastructure required for the promotion and protection of human rights. All human rights cost money and therefore require tax and government revenue to invest in the judiciary, health service, prisons, schools, etc. in order for rights to be realized (see Donnelly 1999; Holmes and Sunstein 2000; Landman and Carvalho 2009). It is also reasonable to argue that greater economic resource allows governments to satisfy competing demands from groups in society and thus create conditions in which the probability of overt conflict and associated forms of human rights abuse to be reduced. In both cases, poor countries struggle to make the kinds of investments that provide strong institutions for rights-protective governance and conflict resolution and as a consequence, may well see greater levels of human rights abuse than their richer counterparts.

Beyond these broader impacts on democracy and human rights associated with the structure of the global economy, **internal** disparities of income can also threaten democracy and the protection of human rights. There are various arguments from the academic literature on political violence, inequality and human rights violations that come together around this key question. At a micro (or individual)-level, there are incentives for the 'haves' in society to engage in rent-seeking behaviour within governmental institutions, to maintain control of their resources and to exclude access to those resources by the 'have nots' in ways that use coercive means that undermine the protection of personal integrity rights (see Heinisch 1998; Henderson 1991: 125; Poe 2004). The distribution, accumulation and defence of resource allocation at the micro-level are historically driven and when aggregated to the macro level, suggest that the means for maintaining these patterns of distribution may well include violations of civil liberties and personal integrity rights. In the context of many lesser-developed countries, there can be state complicity and even collaboration in acts of coercion. In following this line of argument, Landman and Larizza (2009) find that there is indeed a strong relationship between high levels of income and land inequality on the one hand and the violation of personal integrity rights on the other for a global sample of countries between 1980 and 2004. Stiglitz (2012) argues further that persistent inequality threatens democracy as large segments of a disaffected and marginalized population loses its ability to participate in democracy and thus erodes the fundamental principles upon which it is founded: popular sovereignty and collective decision-making (see Chapter 3). Thus, in addition to the structural threats to democracy among the world's poorest countries, there are domestic threats to democracy and human rights that can come from persistent disparities in income distribution.

The economic crisis that began in 2007 among the wealthy democracies and the 'Eurozone' crisis that followed thereafter also need to be seen in this context. Popular movements such as the Occupy Movement are making their case on the grounds of persistent and increasing economic disparity. The '99% versus 1%' discursive construction raises questions about government policies that have redistributed wealth upwards, and some of the more heavy-handed repressive responses in American cities such as Oakland and Davis California have led some to worry about the nature and quality of American democracy. In Europe, the pursuit of economic austerity alongside the bailouts of major banks and high rates of unemployment in countries such as Greece, Spain and Portugal have led to popular protests and a critique of market capitalism and representative democracy. The economic and Eurozone crises in my view are not crises **of** democracy but are crises **for** democracy, which is to say, these crises developed through increasingly unregulated forms of economic activity (e.g. sub-prime mortgage lending, over-exposure and easy extension of credit), absence of accountability among particular governments (e.g. Greece) and rapidly changing economic circumstances that were arguably beyond the control of any one government. They are a problem **for** democracy since democratic governments in the countries affected by the crises now need to respond. Their uncertain and cyclical nature as they move through the electoral cycle means that any response will be partial and subject to ideological differences (e.g. compare the approach of the coalition government elected in the United Kingdom in 2010 to the French approach under President Hollande). Democratic governments need to find solutions to these problems in the face of persistent unemployment that limit the scope for economic opportunity as economies struggle to recover, both of which may bring increased pressure on existing governments and a critique of democracy itself. Austerity programmes are creating problems of service delivery to the poor and marginalized sectors of society, which can undermine fundamental rights commitments found in the 1966 International Covenant on Economic and Social Rights (see Chapter 3).

Climate change

The final large and long-term threat to democracy comes in the form of climate change and environmental sustainability more generally. A number of different studies have identified the current precarious state of a large proportion of the world's population that is directly linked to the environment and the relative scarcity of natural resources (Green Economy Coalition 2012). We saw above that the well-being of at least a billion people has gotten worse, where some estimates suggest that 1.2 billion people live in poverty, of whom 70 per cent depend on natural resources for all or part of their livelihoods (World Bank 2011). This dependence on natural resources means that any further decline in those resources will have a direct impact on the basic survival of a large part of the world's population. In addition, 2.6 billion people lack access to good quality sanitation, 1.3 billion people lack access to electricity and 0.9 billion lack access to clean water (UNDP 2011), which compounds problems associated with water-borne diseases (e.g. high levels of infant mortality) and other ailments linked to poor hygiene and absence of clean water. At current rates of consumption, decline in natural resources is likely to continue for some time, as for 2010 alone, the 'ecological footprint' (i.e. an aggregate measure of environmental damage) was '52% greater than the capacity of the planet to replenish natural resources and absorb pollution and waste' (Green Economy Coalition 2012: 4).

But what do all these trends in poverty and environmental change mean for democracy and human rights. The direct link between poverty, livelihoods and the environment means that the exercise of social and economic rights is limited if not absent for large proportions of the world's population. Constraints on the exercise of these rights can limit the exercise of other rights, such as the right to education and the right to participation. Poor people have less access to basic education, which means levels of literacy required for meaningful participation in politics is naturally reduced or compromised. The 1993 Vienna Declaration and Programme of Action claims in Paragraph 8 that 'Democracy, development and respect for human rights and fundamental freedoms are interdependent and mutually reinforcing'. If this is the case empirically (which we have seen in this volume is a complicated set of relationships), then limited exercise of social and economic rights owing to persistent and growing poverty will limit the exercise of other human rights and ultimately, the quality of democracy itself. Reduced or absent participation and inclusion undermines one of the fundamental principles of democracy as noted above and in Chapter 3. In this way, there is an inter-relationship between and among environmental consumption and decline, poverty and social exclusion and rights and democracy. The quality of democracy itself is thrown into doubt when meaningful participation is restricted only to those who have the material means to do so.

Moreover, the continued competition for natural resources as more and more countries develop economically represents long-term risk and a threat to democracy. So-called resource wars as competing groups and countries fight for continued access to natural resources needed for energy can lead to a new round of violent conflicts in the world and threaten the protection of human rights and democracy. Between 1980 and 2005, for example, there were 73 conflicts in which environmental factors played a key part, including water use, land use, biological diversity and fish resources (WBGU 2008: 31). These different conflicts involved diplomatic crises, protests that included some violence, violent conflicts and systematic and collective use of violence (Ibid., 31). Both the level (or intensity) and the number of conflicts tend to be higher in the lesser developed countries in the world, where a low level of economic development increases the risk of conflict within societies (Ibid., 36, see also Collier and Heoffler 2004; Fearon and Laitin 2003). This interaction between poverty, climate change and conflict represents a significant threat both to the long-term sustainability of democracy and the progressive realization of human rights.

Summary

It is clear that these different threats to democracy and human rights are not necessarily mutually exclusive. Rather, conflict, inequality, terrorism and environmental degradation form a complex web of challenges for democracy and the protection of human rights. Individuals are rights holders and states are duty bearers, while each of these threats on their own and taken together impinge on the ability of the rights holder to exercise his or her rights and challenge the ability of the duty bearers to meet their obligations. Inequalities and the power differentials that are associated with them intersect with democracies in ways that create and reinforce unfair outcomes that in many ways are inconsistent with values of democracy and human rights. Conflict and terrorism present direct threats to the right to life. The response to terrorism limits the exercise of rights in the name of security. Poverty, inequality and environmental degradation can have direct and indirect effects on individuals depending on their relative level of poverty and opportunity. The compromise of rights inherent in the vulnerability of the world's poorest billion people can have long-lasting impact on their well-being, social mobility and meaningful participation in the way they are governed. Any book on democracy and human rights, however optimistic, needs to be realistic and acknowledge these threats and pitfalls and the challenges they represent for the future of governance. The next chapter will examine the benefits and outcomes of democracy before concluding with an overall assessment of the hopes and challenges that the world faces at this critical juncture.

SUGGESTIONS FOR FURTHER READING

Brysk, Alison and Shafir, Gershon (eds) (2007) *National Insecurity and Human Rights: Democracies Debate Counter-Terrorism*. Berkeley: University of California Press.
Enders, Walter and Sandler, Todd (2005) *The Political Economy of Terrorism*. Cambridge: Cambridge University Press.
Lustick, Ian (2006) *Trapped in the War on Terror*. Philadelphia: University of Pennsylvania.
Sands, Philippe (2006) *Lawless World*. New York: Penguin.

Note

1   These types and their definitions are according to the Uppsala Conflict Data Programme at the University of Uppsala in Sweden (http://www.pcr.uu.se/research/ucdp/definitions/) which monitors and analyses conflict around the world.

CHAPTER NINE

Benefits and outcomes

Introduction

We have seen throughout this book that increasingly larger numbers of people around the world have over the last four decades or so expressed a desire and have acted on that desire to establish and maintain democracy, as well as articulate a set of human rights that have become increasingly codified in and adjudicated through international law. The growth of democracy and the proliferation of human rights instruments (quite apart from their actual protection) are indicators of both the attractiveness of these ideas and achievement in their realization; however, what are the benefits and outcomes that ordinary people can expect from their own country making a transition to democracy and establishing a more rights-protective regime? In short, **cui bono**? Who benefits? And to what extent do they benefit? Do all good things come together? Or are their trade-offs between the normative achievements of establishing democracy and the realization of human rights on the one hand and real material benefits and outcomes on the other? There is an emerging global consensus that democracy is good for developmental outcomes and is seen as the preferable political system for the achievement of the eight Millennium Development Goals (MDGS), but is this necessarily the case? In the post-2015 era will the new Sustainable Development Goals include democratic governance as an **end in itself** or also as a **means to an end**?

This chapter seeks to address these questions and considers the benefits and outcomes associated with greater democracy and more rights-protective regimes. First, it begins with a discussion of the non-material and normative benefits associated with democracy and human rights. Second, it discusses the main findings of the democratic peace research, which shows both the international and domestic pacifying effects of democracy. Third, it examines the overall benefits associated with having rights-protective regimes in place, especially with respect to economic distortions prevalent among market capitalist societies. Fourth, it outlines the main economic benefits of democracy with respect to poverty and famine, as well as the human-related elements of sustainable human development. Finally, it considers the mixed record with respect to the environment, where it is becoming evident that democracy makes a positive difference in reducing environmental degradation among the wealthy countries of the world, but among the poor countries, its benefits have not yet been realized.

Democracy qua democracy

Democracy has a number of internal values whose actual **value** to individuals is often intangible and difficult to measure. In talking to individuals in new democracies, there is a palpable sense of exaltation about just being able to move about without the constant fear of repression or suspicion of one's actions. Beyond this micro- and personal sense of democracy, citizens in newly democratized countries value their ability to participate and it is typical during first elections after a prolonged period of authoritarianism that citizen turnout is quite high. The media depict scenes of long queues of voters exercising their rights for the first time, or in the case of a return to democracy, exercising their rights once again. Comparative analysis has shown that there is convergence in turnout rates between established democracies and other states (see IDEA 2002). While turnout itself is a crude measure of participation and subject to influence from mandatory registration and mandatory voting laws across a variety of different countries, it does provide a first insight into a key dimension of participation. Figure 9.1 shows that average global turnout rates over time for presidential and parliamentary elections have seen a secular decline over the last few decades, while the average level of democracy has risen across the same period. For the whole period, the average turnout for both parliamentary and presidential elections is approximately 70 per cent, which in relative terms is remarkably high.

Beyond formal participation through voting, which is also something that is available across a large number of non-democracies in the world, democracy allows for a wide range of alternative forms of participation, such as public inquiries, petitions, social movement activity, voluntary associations, participatory budgeting and other forms of activity in the public sphere in which the separation between the state and the citizen becomes more blurred than in non-democratic systems as multiple entry points are available for influencing government policy. There is great value associated with these kinds of participation and the rights that make them possible, such as freedom of assembly, freedom of association, freedom of speech and freedom of information among others. Moreover, the mere fact

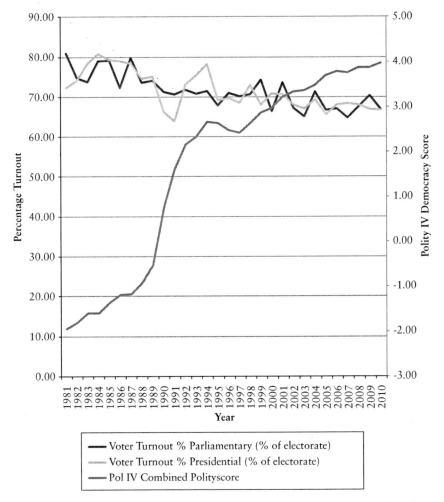

FIGURE 9.1 *Voter turnout for parliamentary and presidential elections and the level of democracy, 1981–2010.*

of knowing that one **can** participate in the political system is of great value to individuals who suddenly find themselves within a new democracy.

Closely associated with participation is the notion of accountability, which concerns the degree to which elected politicians and state officials can be held to account for their actions. This value can be achieved through a variety of ways, including the electoral process itself, through parliamentary committees, the courts and judicial system, special ombudsman offices and other specialized watchdog agencies (see IDEA 2008: 24). Knowing that one can ask questions, find answers and challenge officials in government on the grounds of evidence is a key feature of a mature democracy, and the possibility that officials can be removed or step down from office lends credibility to any system of accountability. While there are many instances in which such challenges have not led to satisfactory outcomes within many democracies, the ability to challenge is available within democracies in ways that are simply not possible in non-democratic regimes, where challenges can be met with silence, misinformation or outright repression. As we saw in Chapter 6, social movements and civil society organizations have the ability to challenge governments through recognized institutional channels as well as through direct forms of protest mobilization and other manifestations of popular discontent. Democracies will naturally limit such activity should it turn violent or in the event that property rights are violated or public order breaks down; however, there is a wide range of activity that is possible among the world's democracies upon which individuals place a very high value.

We saw in Chapter 3, that there is a positive relationship between democracy and human rights, where higher levels of democracy are significantly related to better protection of physical integrity rights (see Figure 3.2). Figure 9.2 shows the time-series trends in democracy and

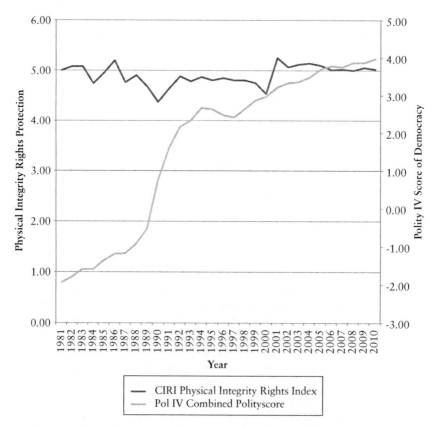

FIGURE 9.2 *Physical integrity rights and democracy, 1981–2010.*

physical integrity rights between 1981 and 2010, where the advance of democracy since 1981 has been steady and positive and the change in human rights has fluctuated considerably with a slight improvement in the early part of this century. The overall correlation between the score of democracy used in the figure and the scale of physical integrity rights is .39 (at the 99% level of statistical confidence), suggesting that while democracies are better at protecting this set of rights, there are still many democracies in the world with continued violations of these rights (see also Diamond 1999, 2008). Across other categories of rights, however, the picture is slightly more positive. For example, the correlation with democracy is higher for such rights as empowerment (.81), assembly and association (.75), freedom of movement (.50), freedom of religion (.47), the rights of workers (.54) and women's social rights (.47). Thus across a collection of different human rights, democracies have a better record than non-democracies, but the relationship between the two falls far short of being perfect.

While higher levels of democratic performance are evident across the world's democracies, within them, there remains great variation across many different measures of performance. Such a variation in the 'quality of democracy' (O'Donnell et al. 2004; Diamond and Morlino 2005; IDEA 2008) belies any quick observation about 'Western' biases in measures of performance or 'Western' superiority among democracies themselves. For example, studies on democratic performance show a certain amount of uniformity among Western democracies, but a remaining degree of differentiation with respect to some key indicators. Women's representation, equal access to the law and income inequality are not all better for Western democracies compared to non-Western democracies, nor are they all the same within the group of Western democracies (Foweraker and Krznaric 2003). Rather, countries such as the United States and Australia do not score very high on these measures compared to other Western democracies. Indeed, income distribution, which for many, is a basic measure of equality and linked to democratic participation is now worse than in the year that preceded the great depression (Stiglitz 2012). The United Kingdom and the United States do not score particularly well on comparative measures of prison population (incarceration rates) where variations in sentencing (particularly in the United States) show disproportionately longer rates for ethnic minority groups (see Foweraker and Krznaric 2003: 327–32). There has been a longstanding problem with the ways in which Australia treats its indigenous population that undermines the notions of equality and inclusiveness. In its report on electoral integrity, the Global Commission on Elections, Democracy and Security (2012) concludes that the pattern of campaign finance and the behaviour of political action committees (PACs and super-PACs) are eroding electoral integrity in the United States. Widespread commentary on the 2000 election debacle in Florida and voter registration issues associated with the 2012 elections have raised grave concerns over infringement of the right to vote that are politically motivated.

In addition to the variation in performance in Western democracies, there are additional differences across many democracies that depend on the kind of institutional design that has been adopted. Institutional design includes the kind of executive-legislative arrangements that are in place, the type of electoral system that is used and the type of political party system that has developed. First, it is possible for countries to have a **presidential system** (as in the United States and all of Latin America), a **parliamentary system** (as in the United Kingdom, Netherlands, Belgium, Norway, Sweden, Italy, among others) or a **mixed system** (as in France, Germany and Portugal). Second, it is possible for countries to have single-member district electoral systems (also known as 'first past the post' as in the United States or United Kingdom), proportional representation systems (as in Italy, Greece, Iceland, Belgium and all of Latin America) or mixed systems that combine features of both (as in Germany and Scotland). Third, it is possible to have dominant party systems, two-party systems, or multi-party systems, where the 'effective' number of parties in the national legislative assembly varies greatly across democracies.

These three main areas of difference among democracies are combined in ways that can have can direct impact on democratic quality and democratic performance. For example, single-member district systems where political parties compete for a plurality of votes in each electoral district tend to produce two-party systems, such as in the United States with the Democratic and Republican Parties and in the United Kingdom with the Labour and Conservative Parties. Many argue that such party systems provide a better framework for governance since the representation of interests is divided into two main parties and the process of government is about the leadership and the opposition. In contrast, proportional representation, where parties win seats in the main legislative chamber according to the proportion of votes they received across electoral districts, tends to produce multi-party systems. In countries such as Germany, coalitions between major parties are formed to create stable governments. Many have argued that multi-party systems such as the German case tend to be more **representative** (and thus uphold a fundamental democratic principle) but are inherently **harder to govern** since multiple interests need to be accommodated through the political process and the need for coalition formation. In contrast, countries with single-member districts and two-party systems are less representative since they do not reflect the underlying proportion of support in the electorate, but are considered better for governance. There is thus a trade-off between **representation** and **governability** that all democracies confront (see Foweraker 1998).

In similar fashion, there are different advantages and disadvantages associated with presidential and parliamentary systems. Within presidential systems, there is a 'dual mandate' from the people to the government. The president and the legislative assembly are elected separately and both therefore have **independent sources of democratic legitimacy**, which at times can lead to conflict between the two branches over policy and, in extreme cases, can lead to constitutional crises and even democratic breakdown (e.g. as in the case of Brazil in 1964 and Chile in 1973; see Cohen 1994). Within parliamentary regimes, there is a **mutual dependence** between the executive and legislative branches, where the prime minister is typically the leader of the largest party, has the confidence of the parliament and there has been a single election to determine who governs. Comparative research has shown that presidential democracies tend to breakdown more than parliamentary democracies, but that among developing countries, parliamentary regimes break down more than presidential ones. Among presidential democracies, the real problem lies in those countries that have **strong presidentialism** (i.e. many unilateral powers that are at the disposal of the president). As we saw in Chapter 4, many 'third-wave' democracies are also presidential democracies and among some, there has been an increasing concentration of power in the office of the president. This problem of strong presidentialism can be compounded in countries where it is combined with a large number of weak parties (see Shugart and Carey 1992; Stepan and Skach 1993). The media stories about the dysfunctionality of American democracy often focus on the frequency of what is known as 'divided government' where one party controls the presidency and a different party controls the Congress. Systematic research has concluded that, despite the popular perceptions, periods of divided government are no less productive and any more conflictual than periods of unified government (see McKay 1994; Landman 2008). Moreover research on presidential democracies with precisely the most difficult combination of institutions for governability (i.e. combined with weak multi-party systems) has shown that across many cases in Latin America, Africa and Asia, presidents and legislators have learnt how to form governing coalitions and to avoid the kind of gridlock and conflict that leads to democratic breakdown (see Ellis et al. 2009).

In addition to the presidential and parliamentary debate, scholars have also examined different outcomes between so-called 'majoritarian' and 'consensus' democracies (see Lijphart 1999, 2012). Majoritarian systems quite simply are those democracies in which a majority rule; a state of affairs that is made possible by particular sets of institutional arrangements and ways of 'doing politics' in which a 'bare' majority holds power. Examples of majoritarian democracies include the United Kingdom, New Zealand and Barbados. Consensus systems, in contrast, share and disperse power where the predominant way of doing politics involves inclusiveness, bargaining and compromise. Examples of consensus democracies include Switzerland and Belgium. In an analysis of 36 democracies across the basic distinction between majoritarian and consensus, Arend Lijphart (1999, 2012) has found that consensus democracies are better across a wide range of policy outcomes, such as government effectiveness, the rule of law, the control of corruption, low inflation and low unemployment (Lijphart 2012: 262– 8). Moreover, consensus democracies are also better for political stability, low internal conflict, lower levels of violence, better protection of civil liberties, income equality and women's representation and empowerment (Ibid., 270–2; 276–7). These findings are in many ways analogous to the findings outlined above with respect to institutional design and show that despite the overall superior performance of democracies for a wide range of indicators of well-being, there remains a large variation in benefits and outcomes across different kinds of democracy. In an assessment of the quality of democracy in South Asia, one of the conclusions that came from the Nepalese assessment was that 'democracy has many stories' (see CSDS 2008; IDEA 2008), and the kind of variation discussed here confirms this basic insight from Nepal.

Democratic peace

There is a longstanding claim that **democracies are more peaceful than other states,** which has become known as the 'democratic peace' proposition. The statement itself needs to be qualified in two important ways. First, it applies to the fact that democratic countries rarely, if ever, fight each other; an empirical observation which for many is 'the closest thing we have to a law in international politics' (see Levy 1989: 270, 2002: 359). Second, it applies to the fact that in any given pair, or 'dyad' of states, the presence of one democracy significantly reduces the probability of inter-state conflict (see Russett and O'Neal 2001). The overall claim (and its further qualifications) about the pacific benefits of democracy is important for our discussions here. The logic of the claim and the research that has been carried out to substantiate it are fairly straightforward. First, there is a normative argument that political elites within democracies adhere to democratic norms, which in turn lead them to prefer non-violent conflict resolution and negotiation to violent conflict. This general normative orientation is then shared by democracies that develop greater trust for one another in the international arena and leads any two democracies not to engage in violent conflict with one another (see Rosato 2003: 586). Second, there are several institutional 'logics' at play involving the inherent element of accountability within democracies that constrain leaders from engaging in warfare or conflict (see above).These institutional factors include public constraints on leaders, interest groups, difficulty in mobilizing the public for war, inability for surprise attacks and relative availability of information within the public domain (Ibid., 586–7).

Both the normative and institutional logics inherent within democracies suggest that they would be less likely to go to war with one another and that the presence of a democracy in any one dyad of states would lower the probability of inter-state conflict. These ideas have been tested and evolved over time from original studies conducted by Babst (1964, 1972) with the development of increasingly complex data sets of all the politically relevant dyads between the late nineteenth century and the late twentieth century. One popular study on the democratic peace conducted by Russett and O'Neal (2001) compiles a database of politically relevant dyads from 1886 to 1992. For inter-state conflict, they use a measure called a 'militarised dispute', which includes all instances when one state threatens to use force, makes an expression of force or actually uses military force against another state. Alongside a measure of democracy, the analysis uses traditional 'realist' measures, such as the contiguity of the countries in each pair, the relative distance between them, the difference in power between them and any alliances that they may have. The results of the analysis show that even after controlling for these realist variables, 'two democracies are 33 per cent less likely than the average dyad to become involved in a militarised dispute'. Russet and O'Neal (2001: 275) argue that this is a conservative estimate of the 'pacific benefits of democracy', and they show further that not only are democracies less likely to fight one another, but they are even less likely to become involved in disputes than autocracies (Ibid., 276).

Christian Davenport (2007) analyses the 'pacific benefits of democracy' at the domestic level and finds general support for this positive benefit of democracy, but qualifies it in several important ways. First, democracy overall does decrease the use of repression, but the decrease is most sensitive to two key features of democracy: electoral participation and competition. In other words, the ability to exercise 'voice' is an important feature of democracy that can help reduce the use of lethal repression at the domestic level; a feature in Davenport's (2007: 179) analysis that is more important than constraints on the executive branch. Second, among different kinds of repression, physical integrity rights violations (see above) are more reduced among democracies than restrictions of civil liberties. Finally, these overall positive trends can be confounded by conflict, where the presence of conflict within democracies can lead to an increase in repression (see Chapter 8 in this volume). Moreover, the pacifying effects of 'voice' are strong in the presence of violent dissent such as that from riots and guerrilla warfare, but are mushy reduced in the presence of all out civil war (Davenport 2007: 178–80).

Economic benefits

We already noted in Chapter 2 of this volume that there are particular economic benefits to democracy that reach far beyond the traditional focus on the annual growth in per capita GDP (see Donnelly 1999). We saw that democracies do not have superior growth rates to non-democracies, but because of the normative and institutional features of democracy, as well as the structure of incentives within democracies, the **quality** of economic benefits is different for democracies. In addition to Amartya Sen's observation that democracies will never experience famine (see Chapter 2), there are strong moral and rational arguments for why democracies ought to be produce better and more equitable economic outcomes. Morally, politicians in democracies ought not to have preferences for citizens to suffer unduly. Rationally, politicians have electoral incentives for more equal economic outcomes (see Meltzer and Richard 1981; Norris 2012). Indeed, if the focus is on **sustainable human development**, with its emphasis on overall well-being of the population, then democracies do outperform non-democracies.

For example, Figure 9.3 shows the difference in the values of the human development index (HDI) for competitive and non-competitive political systems for a global sample of countries between 1980 and 2010.[1] Each curve in the figure is the distribution of the HDI, where the average value is much higher for competitive systems than non-competitive systems. The curves do cross over, such that there are some competitive systems that do not perform as well as non-competitive systems but at an aggregate level, they do. Figure 9.4 shows a comparison of distributions for caloric consumption (itself a measure of the provision of basic nutrition to the population) broken down according to regime type and levels of economic development. The figure shows that rich competitive systems have the highest levels of caloric consumption, followed by rich non-competitive countries, poor competitive countries and poor non-competitive countries. Again, there is some cross-over among the curves, but the overall ranking of systems is statistically significant. Moreover, the interaction between the

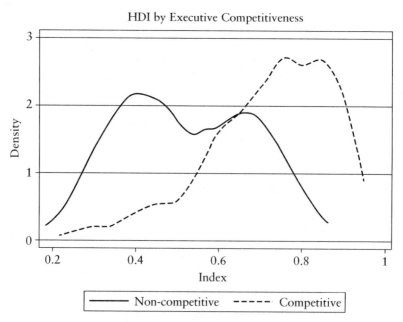

FIGURE 9.3 *Human development and executive competiveness, 1980–2010.*

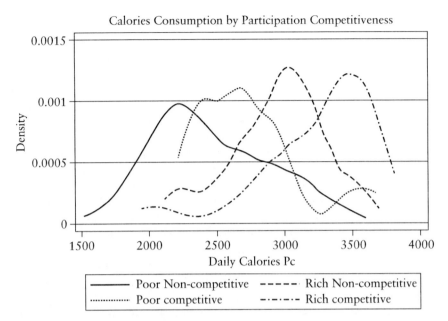

FIGURE 9.4 *Caloric intake and competiveness, 1980–2010.*

level of development and democracy is an important one. Rich countries are better at providing basic nutrition, but within each grouping of countries, it is the more competitive systems that are superior (see also Norris 2012). In this way, among the world's rich and poor countries, democracy still offers better economic outcomes than non-democracy. Both of these sets of findings are upheld in more complex sets of analyses that control for additional factors, such as economic growth, population size and natural resource endowments.

In addition to human development and caloric consumption, Norris (2012) finds additional support for the positive effects of democracy and good governance on longevity, child mortality, the level of health, gender equality in education and education more generally. Across these welfare indicators, Norris finds superior performance for 'liberal democracies' and countries with higher levels of 'bureaucratic governance'. As above, the positive and significant findings are upheld in the presence of other explanatory factors, such as levels of economic growth and income, geographic factors (location, size and natural resource endowments), social structures (e.g. linguistic and religious divisions, human capital, population size and conflict) and cultural background. Thus, the combination of the findings in Figures 9.3 and 9.4 and those from Norris (2012) shows a great deal of support for the proposition that there are a large number of economic benefits to democracy. Across the world, democracy is a form of government that enhances the quality of developmental outcomes and measures of overall well-being.

Environmental outcomes

In the previous chapter, we argued that climate change and environmental degradation presented significant threats to democracy and human rights. But are democracies good for the environment? We saw that they are good for overall levels of well-being, but enhancing human well-being involves a great degree of **consumption of natural resources**, and there have been many arguments about the putative benefits of democracy for overseeing the kinds of sustainable human development that includes guardianship of the world's natural resources. Like the arguments for the democratic peace, those who argue the 'green benefits' of democracy make the case that freedom of speech and press raises awareness levels of democratic citizens, who in turn can put pressure on their respective governments for sound environmental policies. Counter-arguments suggest that democracies are prone to influence from vested interests, some of whom are from businesses operating in the energy and extractive sector, which may prevent democracies from enacting environmentally friendly policies (see, e.g. Whitford and Wong 2009: 191–2).

Testing this set of propositions involves different measures of sustainability and environmental degradation or 'stress'. For example, Whitford and Wong (2009) use measures on sustainability (the 2002 Environmental Sustainability Index or ESI), environmental systems (a combination of air and water quality, biodiversity, human impact on land), environmental stress and human vulnerability. They find that democracy has a positive impact on sustainability and systems, but not on stress and vulnerability. My own analysis for the United Nations Development Programme finds similar mixed results. For example, Figure 9.5 shows that countries with executive competitiveness on average are responsible for less water pollution than non-competitive countries. Figure 9.6 shows that if we take levels of economic development into account, rich competitive countries have lower rates of fossil fuel consumption than rich non-competitive countries, and poor competitive countries have lower rates of fossil fuel consumption than poor non-competitive countries.

This last example shows that levels of economic development are related to environmental degradation, where wealthy countries consume more of the natural environment, but democracy has a mitigating effect on that consumption. Across a variety of studies, the impact of democracy on the environment is mixed, since the consumption of natural resources and the damage that comes from that consumption will always be a function of economic development and political institutions. Moreover, a recent report from the Royal Society in the United Kingdom (2012: 9) entitled *People and the Planet* argues that human development must not be decoupled from the environment, as any large-scale demographic and economic changes will have a necessary impact on the environment. The report sees the need for

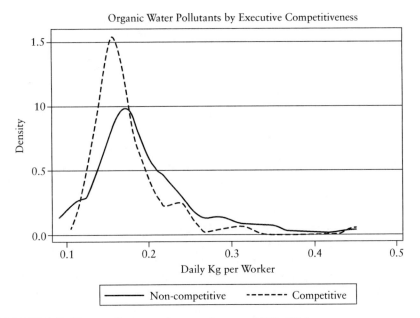

FIGURE 9.5 *Water pollution and competiveness, 1980–2010.*

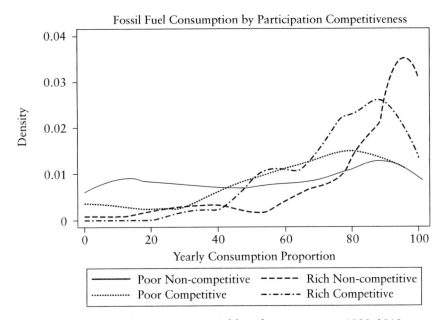

FIGURE 9.6 *Fossil fuel consumption, wealth and competiveness, 1980–2010.*

governments to 'develop socio-economic systems and institutions that are not dependent on continued material consumption growth'. The coupling of people, the environment *and* governance are thus of paramount importance in any consideration of the possible benefits of democracy for the environment.

Summary

The case for democracy in terms of benefits and outcomes for human well-being and citizen life is very strong indeed. This chapter has shown that across a wide variety of tangible and intangible factors, democracies are superior to non-democracies; however, as it has also shown, there are many remaining problems, differences and challenges across democracies. We saw that basic democratic values and principles have personal value to citizens and that democracies have a better record at protecting physical rights and a wide range of other human rights. We have seen that democracies have 'pacific benefits' in reducing inter-state and intra-state conflict. We have seen that democracies have a better record across wide range of economic variables other than a strict focus on annual growth in per capita GDP. And we have seen that within different income bands, democratic countries have a better record for environmental sustainability. This basket of positive benefits of democracy, however, must be tempered by a consideration of the great variation that still exists among democracies. Western democracies are not uniformly superior across all measures of performance. The association between democracy and human rights, despite a normative and theoretical expectation, is nowhere near a perfect one, where many democracies continue to struggle to protect people from physical integrity rights violations and other human rights violations. The kind of institutional design that is chosen can have an impact on democratic performance and represents a trade-off across democracies between the principle of representation and governability.

SUGGESTIONS FOR FURTHER READING

Boix, C. (2003) *Democracy and Redistribution*. New York: Cambridge University Press.

Halperin, M., Siegle, J. and Weinstein, M. (2010) *The Democracy Advantage: How Democracies Promote Prosperity and Peace*. New York and London: Routledge.

Norris, P. (2012) *Making Democratic Governance Work: The Impact of Regimes on Prosperity, Welfare and Peace*. Cambridge: Cambridge University Press.

Russett, B. and Oneal, J. (2001) *Triangulating Peace: Democracy, Interdependence and International Organizations*. New York: W. W. Norton.

Note

1 The analysis presented here comes from a United Nations Development Programme (UNDP) funded project on democratic governance and sustainable human development carried out by Todd Landman, Alejandro Quiroz Flores and Dorothea Farquhar at the Institute for Democracy and Conflict Resolution at the University of Essex. The data that appear in Figure 9.3 through Figure 9.5 are based on that study.

CHAPTER TEN

Hopes and challenges

A tale of three women

I began this book with a series of passages about travelling to 'new' democracies, and it thus seems fitting to conclude the book with another anecdote from travel to another new democracy in the world: Mozambique. The story of Mozambique is a familiar one in many regards. It was colonized by the Portuguese and was part of the struggle for independence and process of decolonization in Africa that took place from the 1960s onwards. It gained its independence in 1975 and was embroiled in civil war until 1992, when a United Nations negotiated settlement was achieved between the ruling Front for the Liberation of Mozambique (Frelimo) and the main rebel group Mozambique National Resistance (Renamo). Frelimo has held power since 1992 through a variety of presidents, but most commentators agree that the country has made a good start in its transition to democracy while at the same time continuing to address its remaining challenges (see EISA 2005; AfriMap 2009). I had the good fortune of spending time in Maputo, the Capital city, in late summer 2012 to engage with civil society organizations working on educational reform and seeking to engage with parliament more effectively as part of a larger DFID-funded project on parliamentary strengthening in Eastern Europe, Africa and the Middle East.

The reason I mention Mozambique, apart from highlighting yet another case in which the appeal of democracy has triumphed, is that I was particularly struck by one thing that one of my Mozambican colleagues said on the last day in the capital:

> People in Mozambique like to get together, have a few beers, a chat and be able to discuss anything they want. It is nice to know that we can move about freely and meet with people and talk without fear of being stopped by the police or watched by the government.

Such an observation seems remarkably simple and even obvious, but for so many people in the world for so long, the simple pleasure of sitting with friends unhindered by the possibility of repression or suspicion from the state and being able to have free and lively discussions on any topic has simply not been possible. Ordinary citizens in the totalitarian states of Eastern Europe were not able to do this. Those in 1970s in Argentina, Brazil, Chile and Uruguay were not able to do it. Those in South Africa were not able to do it. Those in Egypt, Libya and Tunisia were not able to do it. Or those in Burma/Myanmar were not able to it. The simple idea of not being able to walk about unhindered by a fear of the state or a non-state entity infringing one's rights is connected to the kinds of dramatic scenes that the world witnessed in late 2010 and 2011 with the advent of the Arab Spring. This simple notion of the **repressed individual** brings to mind a passage from Georg Groddeck's (1961) *Book of the It*:

> What is repressed does not vanish, it only loses its place. It is pushed into some corner or other where it has no right to be, where it is squeezed and hurt. Then it always stands on tiptoe, pressing from time to time with all its strength towards where it belongs, and as soon as it sees a gap in the wall in front of it, it tries to squeeze itself through. Perhaps it may succeed in so doing, but when it has got to the front it has used up all its strength, and the next good push from some masterful force hurls it back again. It is a most disagreeable situation, and when anything is so repressed, crushed and battered, at length wins freedom you can imagine what leaps and bounds it will be taking (Groddeck 1961: 47).

The events of 2011 in the Middle East and North Africa certainly showed what 'leaps and bounds' can really look like as popular mobilizations toppled the regimes in Tunisia, Egypt and Libya while dissident and opposition forces continue to struggle against authoritarianism in Yemen, Bahrain and Syria. The repressed individual in these cases was not alone and the political opportunities that made possible collective action of the repressed showed that real change is possible. The period since the end of the Cold War and most recently has seen three remarkable individuals, who themselves were repressed under authoritarian rule, rise to political prominence in their own countries. It is also telling that all three of them are women: Michelle Bachelet in Chile, Dilma Rousseff in Brazil and Aung San Suu Kyi in Burma. Michelle Bachelet was elected the first female president of Chile from 2006 to 2010. In 1974, she was taken by the Chilean internal security police (known as the DINA) to the now infamous Villa Grimauldi detention facility in Santiago, where she was tortured as part of Augusto Pinochet's campaign against the political left (her father was a General who served under former president Salvador Allende). She spent many years in East Germany before returning to Chile and serving under President Ricardo Lagos before being elected president (see Politzer 2011). Dilma Roussef was a victim of the Brazilian military regime which held power between 1964 and 1985 and became the first female President of Brazil in 2010. In the early 1970s, she was part of the radical left in Brazil and was in the Tiradentes Prison in São Paulo between 1970 and 1972, where she was tortured by the regime. Found guilty by the regime for subversion, Rousseff resurrected her political career and had many different political positions before being elected President in 2010 (see Roett 2011). Like Bachalet and Rousseff, Aung San Suu Kyi was also an 'enemy of the regime' and had spent many years under house arrest since the 1990s as the leader of the National League for Democracy and was only released in November 2010 and then won a seat in the national parliament in 2012.

Each of these women embodies the notion of the repressed individual. Bachalet and Aung San Suu Kyi had not committed crimes that led to their detention and ill treatment, but at the time of her arrest and detention, Rousseff was part of the armed revolutionary left and was carrying a weapon, neither of which justify the prolonged torture that she endured, but do make her a slightly different case than either of the other two women. All three have suffered state repression for long periods of time, and all three have since risen to occupy positions of political leadership and power. Bachalet and Rousseff despite (or in spite of) their pasts, have become the first female presidents of their countries; a remarkable achievement given the continued prevalence of gender bias in politics across the world, while Aung San Suu Kyi has symbolized freedom through her quiet determination to challenge the Burmese military. At a deeper and more resonant level with the themes that run through this present volume, these three women symbolize what is possible and how even the most repressed individuals can under the proper circumstances achieve remarkable and unforeseen success in politics. They have triumphed over adversity and have entered the political spotlight. Moreover, they represent new symbols for the politically repressed of today and join the ranks of inspirational political leaders such as Mahatma Ghandi, Martin Luther King and Nelson Mandela.

How does the liberation and ascendency of these three women connect to the larger themes of this book? We have seen large-scale and sweeping changes across the world and across many different dimensions of democracy and human rights. In order to bring our discussions to a close, I would like to assess the contribution that has been made by each chapter with respect to the hopes and challenges that now present themselves to the world. The 'thematic couplets' that frame each chapter have been helpful signposts for understanding my own notion 'precarious triumph'. At this point in the twenty-first century, it would have been impossible to imagine 30 years ago that people like Bachelet, Rousseff and Aung San Suu Kyi would (a) be able to survive their incarceration and ill-treatment, (b) rise to prominence within a typically male-dominated opposition and (c) achieve positions of power in transitional countries, two of which now have consolidated democracy. But it is crucial to the premise of this whole book that we understand the basic point that their liberation and ascendency were not inevitable. Rather, they took part in complex and highly contingent political processes that have unfolded in dynamic contexts where larger structural, institutional and socio-economic changes have taken place. They remained steadfast in their determination, but that determination necessarily interacts and is constrained by these dynamic contextual conditions. Such changing contextual conditions have been outlined and examined throughout this book and are now discussed in turn.

Abundance and freedom

There is and there will continue to be a natural affinity between democracy and economic well-being. We saw throughout the book that wealthier societies, on average, are also more likely to be more democratic and to be able to protect human rights better. We also saw that countries that make a transition to democracy under conditions of relative wealth are highly unlikely to reverse their democratic achievements. This is a comforting and often reinforced narrative about the world that creates a certain set of expectations among people who live in countries without democracy, wealth and/or good records of human rights protection. The coupling of economic abundance and individual freedom has repeatedly raised expectations in the post-war boom period of economic development, the period of decolonization, the third wave of democratization, end of the Cold War and during the prolonged Arab Spring since 2011. On the one hand, expectations have been raised that periods of successful economic development will naturally lead to democracy and better human rights protection. On the other hand, expectations have been raised that periods of democratic transition will naturally lead to better economic development and human well-being. The problem with the general finding of a strong relationship between economic abundance and individual freedom is that there will always be exceptions. A telling contrast can be seen between the 2012 US Elections and the 18th Chinese Communist Party Congress. One country is extremely wealthy with a faltering economy and relatively high levels of individual freedom, and one country is becoming wealthier with a rapidly growing economy and relatively low levels of individual freedom. Expectations in both countries are high for their new leadership as both populations desire economic abundance and its many associated benefits. But President Obama himself admitted after the election that democracy is 'messy', while many commentators on Chinese political affairs argue that the regime will struggle to control the desire for freedom as it continues to enrich larger proportions of its society.

In the Middle East and North Africa, the economic critique was coupled with a political critique, which led to regime change and call across many groups and many countries for democracy. But what if the newly constituted regimes of the region are not able to address the question of economic development and the demands of their disproportionately youthful populations? And what happens to the promise of democracy and human rights if agents in the new regime are equally responsible for violating human rights as we have seen in the case of Libya? The vision, fortitude and achievement exemplified by Bachelet, Rousseff and Aung San Suu Kyi runs the risk of being stifled by the adverse and unpredictable events in this region and others undergoing complex processes of transition. President Obama is the first US President to visit Burma, which bodes well for the opposition movement and the National League for Democracy, but will the reforms implemented by the regime go far enough and fast enough to meet and fulfil popular expectations about democracy and human rights? Will a post-Assad regime in Syria be able to represent the different factions in Syrian society and how will the abuses of the regime, the war and the opposition be dealt with in ways that create hope for the next generations?

Beyond these cases and countries, there remain the multiple challenges associated with 'the bottom billion' for whom the type of regime under which they live arguably makes very little difference to their daily lives. Marginalization, social exclusion and global inequality have pushed just over one-seventh of the world's population into a level of poverty that limits their ability to take part meaningfully in their societies. Regimes come and go, but their daily struggle for subsistence remains. If commentators like Thomas Pogge and Paul Collier are correct, then the distribution of wealth has gotten worse not better over the last 30 years and that for this group of people, poverty has deepened. We saw that inequality interacts with power and under certain conditions is intimately related to the violation of civil and political rights as the 'haves' have incentives to use coercive means to exclude access to wealth for the 'have nots' (see Landman and Larizza 2009). For many, poverty and inequality on the scale evident within the bottom billion represent 'structural violations' of human rights in which access to the basic services of the state is extremely limited if not simply unavailable and satisfaction of people's basic needs is not being met. The problem with structural violations is that it there are no 'perpetrators' just victims. Land tenure patterns, policies that exclude and lead to inequality and the power relations inherent in the global economic system make it difficult to find culpability and more importantly long-lasting solutions. The persistence of the bottom billion and its potential for expansion coupled with human rights violations present significant challenges for the growth of democracy in the world.

Democracy and human rights

Many commentators think that democracy and human rights are different sides of the same coin and that advance in one necessarily brings advance in the other. Conceptually, the two share a commitment to well-being and a set of principles around accountability, representation, transparency, participation and inclusion. Empirically, analyses have indeed shown a positive and significant relationship between the two across large samples of countries and time. At both the conceptual and the empirical level, however, there are certain challenges to the naive view that 'all good things go together'. Conceptually, democracy and human rights share certain features, while other features remain quite distinct. Where democracy offers political accommodation, spaces for deliberation and negotiation and the possibility for peaceful resolution of conflicts, human rights are grounded in a strong moral discourse and fortified through the rule of law, which has a particular judgemental and 'adjudicative' way of resolving disputes and finding particular actors and parties in **breach** of their legal obligations. This judgemental, adversarial and confrontational orientation of human rights, while motivated by a shared set of principles, can sometimes be at odds with democracy and its ability to find common ground between and among contending groups.

While there are many studies in political science and international relations that demonstrate the positive and significant relationship between democracy and human rights (Landman 2005a), it is vitally important to understand that such a relationship is very far from perfect. It was popular at the end of the last century to identify the problem of 'illiberal democracy' as a trend among transitional countries that had managed to establish basic democratic institutions, hold several free and fair elections and guarantee at least the chance that the opposition could win power while at the same time fail to provide protection for a wide range of different human rights (Diamond 1999; Zakaria 2003; Landman 2005a). This 'human rights gap' is a significant challenge not only for the new and restored democracies in the world but also for the old and established democracies. The nature of precariousness developed in this book is one that affects all societies, and defenders of human rights need to remain vigilant in all political contexts. Explanations for the gap include weak state institutions and the failure of a human rights culture to grip national consciousness in ways that inculcate human rights values throughout societies.

The post-9/11 'war on terror' demonstrated how quickly long-fought and long-held commitments to human rights can be undermined through appeal to external threat and the priorities of national security. Democratic publics are quick to rush in legislation that centralizes executive authority and provides legal means to subvert rights protections at national and international levels. The international community roundly condemned the Bush Administration's rewriting (or reinterpreting) of international law in ways that justified the use of extraordinary rendition, the detention of 'enemy combatants' and the use of 'intensive interrogation techniques' such as waterboarding (Blakeley 2011). The election of Barack Obama in 2008 led many to expect a reversal of such policies, which by and large has happened, but in their place, President Obama has increased the use of targeted assassination carried out primarily through drones and remote warfare, which many believe runs afoul of international law. In late 2011, President Obama signed the National Defense Authorization Act (NDAA), which codifies into law indefinite military detention without charge or trial. The provisions in the act authorize the president to order the military to pick up and imprison people who are captured anywhere in the world indefinitely. The use of such practices sends strong and contradictory signals to both allies and enemies of the United States in ways that continue to undermine human rights and limit the 'soft power' (Nye 2005) of the world's democracies.

Waves and setbacks

Analysts engage in 'pattern recognition', and one of the hallmarks of the last four decades has been the growth in democracy around the world. Where this growth can be characterized and catalogues in the different 'waves' or not does hide the fact that since 1974, both the number and percentage of countries that are democratic have grown significantly. Any observation of this nature, however, rests on a particular definition of democracy and such counting of democracy typically adopts a thin and 'procedural definition' that focuses on elections and the existence of basic democratic institutions. We can thus celebrate and be somewhat triumphant about the democratic achievements that have been made since 1974, as well as the democratic inspiration that they have spread to countries that have not yet experienced democratic transition. Indeed, now with the advent of new technologies, democratic diffusion not only takes plays among contiguous countries, but the images and narratives associated with the struggle for democracy today can transcend barriers to information that in the past have been more fortified. Pro-democracy movements can observe, learn and absorb lessons from other political contexts and adapt them to their own circumstances in ways that challenge incumbent regimes and make possible democratic advance. The availability and use of social media are thus new factors to take into account in explaining the spread of democratic ideals and the potential for protest mobilization against non-democratic regimes.

Against the positive trends in democratization captured in the quantitative analysis and the hopes that such trends create, there is a wide range of remaining challenges to democratization to which we all must remain aware. The advance of democracy evident in the quantitative figures (see Figure 1.1) is of course for its most minimal features. Experience from a large number of democracy assessments that have taken place since 2000 suggests that there are 'easy' and 'difficult' features in any democratization process (IDEA 2008: 288). The easy achievements are those which occur relatively soon after a democratic transition and key examples are as follows:

- Obtain a broadly agreed constitution with a bill of rights
- Establish some sort of office of ombudsmen and/or public defender
- Hold free elections and establish universal suffrage
- Support the revival of local government
- Ensure the protection of basic freedoms such as party association, press, speech and assembly

The more difficult challenges in democratization processes are as follows:

- The effective inclusion of minorities and women's participation
- Equal access to justice and protection of the right to life
- Meaningful intra-party democracy
- Control of executives
- A reduction in private influence and private interests in the public sphere
- A significant role for opposition parties

The experience of many new and restored democracies around the world has been one of either 'delegative democracy' (O'Donnell 1994) where executives disregard the constitutional limits on the exercise of their authority, or 'rollback' (Diamond 2011) of democracy where executives centralize their authority and undermine democratic values and institutions as well as human rights commitments, as in the case of Russia under Putin and the Central Asian republics of the Former Soviet Union since the mid-1990s. In addition to these challenges, there are long-term questions around elimination of so-called 'authoritarian legacies', access to justice, combating corruption, party finance, freedom of information laws and parliamentary oversight of executives, the security apparatus (military and police) and, in many countries, the extractive industries and foreign direct investment more generally (IDEA 2008: 300–2).

Evidence and explanations

There is still a predominant view that economic modernization is the prime driver for processes of democratization. The theory of 'endogenous democratization' sees socio-economic development as unleashing a wide range of social and political changes that are conducive to democracy and the main propositions of this theory are supported by large-scale statistical analysis. But as argued above, any generalization from such analyses will always carry with it a number of significant outliers and exceptions that make us pause about putting too much emphasis on so-called economic determinism. There are many cases of countries embracing democracy that are not particularly well-developed economically. I began this book with a stylized portrayal of the case of Mongolia, which at the time of its transition had remarkably low levels of national income, and the world has witnessed other such cases where democracy has emerged under conditions of economic scarcity. Indeed, the theory of 'exogenous democratization' posits that the process of economic modernization has very little direct relationship with democracy other than helping it sustain itself once it has been established. Countries that embrace democracy and that are poor are posited to have a lower probability of survival than rich countries that embrace democracy (Przeworski et al. 2000). Thus the case of Mongolia is **improbable** but not **impossible**.

Cases such as Mongolia, among others, have forced us to look for alternative perspectives that account for democratization, and among these, there has been a focus on domestic elites, national opposition groups and social movements and significant international factors, such as coercion, contagion, diffusion and democracy promotion. A moment of transition presents elites in the incumbent regime opportunities to gamble on the future on whether they tolerate and make agreements with opposition forces that pave the way to democracy (e.g. Burma) or maintain authoritarianism and risk international condemnation (e.g. China). Opposition leaders gamble on allying with their more radical counterparts in challenging the incumbent regime and risking violence and civil war, or they can seek engagement with reformist elements in regime and reach some form of accommodation or elite 'pact' (see Przeworski 1991; Higley and Gunther 1994). In this elite-centred account, there are multiple outcomes for democracy (with and without guarantees), continued authoritarianism or conflict, where individual calculations about risk and probability of success are weighed against the desire for maintaining or increasing political power. The outcomes themselves are highly contingent on the strategic interaction between elites in the regime and within the opposition. It is never entirely clear in which direction elites will go and what kinds of choices they will make. This contingency of outcomes and the precariousness of the interactions themselves are important lessons to bear in mind when examining processes of democratization. There is a tendency to assume that particular outcomes were inevitable, while in reality, the outcome that is obtained (i.e. democracy) is one of many.

Agents and advocates

The narrative about elites and 'deal making', which may or may not lead to democracy often ignores the role for popular agency. In this book, I advanced a 'transformational' perspective on the making of democracy that gives fuller weight to social movements, popular mobilization and civil society organizations in the process of democratization. These groups and forms of collective action articulate a wide range of demands and come together in waves of protest that minimize the difference between groups within the opposition and maximize the difference between the opposition and the regime. Popular movements were a key feature in the transitions to democracy in Latin America (see Foweraker 1995; Foweraker and Landman 1997; Foweraker et al. 2003) and Eastern Europe (see Linz and Stepan 1996), while the Arab Spring featured remarkable waves of protest that resulted in regime change in the cases of Tunisia and Egypt. But like the elite accounts of democratization, it is not inevitable that such challenges to incumbent regimes will be successful in (a) toppling leaders and (b) fomenting democratization. Indeed, the case of China and Tiananmen Square is a case of failure to topple leaders or bring about democracy, and the case of the Arab Spring countries has shown that regime change is possible in some countries, but it not clear that democracy will be established. Thus, popular mobilization carries with it a great risk of failure that is contingent on other significant factors.

One key factor that can contribute to the success of popular mobilization for democracy is the degree to which it enjoys support from the international community. Domestic groups often face stiff opposition and harsh repressive crackdowns from the incumbent regime, but if they are successful in forming alliances with 'transnational advocacy networks' (see Risse et al. 1999) and/or powerful pro-democracy states in the international system, then the costs for the regime of resisting the opposition increase considerably. The number of international non-governmental organizations working on human rights issues, campaigning for the release of political prisoners, documenting human rights abuses and advocating for human rights progress has increased dramatically during the third and fourth waves of democratization. The existence of this dense network of agents and advocates provides additional possibilities for challenging unsavoury regimes around the world. In addition, the National Endowment for Democracy in the United States and the European Endowment for Democracy in Brussels are governmental and non-governmental institutions that provide assistance, advice and networks for pro-democracy movements seeking to bring about regime change, while the International Institute for Democracy and Electoral Assistance (IDEA) is an inter-governmental organisation that has expanded its regional presence and offers knowledge and advice on democracy building. The international environment for democracy support is this becoming more robust as governments and popular organizations engage more seriously with the pro-democracy agenda. The key challenge for any of these agencies and organizations is to respect the diversity of democratic forms emerging around the world and to encourage without prescribing pathways to greater democratization.

Truth and justice

It is telling that Dilma Roussef is one the key actors who brought about the establishment of a truth and reconciliation commission in Brazil. As a former prisoner of the regime and president of the country, she sits with a particular moral authority in bringing about this development. The military regime in Brazil left power after 21 years in 1985. In that year, the military selected the next civilian president and it was not until 1989 that Fernando Collor de Mello became the first democratically elected President of Brazil since 1961. Since 1989, Brazil has consolidated democracy, enjoyed the peaceful transfer of power between competing political parties survived the 'perils' of presidentialism in a multi-party democracy (see Linz and Valenzuela 1994), but throughout the post-authoritarian regime, Brazil has used amnesties for perpetrators of past atrocities until the establishment of the truth and reconciliation commission. Alongside Brazil, other countries such as Ireland and Spain are still considering whether they should adopt some kind of truth and justice mechanism to deal with the 'past wrongs' that have been committed. A formal reckoning with the past, public acknowledgement of wrongdoing and some form of redress (e.g. imprisonment of perpetrators, reparations to victims, etc.) can bring new hope and a positive outlook for the future as countries move beyond their own past histories.

The fundamental challenge for any truth and justice process if it is adopted, however, involves the degree to which a punitive and retributive approach is used as opposed to one that is more forgiving and restorative. Justice and punishment, while laudable from a legal and moral justice view, can carry with them certain risks of stirring past resentment, failing to achieve real justice and having selective application by focusing on the primary actors involved in committing atrocities. Retribution has the potential for undermining the hard work required in any democratization process. Restorative processes have the advantage of seeking understanding and healing deep wounds within a society, but run the risk of being too 'soft' on perpetrators and may well be perceived as an inappropriate means to address the problem of past wrongs. No doubt, these kinds of debates will take place in a post-authoritarian Egypt, Tunisia, Libya, among others.

Threats and pitfalls

The precariousness of democracy and human rights stems from a wide range of internal and external threats that are both direct and indirect. Democracies must defend themselves from overt challenges that involve violence, subversion and terrorist methods. Police, security forces and military all exist within democracies and have the responsibility to protect innocent civilians from such overt challenges. These forces in democracies are subjected to civilian control and the rule of law, which is a larger reflection of the constitutional order. That constitutional order across many democracies is further complemented by international legal obligations to respect, protect and fulfil human rights. Democracies struggle with a perceived trade-off between security and liberty in ways that have compromised rights commitments and obligations. There are rights-based approaches to combating terrorism (see OHCHR 2012) and other threats where it is precisely the ability for democracies to uphold the rule of law and treat terrorism in a criminal justice rather than 'war' framing that can preserve the values upon which democracy is based (Landman 2007). On this precise point, former FBI agent Michael German (2005: 14) argues,

> By treating terrorists like criminals, we stigmatize them in their community, while simultaneously validating our own authority. Open and public trials allow the community to see the terrorist for the criminal he [or she] is, and successful prosecutions give them faith the government is protecting them. Judicial review ensures that the methods used are in accordance with the law, and juries enforce community standards of fairness. The adversarial process exposes improper or ineffective law enforcement techniques so they can be corrected. Checks and balances on government power and public accountability promote efficiency by ensuring that only the guilty are punished.

The response to terrorism since 9/11 within the world's democracies carries with it a double threat: (1) the permanent threat of attacks from terrorist groups that are 'home-grown' or foreign-sponsored and (2) the threat from a policy and legislative response that is based on the assumption that human rights commitments must be compromised in some way in order to combat terrorism itself.

Beyond the overt and direct threats to democracy stemming from violent groups and terrorist organizations, there are indirect and less obvious threats to democracy and human rights. Persistent, and in many countries, rising patterns of inequality threaten the social fabric of democracy. Unregulated market capitalism cannot provide the kind of social protections required to alleviate the worst outcomes of market failure. The development of the welfare state in post-war democracies went a long way to establishing what Jack Donnelly (1999) has called 'rights-protective' regimes. The neo-liberal revolution stemming from the 1980s, which is based on the assumption that the market mechanism is the best way to allocate good and services in an economy, has undermined the social safety net. The wave of austerity measures that have been implemented in response to the financial crisis in the United States and the Eurozone have laid bare many of the contradictions associated with free market economics, tax regimes that provide loopholes for the more well-off in society (including such multinational companies as

Amazon Apple and Starbucks) and government spending commitments that are simply unsustainable.

Benefits and outcomes

Our final thematic couplet in this book is based on the premise that the natural appeal of democracy and the full protection of human rights are their promise of the good life, a life without threat, without basic need and without fear. There are benefits inherent to democracy that are difficult to measure and quantify, but that are nonetheless very real for those individuals who live under democratic rule. The freedom and agency that come with democracy for ordinary citizens bring a number of intangible benefits that are embodied in such values as participation, inclusiveness, transparency, accountability and representation. Citizens in democracies can be left alone or can choose to become actively involved at the local and national levels of politics. They do not fear the arbitrary abuse of state power and know that when they have an encounter with the state, laws are in place to protect them from unnecessary intrusion by the state and due process throughout that engagement. Their participation takes place formally and institutionally through the electoral processes, or informally and less institutionally through civil society organizations and social movement activities. Moreover, they enjoy the freedoms to speak out, criticize and make demands on government without fear of repressive reprisals.

The basic framework of participation and accountability provided by democracy and a well-developed rights regime is seen as ultimately beneficial for outcomes not necessarily related to democracy. Alongside its more intangible benefits, we have seen that democracies are better at overseeing equitable forms of human development that take into account key macro-economic indicators beyond simply measures of per capital national income. Democracies, on balance, have higher levels of human development (income, literacy and longevity) and higher levels of caloric consumption than non-democracies. Among wealthy countries in the world, democracies have a better record at protecting the environment. In terms of peace and conflict, democracies have particular sets of 'pacific' benefits at the international and domestic levels, as they are less likely to engage in inter-state conflict and less likely to use harsh repression when facing domestic conflict (Russett and O'Neal 2001; Davenport 2007).

A precarious triumph

As we enter the second decade of the twenty-first century, there is much to celebrate. Fascism and communist totalitarianism have been defeated in Europe, authoritarianism has receded in Southern Europe, South America,

Eastern Europe and parts of Africa and Asia. This decade began with momentous changes in the Middle East and North Africa, the final outcome of which remains unknown but the origins and contours of the challenge to incumbents have been framed in terms of economic justice and political freedom. Any developments such as these at the national and regional levels are naturally embedded in larger power relations at the international level, where the geostrategic interests of the United States, the European Union, Russia and China lead to a wide range of double standards and contradictions with respect to democracy and human rights. The achievements that have been made in the latter half of the twentieth century and the beginning of the twenty-first century must be celebrated and protected at the same time. Forces within states and between states can unravel these otherwise remarkable achievements. In the end, I am most deeply moved by the individuals who have the courage to stand up to oppression in all its forms and to take a stand against injustice. The events and developments that have formed the basis of our discussions in this book have featured a cast of characters that is by now well known. But much of the drama of the past decades has really been made possible by the ordinary people who simply want to have more say in the way that they live their lives. Let us hope that the answers to this simple quest continue to flourish.

REFERENCES

Acemoglu, Daron and Robinson, James A. (2006) *The Economic Origins of Dictatorship and Democracy*. Cambridge: Cambridge University Press.

AfriMap (2009) Mozambique: Democracy and Political Participation. London and Johannesburg: Open Society Institute Network.

Aguilar, Fernandez, P. (1996) *La memoria histórica de la Guerra civil española (1936-39): Un proceso de aprendijaze politico*. Madrid: Alianza Editorial.

Alfredsson, Gudmundur; Eide, Asbjorn (1999) *The Universal Declaration of Human Rights: A Common Standard of Achievement*. The Hague, Netherlands.

Ball, P., Spirer, H. and Spirer, L. (2000) *Making the Case: Investigating Large Scale Human Rights Violations Using Information Systems and Data Analysis*. Washington, DC: American Association for the Advancement of Science.

Ball, P., Asher, J., Sulmont, D. and Manrique, D. (2003) *How many Peruvians have Died? An Estimate of the Total Number of Victims Killed or Disappeared in the Armed Internal Conflict between 1980 and 2000*. Washington, DC: American Association for the Advancement of Science (AAAS).

Barbalet, J. M. (1988) *Citizenship: Rights, Struggle and Class Inequality*. Milton Keynes: Open University Press.

Bates, Robert (2001) *Prosperity and Violence*. New York: Norton.

Becker, Jo and Shane, Scott (2012) 'Secret "Kill List" Proves a Test of Obama's Principles and Will', *New York Times*; http://www.nytimes.com/2012/05/29/world/obamas-leadership-in-war-on-al-qaeda.html?_r=1&pagewanted=all

Beetham, D. (1999) *Democracy and Human Rights*. Cambridge: Polity Press.

Blakeley, Ruth (2011) 'Dirty Hands, Clean Conscience? The CIA Inspector General's Investigation of "Enhanced Interrogation Techniques" in the War on Terror and the Torture Debate', *Journal of Human Rights*, 10 (4): 544–61.

Bob, C. (2005) *The Marketing of Rebellion: Insurgents, Media, and International Activism*. Cambridge: Cambridge University Press.

Boix, C. (2003) *Democracy and Redistribution*. Cambridge: Cambridge University Press.

Boix, C. and Stokes, S. (2003) 'Endogenous Democratization', *World Politics*, 55 (July): 517–49.

Boyle, K. (1995) 'Stock-taking on Human Rights: The World Conference on Human Rights, Vienna 1993', *Political Studies*, 43: 79–95.

Bratton, M. and van de Walle, N. (1997) *Democratic Experiments in Africa: Regime Transitions in Comparative Perspective*. Cambridge: Cambridge University Press.

Breuer, Anita, Landman, Todd and Farquhar, Dorothea (2012) 'Social Media and Protest Mobilization: Evidence from the Tunisian Revolution', Paper prepared for the 4th European Communication Conference for the European Communication Research and Education Association (ECREA), Istanbul, Turkey, 24–7 October 2012.

Brohman, J. (1996) *Popular Development*. Oxford: Blackwell.

Brysk, A. and Shafir, G. (eds) (2007) *National Insecurity and Human Rights: Democracies Debate Counterterrorism*. Berkeley: University of California Press.

Bueno de Mesquita, B., Cherif, Feryal, Downs, George and Smith, Alistair (2005) 'Thinking Inside the Box: A Closer Look at Democracy and Human Rights', *International Studies Quarterly*, 49: 439–57.

Buena de Mesquita, Bruce, Smith, Alastair, Siverson, Randolph N., and Morrow, James D. (2003) *The Logic of Political Survival*. Cambridge, MA: MIT Press.

—(2005) *The Logic of Political Survival*. Cambridge, MA: MIT Press.

Burkhart, R. E. and Lewis-Beck, M. (1994) 'Comparative Democracy, the Economic Development Thesis', *American Political Science Review*, 88 (4): 903–10.

Cammack, P. (1997) *Capitalism and Democracy in the Third World: The Doctrine for Political Development*. London and Washington: Leicester University Press.

Carey, S. and Poe, S. (2004) *Understanding Human Rights Violations: New Systematic Studies*. Aldershot: Ashgate.

Carothers, Thomas (2012) *Democracy Policy under Obama*. Washington, DC: Carnegie Endowment for International Peace.

Centre for the Study of Developing Societies (CSDS) (2008) *State of Democracy in South Asia*. Oxford: Oxford University Press.

Cesarini, Paola (2009) 'Transitional Justice', in Todd Landman and Neil Robinson (eds), *Sage Handbook of Comparative Politics*. London: Sage, pp. 497–521.

Chong, Dennis (1991) *Collective Action and the Civil Rights Movement*. Chicago: University of Chicago Press.

Clark, Phil (2011) *The Gaccaca Courts, Post-Genocide Justice and Reconciliation in Rwanda: Justice without Lawyers*. Cambridge: Cambridge University Press.

Clandinin, D. Jean and Connelly, F. Michael (2000), *Narrative Inquiry: Experience and Story in Qualitative Research*. San Francisco: Jossey-Bass Publishers.

Cleary, Edward (2007) *Mobilizing for Human Rights in Latin America*. Bloomfield, CT: Kumarian Press.

Collier, David and Levitsky, Steven (1997) 'Democracy with Adjectives: Conceptual Innovation in Comparative Research', *World Politics*, 49 (3): 430–51.

Cohen, Jean and Arato, A. (1992) *Civil Society and Political Theory*. Cambridge, MA: MIT Press.

Collier, Paul (2008) *The Bottom Billion: Why the Poorest Countries are Failing and What Can be Done About It*. Oxford: Oxford University Press.

Collier, P. and Heoffler, A. (2004) 'Greed and grievance in civil war', *Oxford Economic Papers*, 56 (4): 563–95.

Cohen, Youssef (1994) *Radicals, Reformers, and Reactionaries: The Prisoner's Dilemma and the Collapse of Democracy in Latin America*. Chicago: University of Chicago Press.

Colomer, J. M. and Pascual, M. (1994) 'The Polish Games of Transition', *Communist and Post-communist Studies*, 27 (3): 275–94.

Crook, Jonathan (2011) The Growing Contribution to Technology and Conflict Resolution, Briefing Papers, Institute for Democracy and Conflict Resolution,

University of Essex. http://www.idcr.org.uk/resources-links/idcr-briefing-papers-series

Cruz, C. (2005) *Political Culture and Institutional Development in Costa Rica and Nicaragua*. Cambridge: Cambridge University Press.

Dahl, R. A. (1971) *Polyarchy: Participation and Opposition*. New Haven, CT: Yale University Press.

Davenport, Christian (2010) *State Repression and the Domestic Democratic Peace*. Cambridge: Cambridge University Press.

Davidson, S. (1993) *Human Rights*. Buckingham: Open University Press.

De Schweinitz, K. (1964) *Industrialization and Democracy: Economic Necessities and Political Possibilities*. New York: Free Press.

Diamond, Larry (1999) *Democracy in Development*. Baltimore: Johns Hopkins University Press.

—(2008) 'The Democratic Rollback: The Resurgence of the Predatory State', *Foreign Affairs*, 87 (2): 36–48.

—(2011) *The Spirit of Democracy: The Struggle to Build Free Societies Throughout the World*. New York: St. Martins Griffin.

Diamond, Larry and Morlino, Leonardo (2005) *Assessing the Quality of Democracy*. Baltimore: Johns Hopkins University Press.

Dipalma, Giuseppe (1992) *To Craft Democracies: An Essay on Democratic Transitions*. La Jolla: The University of California Press.

Donnelly, J. (1989) *Human Rights in Theory and Practice*. Ithaca and London: Cornell University Press.

—(1999) 'Democracy, Development, and Human Rights', *Human Rights Quarterly*, 21 (3): 608–32.

Doorenspleet, R. (2005) *Democratic Transitions: Exploring the Structural Sources of the Fourth Wave*. Boulder, CO: Lynne Rienner.

Ellis, Andrew, Henríquez, J. Jesus Orazco and Zovatto, Daniel (2009) *Making Presidentialism Work*. Stockholm: International IDEA.

Enders, Walter and Sandler, Todd (2005) *The Political Economy of Terrorism*. Cambridge: Cambridge University Press.

Epifanio, Mariaelisa (2011) 'Legislative Response to International Terrorism', *Journal of Peace Research*, 48 (3): 399–411.

European Commission, The European Union's Role in Promoting Human Rights and Democratization in Third Countries, Brussels 8 May 2001 – COM (2001) 252. http://ec.europa.eu/external_relations/human_rights/doc/com01_252_en.pdf

Falk, R. (2000) *Human Rights Horizons: The Pursuit of Justice in a Globalizing World*. London: Routledge.

Fearon, Jame and Laitin, David (2003) 'Ethnicity, insurgency, and civil war', *American Political Science Review*, 97 (1): 75–90.

Fein, Helen (1995) 'Life-Integrity Violations and Democracy, 1987', *Human Rights Quarterly*, 17 (1): 170–91.

Finer, S. E. (1997) *The History of Government*, Vol. I: Ancient Monarchies and Empires. Oxford: Oxford University Press.

Foley, Michael and Edwards, Bob (1996) 'The Paradox of Civil Society', *Journal of Democracy*, 7 (3): 38–52.

Foweraker, Joe (1995) *Theorizing Social Movements*. London: Pluto.

—(1998) 'Institutional Design, Party Systems and Governability: Differentiating the Presidential Regimes of Latin America', *British Journal of Political Science*, 28: 651–76.

Foweraker, Joe and Krznaric, Roman (2000) 'Measuring Liberal Democratic Performance: an Empirical and Conceptual Critique', *Political Studies*, 48 (4): 759–87.

—(2003) 'Differentiating the Democratic Performance of the West', *European Journal of Political Research*, 42: 313–40.

Foweraker, J. and Landman, T. (1997) *Citizenship Rights and Social Movements: A Comparative and Statistical Analysis.* Oxford: Oxford University Press.

—(2004) 'Economic development and Democracy Revisited: Why Dependency Theory is Not Yet Dead', *Democratization*, 11 (1): 1–21.

Foweraker, J., Landman, T. and Harvey, N. (2003) *Governing Latin America.* Cambridge: Polity Press.

Freeman, Michael (1994) 'The Philosophical Foundation of Human Rights', *Human Rights Quarterly*, 16 (3): 491–514.

—(2002) *Human Rights: An Interdisciplinary Approach.* Cambridge, UK and Malden, MA: Polity Press.

Fukuyama, F. (1992) *The End of History and the Last Man.* New York: Avon Books.

—(2006) *America at the Crossroads: Democracy, Power and the Neo-Conservative Legacy.* New Haven: Yale University Press.

Gallie, W. B. (1956), 'Essentially Contested Concepts', *Proceedings of the Aristotelian Society*, 56: 167–98.

Geddes, B. (1990) 'How the Cases You Choose Affect the Answers You Get: Selection Bias in Comparative Politics', *Political Analysis*, 2: 131–50.

German, Michael (2005) 'Squaring the Error', in Shawn Boyne, Michael German and Paul R. Pillar (eds), *Law v. War: Competing Approaches to Fighting Terrorism.* Carlisle, PA: Strategic Studies Institute, pp. 11–16.

German Advisory Council on Global Change (WBGU) (2008) *Climate Change as a Security Risk.* London and Sterling, VA: Earthscan.

Ghandhi, P. R. (2002) *Blackstone's International Human Rights Instruments.* Oxford: Oxford University Press.

Gibson, James L. (1996) 'The Paradoxes of Political Tolerance in Processes of Democratisation', *Politikon: South African Journal of Political Studies*, 23 (#2, December): 5–21.

—(2004) 'Overcoming Apartheid: Can Truth Reconcile a Divided Nation?', *Politikon*, 31 (2): 129–55.

Green, Maria (2001) 'What We Talk About When We Talk About Indicators: Current Approaches to Human Rights Measurement', *Human Rights Quarterly*, 23 (4): 1062–97.

Green Economy Coalition (2012) *The Green Economy Pocketbook: The Case for Action*, Green Economy Coalition; http://www.greeneconomycoalition.org

Greenberg, Karen J. and Dratel, Joshua L. (2005) *The Torture Papers: The Road to Abu Ghraib.* Cambridge: Cambridge University Press.

Groddeck, Georg (1961) *The Book of the It.* New York: Vintage.

Haber, Stephen, Klein, Herbert, Maurer, Noel, and Middlebrook, Kevin (2008) *Mexico since 1980.* Cambridge: Cambridge University Press.

Halperin, M., Siegle, J. and Weinstein, M. (2010) *The Democracy Advantage: How Democracies Promote Prosperity and Peace.* New York and London: Routledge.

Hartlyn, Jonathan (1989) 'Colombia: The Politics of Violence and Accommodation', in Larry Diamond, Juan J. Linz and Seymour Martin Lipset (eds), *Democracy in Developing Countries, Volume Four: Latin America*. Baltimore: Johns Hopkins University Press.

Hasenclever, A., Mayer, P. and Rittberger, V. (1997) *Theories of International Regimes*. Cambridge: Cambridge University Press.

Hassner, P. (2008) 'Russia's Transition to Autocracy', *Journal of Democracy*, 19 (2): 5–15.

Hawkins, Darren (2002) *International Human Rights and Authoritarian Rule in Chile*. Omaha: University of Nebraska Press.

Hayner, P. B. (1994) 'Fifteen Truth Commissions—1974–94: A Comparative Study', *Human Rights Quarterly*, 16: 597–655.

—(2002) *Unspeakable Truths: Facing the Challenge of Truth Commissions*. London: Routledge.

—(2010) *Unspeakable Truths: Facing the Challenge of Truth Commissions*. London: Routledge.

Heinisch, R. (1998) 'The Economic Nature of Basic Human Rights: Economic Explanations of Cross-National Variations in Governmental Basic Human Rights Performance', *Peace and Change*, 23 (3): 333–72.

Held, D. (1996) *Models of Democracy*. Cambridge: Polity Press.

Held, D., McGrew, A., Goldblatt, D. and Perraton, J. (1999) *Global Transformations: Politics, Economics, and Culture*. Cambridge: Polity Press.

Henderson, C. (1991) 'Conditions Affecting the Use of Political Repression', *Journal of Conflict Resolution*, 35 (1): 120–42.

Higley, John and Gunther, Richard (1992) *Elites and Democratic Consolidation in Latin America and Southern Europe*. Cambridge: Cambridge University Press.

Holmes, Jenifer (2009) 'Terrorism', in Todd Landman and Neil Robinson (eds), *Sage Handbook of Comparative Politics*. London: Sage, pp. 463–96.

Holmes, S. and Sunstein, C. (2000) *The Cost of Rights: Why Liberty Depends on Taxes*. New York: W. W. Norton.

Howarth, David (1998) 'Paradigms Gained? A Critique of Theories of Democratization in South Africa', in David Howarth and Aletta Norval (eds), *South Africa in Transition: New Theoretical Perspectives*. London: Macmillan, pp. 182–214.

Human Rights Watch (2011) *World Report*. New York: Human Rights Watch.

Huntington, Samuel (1968) *Political Order in Changing Societies*. New Haven: Yale University Press.

—(1991) *The Third Wave: Democratization in the Late Twentieth Century*. Norman, OK: University of Oklahoma Press.

—(1996) *The Clash of Civilizations and the Remaking of the World Order*. New York: Free Press.

Ignatieff, M. (2001) *Human Rights as Politics and Idolatry*. Princeton, NJ: Princeton University Press.

Ingram, Attracta (1994) *A Political Theory of Human Rights*. Oxford: Oxford University Press.

Institute for Democracy and Electoral Assistance (IDEA) (2009) *Democracy in Development: Global Consultations on the EU's Role in Democracy Building*. Stockholm: International IDEA.

Institute for Reconciliation and Justice (2011) *SA Reconciliation Barometer 2010*. Cape Town, South Africa: Institute for Reconciliation and Justice.

International IDEA (2002) *Voter Turnout since 1945: A Global Report*. Stockholm: International IDEA.

—(2005) *Ten Years of Supporting Democracy Worldwide*. Stockholm: International IDEA.

—(2008) *Assessing the Quality of Democracy: A Practical Guide*. Stockholm: International IDEA.

Ishay, Micheline (2004) *The History of Human Rights: From Ancient Times to the Globalization Era*. La Jolla: University of California Press.

—(2008) *The History of Human Rights: From Ancient Times to the Globalization Era*. Berekeley, CA: University of California Press.

International Federation of Human Rights Leagues (FIDH) (2002) 'Terror and Impunity: A Planned System', last updated 9 August 2004, http://www.fidh.org/Terror-and-Impunity-A-Planned; last accessed 24 October 2012.

Keane, John (2004) *Violence and Democracy*. Cambridge: Cambridge University Press.

Keck, Margaret and Sikkink, Kathryn (1998) *Activists beyond Borders: Advocacy Networks in International Politics*. Ithaca, NY: Cornell University Press.

Key, V. O. (1955) 'A Theory of Critical Elections', *The Journal of Politics*, 17 (1): 3–18.

Kitschelt, H. (1986) 'Political Opportunity Structures and Political Protest: Anti-nuclear Movements in Four Democracies', *British Journal of Political Science*, 16 (January): 57–85.

Lagos, Marta (1997) 'Latin America's Smiling Mask', *Journal of Democracy*, 8 (3): 125–38.

—(2003) 'Latin America's Lost Illusions: A Road with No Return', *Journal of Democracy*, 14 (2): 163–73.

Landman, Todd (1999) 'Economic Development and Democracy: The View from Latin America', *Political Studies*, 47 (4): 607–26.

—(2000) *Issues and Methods in Comparative Politics: An Introduction*. London: Routledge.

—(2004) 'Measuring human rights: Principle, practice and policy', *Human Rights Quarterly*, 26: 906–31.

—(2005a) *Protecting Human Rights: A Comparative Study*. Washington, DC: Georgetown University Press.

—(2005b) 'Review article: The political science of human rights', *British Journal of Political Science*, 35 (3): 549–72.

—(2006) *Studying Human Rights*. London and New York: Routledge.

—(2007) 'The United Kingdom: Terror and Counter-Terror Continuity', in A. Brysk and G. Shafir (eds), *National Insecurity and Human Rights: Democracies Debate Counterterrorism*. Berkeley: University of California Press, pp. 75–91.

—(2008) *Issues and Methods in Comparative Politics: An Introduction*, 3rd edition. London: Routledge.

—(2009) 'Measuring human rights', in M. Goodhart (ed.), *Human Rights: Politics and Practice*. Oxford: Oxford University Press.

—(2012a) 'Framing the Fight: Public Security and Human Rights in Mexico', in George Philip and Susuna Berruecos (eds), *Mexico's Struggle for Public Security: Organized Crime and State Responses*. London: Palgrave Macmillan, pp. 99–118.

—(2012b) 'Phronesis and Narrative Analysis' in Bent Flyvbjerg, Todd Landman, and Sanford Schram (eds), *Real Social Science: Applied Phronesis*, Cambridge: Cambridge University Press, 27–47.

Landman, Todd and Carvalho, Edzia (2009) *Measuring Human Rights*. London: Routledge.

Landman, Todd and Larizza, Marco (2009) 'Inequality and Human Rights: Who Controls What When and How', *International Studies Quarterly*, 53 (3): 715–36.

Levine, Daniel (1989) 'Venezuela: The Nature, Sources and Prospects for Democracy', in L. Diamond, J. Linz and S. M. Lipset (eds), *Democracy in Developing Countries, Volume Four: Latin America*. Baltimore: Johns Hopkins University Press, pp. 247–90.

—(2011) *The Agony of Venezuela's Democracy, Demdigest*. Washington, DC: National Endowment for Democracy, 4 March 2011 [Democracy Digest – http://www.demdigest.net/blog].

Levy, J. S. (1989) 'Domestic Politics and War', in R. I. Rothberg and T. K. Rabb (eds), *The Origin and Prevention of Major Wars*. Cambridge: Cambridge University Press.

Li, Q. (2005) 'Does Democracy Promote Transnational Terrorism?', *Journal of Conflict Resolution*, 49 (2): 278–97.

Li, Q. and Reuveny, R. (2003) 'Economic Globalization and Democracy: An Empirical Analysis', *British Journal of Political Science*, 33: 29–54.

Lijphart, Arendt (1999) *Patterns of Democracy: Government Forms and Performance in Thirty Six Countries*. New Haven: Yale University Press.

—(2012) *Patterns of Democracy: Government Forms and Performance in Thirty Six Countries*, 2nd edition. New Haven: Yale University Press.

Lipset, S. M. (1959) 'Some Social Requisites for Democracy: Economic Development and Political Legitimacy', *The American Political Science Review*, 53: 69–105.

—(1960) *Political Man: The Social Bases of Politics*. Baltimore: Johns Hopkins University Press.

Lindberg, S. (2006) *Democracy and Elections in Africa*. Baltimore, MD: Johns Hopkins University Press.

Linz, Juan and Stepan, Alfred (1996) *Problems of Democratic Transition and Consolidation: South America, Southern Europe, and Post-Communist Europe*. Baltimore, MD: Johns Hopkins University Press.

Marshall, T. H. (ed.) (1963) 'Citizenship and Social Class', in *Sociology at the Crossroads and Other Essays*. London: Heinemann.

Marshall, Monty G. and Gurr, Ted Robert (2005) *Peace and Conflict 2005: A Global Survey of Armed Conflicts, Self-Determination Movements, and Democracy*. College Park, MD: Center for International Development and Conflict Management, University of Maryland.

McAdam, D., McCarthy, J. D., and Zald, M. N. (1996) *Comparative Perspectives on Social Movements*. Cambridge: Cambridge University Press.

McKay, D. (1994) 'Review Article: Divided and Governed? Recent Research on Divide Government in the United States', *British Journal of Political Science*, 24: 517–34.

Meier, Gerald and Stiglitz, Joseph (2001) *Frontiers of Development Economics: The Future in Perspective*. New York: Oxford University Press.

Meltzer, Allan H. and Richard, Scott F. (1981) 'A Rational Theory of the Size of Government', *Journal of Political Ecoomy*, 89 (5): 914–27.

Mendus, S. (1995) 'Human Rights in Political Theory', *Political Studies*, Special Issue 43: 10–24.

Mitchell, N. J. and McCormick, J. M. (1988) 'Economic and Political Explanations of Human Rights Violations', *World Politics*, 40: 476–98.

Moore, B. (1966) *The Social Origins of Dictatorship and Democracy: Lord and Peasant in the Making of the Modern World*. Boston, MA: Beacon Press.

Moravcsik, A. (2000) 'The Origins of Human Rights Regimes: Democratic Delegation in Postwar Europe', *International Organization*, 54 (Spring): 217–52.

Muravchik, Joshua (1992) *Exporting Democracy: Fulfilling America's Destiny*. Washington, DC: American Enterprise Institute (AEI) Press.

Nickel, J. W. (2007) *Making Sense of Human Rights*, 2nd edition. Malden, Oxford and Victoria: Blackwell Publishing.

Nowak, M. (2003) *Introduction to the International Human Rights Regime*. The Raoul Wallenberg Institute Human Rights Library, Vol. 14, Leiden/Boston: Martinus Nijhoff Publishers.

Norris, Pippa (2012) *Making Democratic Governance Work: The Impact of Regimes on Prosperity, Welfare and Peace*. Cambridge: Cambridge University Press.

Nye, J. E. (2009a) *Soft Power: The Means to Success in World Politics*. Washington, DC: Public Affairs.

—(2009b) 'Get Smart: Combining Soft and Hard Power', *Foreign Affairs*, 88 (4): 160–3.

O'Donnell, G. (1973) *Economic Modernization and Bureaucratic Authoritarianism*. Berkeley, CA: Institute of International Studies.

—(1994) 'Delegative Democracy', *Journal of Democracy*, 5 (1): 55–69.

O'Donnell, Guillermo, Cullell, Jorge Vargas and Iazzetta, Osvaldo M. (2004) *The Quality of Democracy: Theory and Applications*. South Bend: University of Notre Dame Press.

O'Donnell, Guillermo, Schmitter, Philippe, and Whitehead, Laurence (eds) (1986) *Transitions from Authoritarian Rule*. Baltimore, MD: Johns Hopkins University Press.

Olson, M. (1965) *The Logic of Collective Action*. Cambridge, MA: Harvard University Press.

Olsen, Tricia D., Payne, Leigh A. and Reiter, Andrew G. (2010) *Transitional Justice in the Balance: Comparing Processes*, Weighing Efficacy. Washington, DC: United States Institute for Peace.

Pape, Roger (2003) 'The Strategic Logic of Suicide Terrorism', *American Political Science Review*, 97 (3): 343–61.

Payne, L. (2000) *Uncivil Movements: The Armed Right Wing and Democracy in Latin America*. Baltimore, MD: Johns Hopkins University Press.

Peeler, J. A. (1992) 'Elite Settlements and Democratic Consolidation: Colombia, Costa Rica, and Venezuela', in J. Higley and R. Gunther (eds), *Elites and Democratic Consolidation in Latin America and Southern Europe*. Cambridge: Cambridge University Press, pp. 81–112.

Philip, George and Berruecos, Susana (eds) (2012) *Mexico's Struggle for Public Security: Organized Crime and State Responses*. London: Palgrave Macmillan.

Philip, George and Panizza, Francisco (2011) *The Triumph of Politics: The Return of the Left in Venezuela, Bolivia and Ecuador*. Cambridge: Polity Press.

Poe, S. C. (2004) 'The Decision to Repress: An Integrative Theoretical Approach to the Research on Human Rights and Repressoin', in S. Carey and S. C. Poe (eds), *Understanding Human Rights Violations: New Systematic Studies*. Aldershot: Ashgate, pp. 16–42.

Poe, S. C. and Tate, C. N. (1994) 'Repression of Human Rights to Personal Integrity in the 1980s: A Global Analysis', *American Political Science Review*, 88 (4): 853–72.

Poe, S. C., Tate, C. N. and Keith, L. C. (1999) 'Repression of the Human Right to Personal Integrity Revisited: A Global Cross-national Study Covering the Years 1976–93', *International Studies Quarterly*, 43: 291–313.

Politzer, Patricia (2011) *Bachelet en tierra de hombres*. Debate.

Przeworski, Adam (1991) *Democracy and the Market*. Cambridge: Cambridge University Press.

Przeworski, Adam and Limongi, Fernando (1997) 'Modernization: Theories and Facts', *World Politics*, 49 (January): 155–83.

Przeworski, A., Alvarez, M. E., Cheibub, J. A., and Limongi, F. (2000) *Democracy and Development: Political Institutions and Well-being in the World, 1950–1990*, Cambridge: Cambridge University Press.

Reynolds, Andrew, Stepan, Alfred, Zaw, Oo, and Levine, Stephen (2001) 'How Burma Could Democratize', *Journal of Democracy*, 12 (4): 95–108.

Riessman, C. K. (2008) *Narrative Methods for the Human Sciences*. Thousand Oaks, CA: Sage.

Risse, T., Ropp, S. C. and Sikkink, K. (eds) (1999) *The Power of Human Rights: International Norms and Domestic Change*. Cambridge: Cambridge University Press.

Roett, Riordan (2011) *The New Brazil*. Washington, DC: The Brooking Institution.

Roldán, Mary (2002) *Blood and Fire: La Violencia in Antioquia, Colombia, 1946–1953*. Durham and London: Duke University Press.

Roldán, Mary (2010) 'End of Discussion: Violence, Participatory Democracy, and the Limits of Dissent in Colombia', in Enrique Desmond Arias and Daniel M. Goldstein (eds), *Violent Democracies in Latin America*. London and Durham: Duke University Press, pp. 63–83.

Roman, David (2011) *Lustration and Transitional Justice: Personnel Systems in the Czech Republic, Poland and Hungary*. Philadelphia: University of Pennsylvania Press.

Rosato, Sebastian (2003) 'The Flawed Logic of Democratic Peace Theory', *American Political Science Review*, 97 (4): 585–602.

Rueschemeyer, D., Stephens, E. H. and Stephens, J. (1992) *Capitalist Development and Democracy*. Cambridge: Polity Press.

Russett, B. and O'Neal, J. (2001) *Triangulating Peace: Democracy, Interdependence and International Organizations*. New York: W. W. Norton.

Rustow, Dankwart (1970) 'Democratic Transition: Toward a Dynamic Model', *Comparative Politics*, 2 (3): 337–63.

Sa'adah, Anne (1998) *Germany's Second Chance: Truth, Justice and Democratization*. Cambridge, MA: Harvard University Press.

Sandercock, Leonie and Attili, Giovanni (2012) 'Unsettling a settler society: film, phronesis and collaborative planning in small-town Canada', in Bent Flyvbjerg, Todd Landman and Sanford Schram (eds), *Real Social Science: Applied Phronesis*. Cambridge: Cambridge University Press, pp. 137–66.

Sandoval Villalba, Clara (2011) *Transitional Justice: Key Concepts, Processes, and Challenges*, IDCR Briefing Paper 7, University of Essex: Institute for Democracy and Conflict Resolution.

Sands, Philippe (2006) *Lawless World America and the Making and Breaking of Global Rules*. New York: Penguin.

Sen, Amartya (1999) *Development as Freedom*. Oxford: Oxford University Press.

Shugart, M. and Carey, J. M. (1992) *Presidents and Assemblies: Constitutional Design and Electoral Dynamics*. Cambridge: Cambridge University Press.

Sikkink, Kathryn (2011) *The Justice Cascade: How Human Rights Prosecutions Are Changing World Politics*. New York: Norton.

Shvetsova, L. (2010) 'What's the Matter with Russia?' *Journal of Democracy*, 21 (1): 152–9.

Simmons, Beth (2009) *Mobilizing for Human Rights: International Law in Domestic Politics*. Cambridge: Cambridge University Press.

Singer, Max (1997) 'What is Happening in History?', *PS: Political Science and Politics*, 30: 28.

Sitoe, Eduardo, Matsimbe, Zafanias, and Pereira, Amilcar (2005) *Parties and Political Development in Mozambique*, EISA Research Report, 22 [http://www.eisa.org.za/PDF/rr22.pdf]

Skidmore, Thomas (ed.) (1993) *Television, Politics and the Transition to Democracy in Latin America*. Baltimore: Johns Hopkins University Press.

Smith-Cannoy, Heather (2012) *Insincere Commitments: Human Rights Treaties, Abusive States and Citizen Activism*. Washington, DC: Georgetown University Press.

Stepan, A. and Skach, C. (1993) 'Constitutional Frameworks and Democratic Consolidation: Parliamentarism and Presidentialism', *World Politics*, 46 (October): 1–22.

Stiglitz, J. E. (2002) *Globalization and Its Discontents*. New York: Allen Lane/The Penguin Press.

—(2012) *The Price of Inequality: The Avoidable Causes and the Invisible Costs of Inequality*. New York: Allen Lane.

Tarrow, Sidney (1994) *Power in Movement: Social Movements, Collective Action, and Politics*. Cambridge: Cambridge University Press.

—(2005) *The New Transnational Activism*. Cambridge: Cambridge University Press.

Themnér, Lotta and Wallensteen, Peter (2012) 'Armed Conflict, 1946–2011', *Journal of Peace Research*, 49 (4): 565–75.

United Nations (2004) 'The Rule of Law and Transitional Justice in Conflict and Post Conflict Societies: Report of the Secretary General', New York: United Nations, S/2004/616.

United Nations Development Programme (UNDP) (2011) *Human Development Report*. New York: United Nations Development Programme.

Whitehead, Laurence (1996) *The International Dimensions of Democratization*. Oxford: Oxford University Press.

Whitford, Andrew B. and Wong, Karen (2009) 'Political and Social Foundations for Environmental Sustainability,' *Political Research Quaterly*, 62 (1).

Wilson, Richard (2001) *The Politics of Truth and Reconciliation in South Africa*. Cambridge: Cambridge University Press.

World Bank (2011) *World Development Report*. Washington, DC: World Bank.

Zakaria, Fareed (2003) *The Future of Freedom: Illiberal Democracy at Home and Abroad*. New York: W.W.Norton.

Zanger, S. C. (2000) 'A Global Analysis of the Effect of Regime Changes on Life Integrity Violations, 1977–93', *Journal of Peace Research*, 37 (2): 217–33.

INDEX

advanced democracies   28
African Charter on Human
        and Peoples' Rights
        in 1979   31, 33
African Court of Human and People's
        Rights in 2006   33
1969 American Convention on Human
        Rights   32
1776 American Declaration of
        Independence   28
The American Founding   40
amnesties   104–5
Anti-Terrorism, Crime and Security
        Act 2001   118
2004 Arab Charter on Human
        Rights   33
Arab Revolutions of 2011   11
Arab Spring   40, 42, 58, 65–6, 74–5,
        78, 94–5, 146, 154
Arab Spring of 2011   38, 42
armed conflict *see* conflict
Aung San Suu Kyi (Burma)   147
austerity programmes   125

Babst   136
Bachelet, Michelle (Chile)   146
Bob, Clifford   91
Book of the It (Groddeck, Georg)   145
boomerang model   90
The Bottom Billion (Collier, Paul)   122
Brazil   15, 41, 75, 98, 100,
        102, 155

Capitalist Development and Democracy
        (Rueschemeyer, Stephens and
        Stephens)   67
1945 Charter of the United
        Nations   32
Chile   2, 8, 15, 46, 73, 78, 88,
        102–3, 146

18th Chinese Communist Party
        Congress   149
citizenship   25–6
civil and political rights   33
    large-scale quantitative
        analysis   38–9
civil war   114
Clash of Civilizations
        (Huntington, Samuel)   65
climate change   125–6
Collier, Paul   149
Colombia   48, 57, 115
conflict
    civil war   114
    Colombia   115
    Peru   114–15
    types   115–16
consensus democracies   135–6
1787 Constitutional Convention in
        Philadelphia   40
contagion   76, 78
contestation   27
contestation for power needs
        systems   70
1979 Convention on the Elimination
        of Discrimination against
        Women (CEDAW)   34
1984 Convention against Torture
        (CAT)   33
1989 Convention on the Rights of the
        Child (CRC)   34, 37
Copenhagen criteria for membership of
        the EU   32
Council of Europe (COE)   32, 48
Crowds and Power
        (Canetti, Elias)   84
cycle of protest   86–8

Davenport, Christian   137
delegative democracies   39, 152

democracy
    and development 14
    and human rights 149–51
democratic peace
    inter-state conflict 136–7
    normative and institutional
        logics 136
    pacific benefits of democracy 137
democratisation of technology 83
democratization
    difficult challenges 152
    easy achievements 152
    theory of endogenous
        democratization 152–3
    theory of exogenous
        democratization 153
'dependency' theory 122–3
Diamond, Larry 28, 46
diffusion process of democracy 78–9
distributive justice 108–9
domestic mobilization 83
    authoritarian conditions 88–9
    Burma case 89
    civil society groups 86–7
    cycle of protest 86
    economic failure 85
    formation and aggregation of
        groups 87
    free-rider problem 84–5
    grievance 84
    Polish and Chilean cases 88
    political opportunities 86
    private and selective incentives 85
    rationality 84–5
    social movement activity 87
domestic struggles 83
domestic terrorism see terrorism
Donnelly, Jack 30, 156

East Asian Tigers 15
ecological footprint 125
economic abundance 12–13, 16, 22,
        148–9
economic benefits
    caloric consumption 139
    fossil fuel consumption and
        wealth 141
    human development 138
    water pollution 141

Economic Community of West African
        States (ECOWAS) 54
economic crisis 124
economic globalization 121–5
    arguments for 122
    economic and Eurozone crisis 124
    global comparative analysis 123
The Economic Origins of Dictatorship
        and Democracy (Acemoglu
        and Robinson) 67
economic, social and cultural
        rights 33
Egypt 4–5, 22, 58–9, 71, 74,
        85, 154
electoral participation 130–1, 157
elite accounts of democratization 5,
        16, 20, 48, 50, 55, 67–8, 71,
        74, 85–6, 136, 153–4
The End of History and the Last Man
        (Fukuyama, Francis) 63, 66
Europe 48–9, 56, 76, 78, 85, 101,
        118, 124, 154
European Convention on Human
        Rights, 1950 32
European Court of Human
        Rights 118
European Endowment for Democracy,
        Brussels 154
European Union (EU) 32
Eurozone crisis 124
extra-systemic conflict 115

Facebook 94
fomenting democratization 154
1789 French Declaration of the Rights
        of Man and the Citizen 28
FrontlineSMS (organization) 94
fulfilling human rights 31–2

game theory of democratization 71–3
    Chile 73–4
    Egypt and Libya 74
    payoffs and choices 73
    Poland 73
    Tunisia 74
General Agreement on Tariffs and Trade
        (GATT) 122
German, Michael 156
Germany 41, 134

Global Commission on Elections,
    Democracy and
    Security   133
global income   122
grievance   84, 95

Hawkins, Darren   73
human development index (HDI)   138
human rights
    categories   33
    and democracy   40–1
    list of   34–6
    treaties of   37
human rights gap   150
Human Rights Watch   107–8

Ignatieff, Michael   37
illiberal democracy   28, 150
income distribution   122, 124, 133
income, internal disparities of   123–4
India   18, 48
Industrialization and Democracy
    (de Schweinitz)   19
initial democratization,
    pathways to   69
Institute for Justice and Reconciliation
    in South Africa   110
institutional design   134
inter-connectedness   121
inter-governmental organizations
    (IGOs)   89–90
1966 International Convention on
    the Elimination of all Forms
    of Racial Discrimination
    (CERD)   34
1966 International Covenant on
    Civil and Political Rights
    (ICCPR)   33
1966 International Covenant on
    Economic and Social
    Rights   125
1966 International Covenant on
    Economic, Social and Cultural
    Rights (ICESCR)   33
International Criminal Tribunal for
    Rwanda (ICTR)   103
International Criminal Tribunal for
    the Former Yugoslavia
    (ICTY)   103

International Institute for Democracy
    and Electoral Assistance
    (IDEA)   30, 154
international intra-state
    conflict   115
international law of armed conflict
    (ILAC)   97
international mobilization
    coercion   92
    export of democracy   92–3
    goals   89
    inter-governmental organizations
        (IGOs)   89–90
    International Institute for
        Democracy and Electoral
        Assistance (IDEA)   93
    international non-governmental
        organizations (INGOs)   90
    motivations   91
    Nigeria and Mexico cases   91
    promotion of democracy   93
    smart phone technology-internet
        integration   93–4
    social media   94
    tools and instruments   91–2
international non-governmental
    organizations (INGOs)   90
international terrorism *see* terrorism
inter-state conflict   115
intra-state conflict   115
Islamist terrorism   116

Jacksonian Democracy   45

Karman, Tawakkol   42

Lagos, Marta   17
Landman, Todd   124
Larizza, Marco   124
liberal democracy   27–9
Liberation of Mozambique
    (Frelimo)   145
Lijphart, Arend   135
Lipset, Seymour Martin   12–13,
    15, 63
    Political Man   62
local mobilization *see* domestic
    mobilization
Logic of Collective Action   84

lower-class mobilization for
         inclusion   70
lustration   49, 98, 101

macro-historical change   66–70
Magna Carta of 1215   117
majoritarian democracies   135
Maputo   145
Mexico   2–3, 17, 57–8, 75
Millennium Development Goals
         (MDGs)   1, 13, 38, 93, 129
Mobilizing for Human Rights
         (Cleary, Edward)   49
modernization   15
   limitations   64
   protection of human rights   63–4
   revisions   64–5
modern world, routes to   68
Mongolia   1, 16, 153
Movement for the Survival of the Ogoni
         Poeple (MOSOP), Nigeria   91
Mozambique   145
Mozambique National Resistance
         (Renamo)   145
multiparty systems   134

National Defense Authorization Act
         (NDAA)   151
National Endowment for Democracy,
         United States   154
National Human Rights Institutions
         (NHRIs)   99
natural resources, decline in   125
neo-liberal economic theory   123
Norris, Pippa   139
North Atlantic Treaty Organization
         (NATO)   21, 49, 58, 74,
         78, 92

Occupy Movement   124
older democracies   50
O'Neal, J.   137
Organization for Security and
         Cooperation in Europe
         (OSCE)   32
outliers   21–2, 40

pacific benefits of democracy   137
participation   27

Patriot Acts of 2001 and 2004   118
People and the Planet
         (Royal Society report,
         United Kingdom)   140, 142
personal integrity rights   39–40
Peru   53, 114–15
Peruvian Truth and Reconciliation
         Commission (CVR)   105
physical integrity rights   114, 132–3
Pogge, Thomas   149
Poland   73, 88
political freedom   13–14, 16, 148–9
   economic benefits   17
   economic justice and   158
   political transformations   22
Political Order in Changing Societies
         (Huntington, Samuel)   64
Polyarchy (Dahl, Robert)   26
popular movements   75, 124, 154
post-Cold War democratization   49
poverty   125–6
Power of Human Rights (Risse,
         Ropp and Sikkink)   79
President Obama   92, 119–21,
         148–9, 151
presidential vs parliamentary
         systems   134–5
'prisoners' dilemma   71
procedural democracy   26–7
pro-democracy movements   151
proponents of human rights   29
proportional representation   134
protecting human rights   31
protection of cultural rights   29
Przeworski, Adam   16
Putin, Vladimir   56

quality of democracy   47, 55, 93, 114,
         126, 133, 136

rationality   84–5
The Rebel's Dilemma
         (Lichbach, Mark)   85
Reif, David   38
reparations   108
resource wars   126
respecting human rights   31
restorative justice   109, 155
retributive justice   107–8, 155

revised modernization   65
rights-protective governance   30, 67,
        123, 156
Rio + 20 Nations Conference on
        Sustainable Development
        in 2012   114
rollback of democracy   152
Roussef, Dilma   155
Rousseff, Dilma (Brazil)   146–7
Rueschemeyer, D.   19
Russet, B.   137
Russia   56
Rustow, Dankwart   76

satisfaction with democracy   17
Sen, Amartya   14, 137
Singer, Max   63
single-member district systems   134
smart phone technology-internet
        integration   93–4
social and economic rights, poverty and
        livelihoods   125–6
social democracy   29–31
*The Social Origins of Dictatorship
        and Democracy* (Moore,
        Barrington)   19, 67
solidarity rights   33
South African Truth and Reconciliation
        Commission (TRC)   105
stable democracies   12
stable dictatorships   12
The Stages of Economic Growth
        (Rustow, Dankwart)   62
Stiglitz, Joseph   124
structural violations   149
struggle for rights   75
Sukey (organization)   94
support for democracy   17–18

terrorism
    9/11 attacks   117
    anti-terrorism acts   118
    comparative and statistical
        analysis   117
    detainees, Guantanamo Bay
        facility   119
    liberties   117–18
    lower costs and bigger
        gains   116–17

restrictions   118
    US domestic anti-terror
        policy   118–21
Terrorism Act 2000   118
theory of endogenous
        democratization   152–3
theory of exogenous
        democratization   153
theory of free markets   122
The Third Wave (Huntington,
        Samuel)   45
threats
    climate change   125–6
    conflict   114–16
    economic globalization   121–5
    terrorism   116–21
Tilly, Charles   94
toppling leaders   154
transnational advocacy
        network   90
trials   103–4
truth
    amnesties   104–5
    challenge   155
    choice   99–102
    justice   107–11
    lustration   49, 98, 101
    mandate   102–5
    methods   105–7
    narratives   106
    reparations   108
    trials   103–4
    truth commissions   104
truth commissions   104
Tunisia   22, 58–9, 74, 85, 94–5
Twitter   94
two-party systems   134

United Nations Development
        Programme   140
1948 Universal Declaration
        of Human Rights
        (UDHR)   31–3, 38
unregulated market capitalism   156
unstable democracies   12
unstable dictatorships   12
US domestic anti-terror
        policy   118–21
2012 US Elections   149

Venezuela   29, 55

1993 Vienna Declaration and
        Programme of Action   125

Villaba, Sandoval   107

voter turnout rate, parliamentary and
        presidential elections   130–1

war on terror   121, 150

waves of democracy   47–8

Western democracies   133

Whitford, Andrew B.   140

Why Men Rebel
        (Gurr, Ted Robert)   84

Wong, Karen   140

World Trade Organization
        (WTO)   122

Zakaria, Fareed   28